On 20 July 1978 I erected my Base Camp in the upper Diamir Valley at the foot of the 3500 metre West Face of Nanga Parbat. My plan was to make the first absolutely solo ascent of an eight-thousander by a new route. On 6 August I bivouacked at the foot of the face (B1). The next day I climbed with fifteen kilos of luggage in my rucksack — sleeping bag, special tent, foam mattress, crampons, axe, rope, one rock piton, one ice screw, and food for ten days — over the avalanche-prone lower section of the face to a point just above the big Icefall in the centre of the picture. In six hours I had gained 1600 metres of height. I bivouacked under an ice overhang (B2) and on 8 August climbed diagonally left under the rocky summit trapezium (B3). After strenuous trail-breaking and steep rock climbing I reached the summit at four o'clock on 9 August. Just before dark I was back in my tent in the Western Basin (B4). Next day — snowstorm. I rationed the food and sat it out. Part of the descent route had been rendered impossible by an earthquake. That gave me no choice but to climb down the more dangerous direct line (11 August).

Front endpaper

Nanga Parbat from the east in early morning light. The Chongra Peaks are on the right, from which a sharp ridge leads to the prominent Rakhiot Peak; from there it continues up to half in light, half in shade. It was over the Silver Saddle (Silbersattel) that Herman Buhl came when he made the first ascent of Nanga Parbat on 3 July 1953. Seen in profile to the left is the South-east Ridge; behind it runs the Rupal Face route climbed by my brother Günther and I in 1970.

*Loneliness is a force
that can kill you
if you are unprepared for it,
but it will carry you beyond your own horizon
if you understand how to use it to your advantage.*

REINHOLD MESSNER

SOLO NANGA PARBAT

Translated by Audrey Salkeld

KAYE & WARD . LONDON
OXFORD UNIVERSITY PRESS . NEW YORK
VISION BOOKS . NEW DELHI

First published in Great Britain by
Kaye & Ward Ltd
21 New Street, London EC2M 4NT
1980
First published in the USA by
Oxford University Press Inc.
200 Madison Avenue, New York, N.Y. 10016
1980
First published in India in 1980 by
Vision Books Pvt. Ltd.,
36-C, Connaught Place, New Delhi 110001
Copyright © BLV Verlagsgesellschaft MbH, Munich 1979
English translation Copyright © Kaye & Ward Ltd 1980

All rights reserved. No part of this publication may be
reproduced, stored in a retrieval system, or transmitted,
in any form or by any means, electronic, mechanical,
photocopying, recording or otherwise, without
the prior permission of the copyright owner.

ISBN 0 7182 1250 9 (Great Britain)
ISBN 0-19-520196-5 (USA)
Library of Congress Catalog Card No. 80-7441 (USA)
Printed in Great Britain by
Butler & Tanner Ltd, Frome and London
Set in Monotype Bembo by Gloucester Typesetting Co Ltd

CONTENTS

NANGA

One Man and One Eight-Thousander	9
Black Loneliness	35
Solo	40

TIKE

My Dreams Realized	63
Walking Alone	82
Night of the Long Shadows	108
Breaking Loose	125

DIAMIR

White Loneliness	146
Strange Voices	162
Saved from the Ice	166
Lost for Words	181
An Encounter with Death	198
Being Alone	211

NANGA PARBAT HISTORY

Nanga Parbat Chronicle		231
Expeditions to Nanga Parbat		237
Successful Ascents		241
1932–9	The Great Tragedies	243
1953	Hermann Buhl's Summit Climb	248
1961–2	The Diamir Flank	254
1963–70	The Rupal Face	258
1969–71	Czechoslovakians on the Buhl-Route	265
1976	Four Graz Mountaineers on Nanga Parbat	266
1978	Austrians on the Diamir Flank	272

*The self-destruction of the sahib has reached a point
where he wants to know everything and no longer sees what's in
    front of him;
where he only believes in technology;
where he wants to rationalize everything;
where out of fear of being lonely, he seeks crowds and
    then feels isolated amongst them;
where he denies the existence of death
and all the time thinks and thinks and thinks ...*

        Dawa Tensing, Sherpa from Pangboche.

NANGA

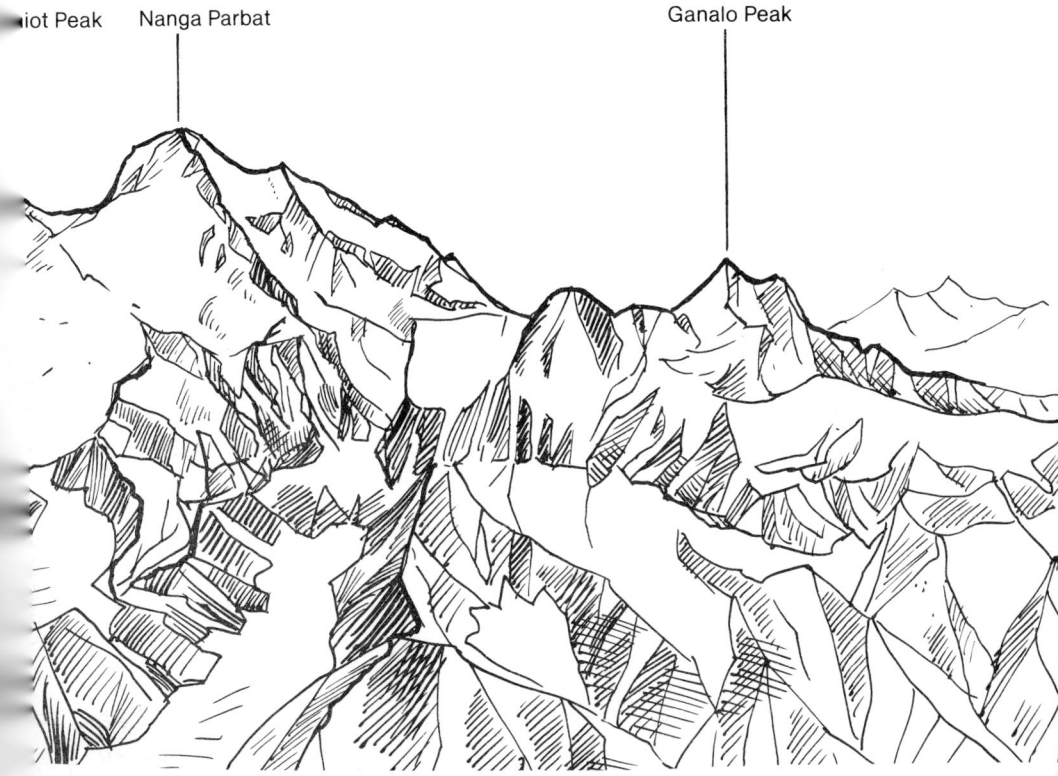

Ich kann es nicht, wieder nicht, meine Einsamkeit ist zur Verzweiflung angewachsen. Ich bin sicher, daß ich am Fuße des N.P. in besserer seelischer Verfassung sein würde, weiß jetzt aber auch, daß ich in meinem derzeitigen Zustand nicht bis dorthin komme. Es ist weniger die Angst vor der Tour, als vielmehr eine innere Leere, die noch mit Schmerz erfüllt. Nie im Leben habe ich mich so allein gefühlt wie jetzt. Der Wunsch, mit Ushi zu sprechen, mit ihr zu sein ist so groß, daß ich gleich in die Nacht hinausgehen muß, um laut reden zu können, von ihr, zu ihr.

Ich habe mich entschlossen vorerst aufzugeben und noch die Schneelage zu

I kept a diary in 1973 on my first attempt and in 1978 when I completed my solo climb.

ONE MAN AND ONE EIGHT-THOUSANDER

I have climbed a steep section of mountain and now, breathless inside my tent, the realization hits me that I cannot get back down again. I lie rigid, unable to move, and am sweating profusely even though it is so cold. Hoar frost coats the drab fabric above my head. I mutter to myself, call out, yet cannot hear the sound of my own voice. Panic has me in its clutches and all I want to do is to scream.

It came suddenly upon me in a moment between sleeping and waking when I was pondering the route ahead. In a moment I saw just how alone I am. So alone. The muscles in my stomach tighten with fear.

I am a speck on this vast mountain face, I cannot see back to the start of my climb. Below me the dizzy void has no end.

Within seconds terror has reduced me to a weak, shivering bundle, I want to crawl away and weep, and never, never have to look down again. My fingers will no longer grip, my legs no longer support my weight. I want to close my eyes but they remain open. It is still night; I can see the stars through the frozen tent fabric. A long time passes before I am able to relax even a little. Then I massage my arms and legs.

Despair at being alone floods my whole body. I cannot explain what suddenly triggered it off, but it won't go away. Fear of being here, fear of going on, fear of being alive even. It is not falling that I'm scared of, it is as if I had lost my own self in this vast emptiness.

'This is sheer madness,' I say to myself, 'I'll give up,' and immediately I feel drowsy. It is as if I had to make the decision to retreat just in order to get some sleep. When I finally say, 'I'll pull out, go back home,' it is five in the morning and the first light streaks the sky. I crawl deeper into my sleeping bag and drift back to sleep. However, my peace of mind does not last long. Once more I see the rock spur soaring above me, the

> It wasn't just ice avalanches that tumbled down the Diamir Flank, there were also frequent stonefalls.
> On my first solo bid there was a rockfall.

Diamir Flank of Nanga Parbat. This name 'Diamir' is from the Sanskrit and means 'Naked Mountain'. Perhaps I should give it one more try. 'Nanga solo,' I whisper to myself. Then, 'What's the point?' I want to go down yet all the time I am thinking of going on, climbing higher. I bury my face in my hands but I am still aware that it is a fine day. One way or another I must get out of this place before the first avalanches come down. 'Better get out of bed,' I command myself.

Having made the 'final decision' to retreat gives me the strength to sit up in my sleeping bag. Ponderously I peel off the warm down shell and, grumbling, reach for my boots which I had stuffed under the end of my sleeping mat. I put my hands inside them — frozen solid. I lie down again and take the boots into my warm sleeping bag to thaw out. All these little chores, I know, serve only to delay my failure. I have to justify it to myself. I busy myself with my altimeter for a while. It doesn't help. The weather is good, true, but there's a lot of snow on the face. I can't contemplate cooking. Why bother? In two hours I can be back down below the snowline, and if I hurry, the going will still be crisp. Down there I'll find water and wood.

One half of me is glad that I've decided to go down, but at the same time I hate myself for it. I am still miserably tormented. I want to leave, but continue making preparations for the climb. I am frightened; frightened that I might not be able to endure the loneliness up there, of breaking down. I am torn between desire and fear.

Suddenly I hear a cracking sound above me. Stones have come off from somewhere. I hear the fragments rattling down the face in great leaps and bounds, and become absorbed in their changing sounds: a singing and piping in the air, the crashing into rock or ice, the explosion of the shattered pieces. Involuntarily I crawl out of the sleeping bag, open the tent door and peer outside. It is broad daylight. Below, clouds of dust are rising in the wake of the stone avalanche. Occasional dark spots appear amongst the billows, lumps of rock. These fall faster, break again, and new, thicker dust clouds well upward.

To my left, between the Mummery Rib and the Kinshofer-Route, the face, swept by a shower of stones, is alive with movement. I realize

SOLO NANGA PARBAT

immediately that I am well out of reach and look upwards again. From this viewpoint the way ahead does not seem as steep as it did. Above the sharp pyramid of Ganalo Peak the sky is bright. Below, the tangled ice cascade of the Diama Glacier looks like waves in a sea that has all of a sudden solidified; blue-white the foam and dark in the hollows. From up here I can see clearly the many laborious detours I was forced to make yesterday to get round its obstacles. And I can see the stages of the climb that lie ahead. It will take another two or three days to the summit from this bivouac beneath the upper Mummery Rib.

I see in flashbacks the experiences of the past few days. The march-in through the desert-like Indus Valley; the deep snow in the upper Diamir Basin; the restless days spent acclimatizing at the foot of the mountain. Three porters accompanied me as far as Base Camp only. No-one waits for me now. I wonder if my tent is still standing down there? I read what I wrote in my diary the day before yesterday, and it becomes obvious to me that I ought never to have started on this venture.

'*1 June, 1973.* Long after midnight and I cannot sleep. The few mouthfuls of food I managed to force down last evening weigh heavily on my stomach. I think of Uschi and sob violently. This oppressive feeling that robs me of hunger and thirst won't go away. It is not my Grand Plan that prevents me from eating and sleeping, it is this separation from my wife. I am not mentally ready to see such a big undertaking through to the end.'

'It's 3 June today,' I tell myself as I gather up my things from inside the open tent. I keep taking a look outside. Like massive ramparts, vertical ice pinnacles — seracs — bar the way ahead. I see them change from a warm night grey to the cold blue of morning. It is as if I only needed to busy myself to regain strength and courage. If I were to hurry, I say to myself, then in four or five hours I could get high enough to be beyond the reach of avalanches. The challenge is hard to resist. The sky is neither cloudy nor clear, but hazy. So too is the glacier, receding far below between the steep-sided foothills, hazy and grey, barely discernible from the two moraines to left and right. The weather, the sky, the ice — everything has changed overnight.

'You don't have to do it,' I tell myself, 'no-one is forcing you.' I want

The last of my anxieties did not evaporate until after I had crawled out of my tent. As I dismantled it I resolved to keep on going.

to go back. Fear in the belly! It's as if the fear goes up and down inside me. From head to belly, belly to head.

All the while the tent is still standing I don't have to face the decision. I gnaw on a hard piece of bread. Putting on my boots and zipping up my anorak, I am seized by a feeling of aggression. All my actions become careful and deliberate as if I wanted to conserve every ounce of energy. But for what purpose?

Shortly before I am ready to leave, I calm down. A truce seems to have been declared between the two conflicting forces within me. No decision can be taken until the tent is down. It is not apathy that afflicts me like this, it is the fear of being alone and it hits me whenever I am unoccupied, whenever I am waiting. If it took hold of me higher up, it could finish me.

When the tent is rolled up, I strap it onto the tightly-packed rucksack. For a long moment I stand there and stare at the red bundle in the snow, as if it held the answer to which way I should go. But there is no-one who can make this decision for me; no-one to say yes or no, to nod or shake his head; no friendly face, no encouraging look.

I am warmly dressed. The one-piece storm suit I wear as an outer-layer gives me a sense of security. Only my feet are still cold. My hands are stuffed deep into down mittens. My hesitation no longer seems a sign of weakness in myself, it is more like an all-pervading presence. Only as I hoist the rucksack strap over my shoulder and swing the twenty-kilo

SOLO NANGA PARBAT

pack onto my back, do I finally know what I want to do. I will continue — at least to a height of around 6500 metres. From such a height, I reckon, I could still get down in a single day, and the avalanche danger would still not be too great. With a shrug of my shoulders to settle the rucksack into a comfortable position, I pick up my axe and take the first few steps.

Meanwhile it has grown lighter. The sky is a ghostly colour, something between violet and grey. At first I climb purposefully like someone who knows what he wants. The packed snow is firm. It bears my weight well yet allows me to get a grip with the edge of my heavy climbing boots. It doesn't occur to me to put on my crampons. The rocks at the start of the Mummery Rib seems to be dry and it would only take unnecessary time putting them on and then taking them off again. Things are going well again, I am cheerful.

'What can happen to me anyway?' How was it possible that all night long I was so beset with doubts? Suddenly I notice that my steps are taking me down, down in the direction of the ice 'hose', down towards Base Camp. But I thought I wanted ... had decided to go on ... My body takes me where *it* has to go, and I let myself be taken.

It takes only a few hours to cover the stretch that took the whole day yesterday. I leap over crevasses, balance across ice bridges, and run downhill across the flat ice slopes. The way seems easy, I am so happy. Before the sun is fully up, I am sitting in Base Camp.

In the morning light, the concave face seems smaller. Even so it is formidable, filling the end of the valley, a barrier for ever and everyone. Its rocky shoulders hunched left and right of the main summit, stand out starkly against the blue of the sky. The light changes from one second to the next. A cloud draws in front of the sun and instantly everything appears frozen in ice. I shiver involuntarily and can't help remembering 1970, when after climbing the Rupal Face, my brother and I had to come down this side. My brother, Günther, was slower than I, and I went ahead to scout out a route. How often I felt like giving up during that dreadful descent! I just wanted to lie down and not take another step. For three long days we toiled down. There were many moments of despair in that 4000 metres from summit to here. But we made it to the

Flying back from Gilgit to Rawalpindi in June 1973, I went right past Nanga Parbat. The Diamir Flank, in all its steepness, stood there for me to see. That time I only reached the foot of the Mummery Rib (lower edge of the picture).

bottom. And then it happened; on the upper Diamir Glacier my brother vanished, lost under an avalanche at the very foot of the face.

Between then and now I have come to terms with these experiences; I have not pushed them from my mind but have absorbed them. They belong to me, to my life. Since 1971, when I went back to search for my brother, and saw everything again, I have been able to accept that it had to be like that. Even if my brother's body is never found. I was often plagued by terrible dreams on that trip, both during the march-in and at Base Camp, I would see Günther crawling towards me across the glacier. With the shock and joy of finding him, I would wake up. 'Destiny Peak' is one of the names given to Nanga Parbat.

Albert Frederick Mummery made the first attempt to climb the Diamir Face way back in 1895. It was the very first time anyone had ever tried to storm an eight-thousander. First of all he studied the South Face of Nanga Parbat from the Rupal Valley, a savage 4500 metre mountain wall. Then, moving his Base Camp around into the Diamir Valley, he set off, first with two, then with a single Gurkha porter in a bid to reach the summit. He took a line in the centre of the face directly under the main summit. Following a steep rock spur he made good progress. Then Raghobir, his companion, began suffering from the effects of altitude. Retreat. A few

It was in May 1973 that I first set off for Nanga Parbat with the serious intention of attempting the 8125 metre high mountain by myself. On that occasion my equipment was light, but not refined to the very last detail. And there was, that time, a lot of snow in the Diamir Valley and on the face. Perhaps I would still have succeeded, despite all that, had I had the mental strength to be able to endure weeks on my own in an extreme situation. I reached about 6000 metres and then climbed hastily down again, as if I was fleeing from my own fear. I had chosen a direct route up the Diamir Face (next double-page). I reached a point just under the line of shadow, which the Mazeno Ridge in the foreground throws upon the concave Diamir Face. I had climbed down this face in 1970, after the first ascent of the Rupal Face, with my brother who was suffering from altitude sickness. It took us three long days, and all the time we were terrified that we would never find a way out of this tumbled labyrinth of rock and ice. But we did, we made it without bivouac protection, with nothing to eat or drink, we reached the foot of the face. Then my brother was lost under an avalanche.

In 1970 when I trudged down the Diamir Valley, I lost consciousness at one point. At that time I didn't know the way and, with frostbitten hands and feet, was hardly in a condition to walk. It was only when I reached the high village of Nagaton that I met the first Pakistani hillfarmers. A year later I went back to the Diamir Valley to search for traces of my vanished brother. Uschi came with me that time and we were married the following year. Our search was fruitless. On this expedition I met again the local people who had helped me in 1970, and learnt to appreciate the ruggedness of the western basin of Nanga Parbat with fresh eyes. In 1970 I was too completely played out to register impressions properly. And I only began to cope with the pain of losing my brother after this expedition to search for him. In 1973 I confidently set off on a solo attempt. I was at that time completely stable emotionally, and quickly reached the foot of the face. After a short acclimatization phase, I set off up the Diamir Face, following the Mummery Rib (at the junction of the light and shade). I climbed less than a third of the way. When I returned to Base Camp a large amount of my equipment was missing; and in any case I wanted nothing better than to get home.

SOLO NANGA PARBAT

days later Mummery and two Gurkhas disappeared whilst endeavouring to cross the Diama Col on the North Ridge of Nanga Parbat. They were never found.

After Mummery's disappearance things were quiet on Nanga Parbat. Avalanches continued to thunder down its mighty flanks, storms to howl around its lonely summit as they had always done. Local farmers spun their legends around each strange phenomenon they could not otherwise comprehend. There was no more thought of finding a route to the top. In 1913 an English traveller, Candler, circumnavigated the mountain but he didn't set foot on the actual peak. A year later the tireless Himalayan pioneer, Dr Kellas, visited Nanga Parbat, but he too departed without making any attempt upon it.

At the beginning of 1930 Dr Willo Welzenbach became preoccupied with the idea of climbing Nanga Parbat. He had formed the view that Nanga Parbat was the easiest of the eight-thousanders. Like Mummery, he wanted to climb it from the Diamir side, but events took a different turn.

In 1932 Willy Merkl, the outstanding German climber, took over leadership of a new Nanga Parbat expedition from Willo Welzenbach, who had to withdraw for business reasons. Merkl selected the north side of the mountain for his attempt, which in the event was defeated by the depth of new snow. Merkl, however, was convinced that he had discovered the ideal route on the mountain and two years later he launched another big expedition: nine climbers, a base camp supervisor, three scientists and two transport officers, as well as thirty-five of the best Sherpas and 500 porters! Four camps were quickly established. Despite a fatal incident — Alfred Drexel died of acute pulmonary oedema — the expedition pushed on. On the Silver Plateau, immediately below the summit, the summit team were caught in a blizzard. Retreat. Three sahibs — Wieland, Welzenbach, Merkl — and six Sherpas died of exposure and exhaustion.

In 1937 an avalanche engulfed a camp under Rakhiot Peak, burying sixteen men. A small expedition led by Paul Bauer immediately flew out to India, but could only dig out part of the destroyed camp and recover the diaries. In 1938 a three-motor Junkers aircraft was employed to trans-

Mummery, one of the ablest of British alpinists, discovered the climbing potential of Nanga Parbat; Welzenbach (right) popularized it in German-speaking circles.

port luggage from a base in Srinigar. Climbing the 'Moor's Head', Bauer and his expedition comrades found the bodies of Merkl and his porter Gay-Lay. They abandoned their attempt.

Despite a massive outlay of money and a desire to plant the swastika flag on the summit of Nanga Parbat, success to date had been only modest. People were already beginning to question such a costly enterprise: 'The climber places his faith fundamentally in his axe and his rope. Heaven forbid that the borders of possibility, of sporting admissibility, be rigidly defined; but there is a strong opinion among true mountain lovers that the line has to be drawn somewhere. In British climbing circles there had already been a move away from the all-too-big and all-too-expensive Everest expeditions; the history of German Himalayan expeditions shows a reverse development. Beginning with an assault on Kangchenjunga (Kantsch) in 1929 which was celebrated for its simplicity, it culminated in the giant expeditionary force which went to Nanga Parbat in the year 1938. Perhaps that was not representative of true mountaineering development. For a long time the struggle for Nanga Parbat had not been a free adventure undertaken by a spirited bunch of friends; the expenditure alone showed that it had grown into an issue of state in the Germany of the day.'★

In 1939 Mummery's old direct route and a possible route via the North

---

★ Rudolf Skuhra, *Sturm auf die Throne der Götter* (p. 190).

SOLO NANGA PARBAT

Summit were reconnoitred. A small expedition with Peter Aufschnaiter and Heinrich Harrer was forced to give up on account of avalanche danger and stonefalls. 'Not only the technical difficulties, but also the objective dangers of this face are questionable.'

The 'Willy–Merkl–Memorial–Expedition 1953' finally brought the dreams of two generations of German mountaineers to fruition: Nanga Parbat was climbed. Hermann Buhl, a Tyrolean, achieved this seemingly impossible feat. Dr Herrligkoffer had in his characteristically dogged way, against all odds, produced all the necessary finance and completed the administration. His team worked hard to a height of 6900 metres and set up the requisite conditions for Hermann Buhl's epic climb — some 1400 metres of ascent without oxygen, taking from two in the morning to seven at night and involving in places difficult rock climbing. He spent some forty hours in the 'Death Zone', an achievement for which there is no comparison.

In the period between 1895 and 1953, some 200 expeditions were organized to the Himalaya and Karakorum, yet only three 8000 metre peaks were climbed. Climbers possessed endurance and remarkable courage, but their equipment was heavy and their experience still slight. Only after the Second World War did ropes, clothes, sleeping bags and tents come to be made from synthetic fibres, and pegs, karabiners, oxygen apparatus and crampons from light metal. In the space of fifteen years, all the fourteen 8000 metre peaks were climbed.

Technical advances aside, from the development of climbing techniques and modern transport onwards, all Himalayan expeditions adopted the tactic employed by de Saussure when he climbed Mont Blanc in 1787: in order to spare time and effort, qualified local porters, were hired such as Baltis, Gurkhas, Hunzas and Sherpas. 'To scale an Himalayan eight-thousander calls for qualities other than those needed in our own East and West Alps. It is the difference between mustering mental and physical skills for days, or months, at a stretch. In the Himalaya, it is not so much a matter of some momentary output of supreme willpower, as is so often the case for the hardest faces in the Alps, but rather of steadfast endurance in order to maintain a constant readiness for struggle. The most decisive factor in the Himalaya is the collaboration of like-minded

NANGA

individuals, a community of labour which devotes itself, not to personal ambition, but is loyal to the main goal.'*

How often I have read that. It is not a sentiment for which I have much sympathy. I have always been far too much of an individualist to happily accept this system. Nor indeed could I see the fascination of the eight-thousanders — until that first day I saw Nanga Parbat. That was the first eight-thousander I climbed.

Later I saw Annapurna, Dhaulagiri, climbed Manaslu, saw K2, Broad Peak, and, again, Nanga Parbat. And only then was I really under their spell, and it occurred to me that the time could not be far off when it should be possible to climb an 8000 metre peak as a single rope, or even alone. Certainly without high-level porters and a chain of camps, but with just the everyday things like rope, axe and tent. Thus, expeditions would cease to be technological onslaughts, and the dignity of the mountains would be preserved. Many climbers can only see the negative aspects of such ventures — the monstrous new possibilities of danger inherent in them — the intoxication of expanded possibility is beyond their grasp.

The huge dimensions of the Himalaya makes it impossible to storm a summit from the nearest village, as for instance you can Montblanc from Chamonix. The pioneers believed porters and high-level porters were absolutely necessary. Without them, everything would founder from the start. Yet, the larger the number of participants, of high-level and approach-march porters, the longer time is spent in preparing for the final assault and the more expensive and long-winded is the expedition. Naturally there were some attempts that broke with tradition to a greater or lesser extent. In 1954 the Austrians Herbert Tichy, Sepp Jöchler and Helmet Heuberger successfully climbed Cho Oyu (8189 metres) with four intermediate camps and eleven high-level porters. In 1957 Austrians Markus Schmuck, Fritz Wintersteller, Kurt Diemberger and Hermann Buhl climbed Broad Peak (8047 metres) with only three camps and no high-level porters. But another eighteen years went by before an eight-thousander was possible in pure alpine-style. In August 1975 Peter Habeler and I, after a twelve-day acclimatization period, with no porters, no pre-

* Willy Merkl, *Ein Weg zum Nanga Parbat* (p. 183).

SOLO NANGA PARBAT

established high camps, and no oxygen, climbed 8068 metre Hidden Peak.

What was now lacking was to climb an eight-thousander solo, the final juxtaposition of man and mountain: one man, one 8000 metre mountain.

Back in 1929, a young American, E. F. Farmer, attempted to climb Kangchenjunga alone, and in 1934 the Englishman, Maurice Wilson, even attempted Everest. Neither of them returned.

Once more I look up at the Diamir Flank. I, at least, have come back — but I didn't get to the top. The challenge remains. An idea like that doesn't die.

Nanga Parbat rises 125 kilometres north of Kashmir's main town, Srinagar; it forms the western corner buttress of the Himalaya. After Mount Everest and K2, it is the best-known of the eight-thousanders. The names 'Diamir' or 'Nanga Parbat' were attributed to the mountain by Adolf Schlagintweit as long ago as 1856. It is, by its Kashmiri name, Nanga Parbat, known to every child throughout the Himalaya; its other name, Diamir, or King of the Mountains, is less used. Above the arid Indus Valley, Nanga's northern flanks rise almost 7000 metres. Here, from where I sit, it looks like a huge bat with wings outstretched.

The concave middle section of the face is broken by icefalls. Like tumbled stairs, they rest one above the other. 100, 200 metres high, the ice masses end abruptly in vertical cliffs. These 'calve' almost daily, great blocks of ice breaking away, with the result that a climb up the lower section of the face is like a game of Russian roulette. All the avalanches funnel down into the semicircular basin at the foot of the mountain, from which there is no escape. Ice avalanches are part of the daily order on the Diamir Flank. Only a few spurs of rock rise, like islands, out of the vertical wasteland of snow and ice.

Though I made a vow to myself never again to attempt it, the idea won't leave me. I take off my dark glasses and look up at the delicate yet, appalling summit. It is so far away, yet so near. My inability to judge its true dimensions is maddening. I really don't know how big it is, this Nanga Parbat.

I had climbed perhaps a third of its height and that had taken me only one day. From Base Camp the Mazeno Wall looks almost as imposing and every bit as high as the Diamir Face, and yet I know it is 1000 metres lower than the summit of Nanga Parbat, and 1000 metres in the 'Death Zone' is a lot. Even the Mazeno Wall is three times as high as the North Face of the Droites in the Montblanc region, and that ranks amongst the fiercest of the great Alpine faces.

The natural amphitheatre of the Diamir Valley is so huge that it is impossible to take it all in. There is nothing to which it can be compared. Picture two Eiger North Faces set one upon the other and they would not reach the summit of Nanga Parbat. Moreover, my Base Camp here is already higher than the Eiger summit.

Gradually night falls. As I amble around sniffing the evening breeze, I can feel the vast scale of this place. The mountain seems infinitely huge, and once more I am unable to believe it could ever be climbed alone. The stumbling block is always my incapacity to bear utter solitude.

'I'll go home tomorrow,' I promise myself, 'and perhaps I never will come back again.' The mountains look glassy and cold as the first stars come up over the summits. The brown wooded hills on the western horizon are bordered by the dull white snowcaps of the Mazeno outliers and the Ganalo ridge. That is the way I came in. A few days' walk in the heat and dust and I will be back in Gilgit, where the nearest airstrip is.

The two boys who have promised to be my porters for the return march are sitting in the shelter of some stone walls and drinking tea.

'Want some?' they ask me.

'*Tike*', I reply and join them. Sitting beside their fire I absorb their Asiatic calm, their quiet acceptance of fate. They have a firm belief in the unalterability of events, and so are spared eternal questioning into the meaning of things. My preoccupation with facts and my powers of rational reasoning — what are they worth compared to their ancient wisdom?

It is late before we leave the glimmering fire and grope our way out of its warm circle of light to the tent. The moon breaks through the driving clouds high above the summit ridge of Nanga Parbat.

We make good time over the return march and in only two days I am in Gilgit. The first thing I do is send a telegram to my wife. Leaving the office, I begin to be bothered by doubts and emotions that till now

Before setting off for my first attempt to climb an eight-thousander solo, in 1973, I tested the remote-control on my camera. The result was this departure shot with Uschi. At that time we had a little flat in St Peter in Villnöss, and lived closely amongst the village community. That winter I bought the old parsonage on the hill of St Magdalena. It had been a schoolhouse in the nineteen-twenties before it was closed for hygenic reasons and put up for sale by the local authorities. Uschi and I fell in love with its situation and bought it despite its dilapidated condition. She began work on the renovations and garden whilst I was away on Nanga Parbat on my own. We got on well with our neighbours and the local farmer presented me with some hard flat loaves (which are baked slowly in 'bread rooms') and I took them with me on the expedition. This bread is not heavy and lasts for years. In 1978 on my successful climb of Nanga Parbat, I also had some of this fladenbrot *with me.*

I have always taken only the barest essentials with me on my solo attempts on eight-thousand metre peaks (1973 — Nanga Parbat; 1974 — Broad Peak; 1978 — Nanga Parbat). I always arrived in Parkistan as a tourist with hand luggage and twenty kilos baggage allowance. This had great advantages: it shortened the time taken trekking into the mountains and I could easily manage the few porters required. This made good sense especially in the wild Diamir Gorge (previous double-page). On my first attempt I had three porters, with a fourth for part of the way; returning I needed only two. On the flight back from Gilgit to Rawalpindi, I saw Nanga Parbat rising over the seas of morning mist (above). It was a fascinating sight and I was torn between the desire to climb one of the world's highest mountains on my own, and the wish to return to my own village and get to work putting my 'nest' into shape. When I did get home I spent half a year working on it. I was bricklayer, carpenter, roof-tiler and donkey-man. Together, Uschi and I succeeded in giving the house back its original character. For several years after that I would come back here to roost. In 1978 when I set off for Nanga Parbat again, this homing instinct had gone. I have become a true gypsy, like the nomads in Afghanistan, Pakistan and the Saharan Tuareg.

SOLO NANGA PARBAT

have been only in my unconscious mind. Suppose Uschi has gone back to Munich, suppose she has left Villnöss, left me . . .

In the PIA office I try and book a flight to Rawalpindi. I am told that the plane which brought me to Gilgit had to make a forced landing on its way back and is now out of commission.

'You may have to wait a long time for a flight,' the man in the office tells me. Nevertheless I decide to wait, for if I were to set off alone down the Indus Valley in my present state of mind, without Uschi, I should go mad. The afternoon is sultry, overcast; I try and read, but can only manage a few lines at a time. Nor can I sleep. My mind is so completely preoccupied with Uschi. I try to analyse my feelings for her.

This expedition has proved to me that basically I can do without everything — except her. She is the only person in the world that I care intimately for, and when I think of the possibility that she isn't there any more, I am desolate, bereft. I know that I am unable to reveal the extent of my love for her; it has taken this separation to show me that.

Contrary to predictions, the first plane flies in a day later. I breathe a sigh of relief. We can go.

Suddenly in the distance, I see the summit of Nanga Parbat above the clouds. The pilot is heading straight towards it. There is the Rakhiot Peak and there, nearby, the Moor's Head; immediately above it, the Silbersattel. This is the plateau at a height of 7500 metres, a glacier of several square kilometres, where the 1934 tragedy began. The summit team thrust their way across these very slopes, and from there it was not far to the top! A narrow snow and rock crest leads over the fore-summit to end at the Bazhin Gap. Behind it stands the main summit — a snow-crowned pyramid. It drops away on all sides like the layered tiles of a roof. The lower part of the massif is hidden in mist, but the top is completely clear. We fly over the ridge to the south. Suddenly the Diamir Flank is to our left. I tremble all over. It's not agitation, it's as if some force were passing through me. I feel that I am in contact with this face, even through the oval windowpane, across the many kilometres between. I am an integral part of it and it of me. I know then that I shall return. Some power compels me to rise to my feet. I seem to hear someone saying *'tike'*. Then I am myself again.

Marching-in in 1973 I employed only three porters, for the return journey through the Diamir Valley I mostly kept only two.

We glide over the foothills to the south. I turn and gaze back intently. Nanga is no more to be seen.

BLACK LONELINESS

Almost exactly four years later, in 1977, I find myself once more on the road to Nanga Parbat. This time my young brother, Hansjörg, is with me. He has spent several months wandering around India before joining my Dhaulagiri-Expedition in Kathmandu. Now, on our way home, we

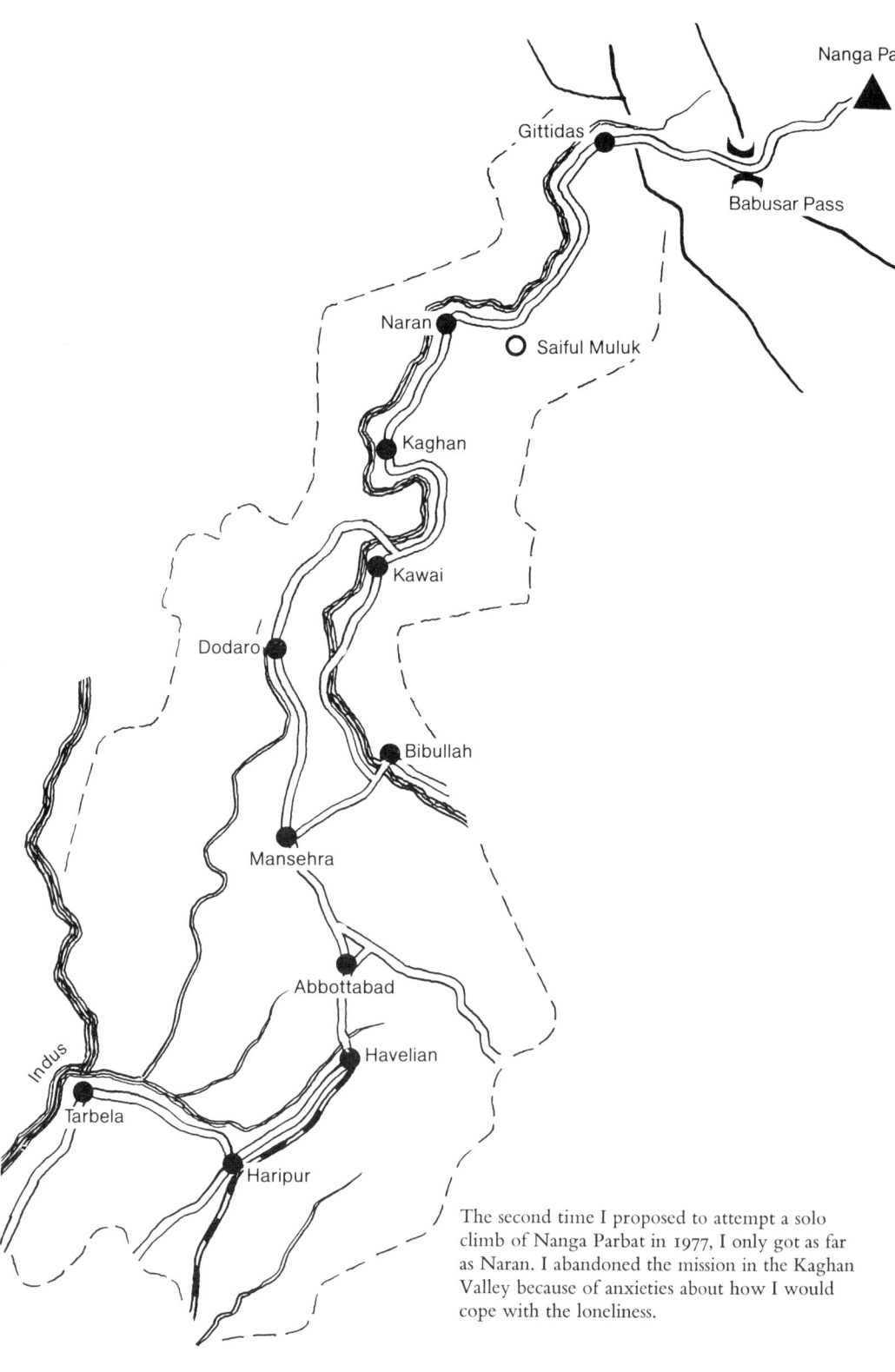

The second time I proposed to attempt a solo climb of Nanga Parbat in 1977, I only got as far as Naran. I abandoned the mission in the Kaghan Valley because of anxieties about how I would cope with the loneliness.

NANGA

plan a detour to Nanga Parbat. The idea of climbing an eight-thousander alone is still very much with me. This will be my third attempt. My second was on Broad Peak in 1974, but now, for technical and personal reasons, I want to have another try at Nanga. Its rock spurs and compact glacier system reach right down to the green valley floor, so the danger of falling into a crevasse on the approach is consequently slight. Despite the fact that the height gain from its base to its summit is greater than that of most other eight-thousanders, I still feel instinctively that this is *the* mountain for a solo climb. There may be no rational grounds for such a conviction, but emotionally I am sure of it.

This time, however, I do not get as far as on my first attempt. Suddenly, as we travel through the Kaghan Valley, I am overwhelmed by such bleak despair that we have to turn back. Soloing an eight-thousander has become in an instant a matter of no import; Uschi, I now know has left me for good and the passion I felt for this project has dissolved in a wave of indescribable loneliness.

Through sleepless nights and by day on the road, as I gaze blankly around at the sparcely-wooded ridges, all I can see is the image of Uschi walking away. She doesn't cast a glance at me. Whatever I do, whereever I go, wherever I look — there she is, going in the opposite direction. I watch as she grows smaller and smaller until she vanishes completely or I awake from my dream. On the journey home — in the aeroplane, in the hotel — these feelings never leave me. And sometimes I come to her and say that I don't ever want to leave her again, this time I'll stay at home. But she doesn't answer, and a feeling of infinite sadness tears me apart. Perhaps, I try and tell myself, my anxieties will prove unfounded, but it is weeks since I have heard a word from Uschi and the despair will not leave me.

At Munich Airport she is there to meet me. For the final separation. It's what I have known all along, but not wanted to believe. Now, with the brute force of an avalanche, everything collapses around me and in the same instant I am filled with a sad weariness. No more anger. No more self-reproach. The loneliness alone endures. I look across at her and it is as if those mysterious turquoise eyes shatter me into tiny pieces. Quite clearly I can feel that there is an emptiness within me, that she has

SOLO NANGA PARBAT

taken everything away from me. Everything. And I know that she has the strength to go wherever she wants to go.

The shock of finding myself suddenly alone and empty drives me into a tangle of emotions. Months pass and I no longer know what I do. I don't sleep, I have no control over myself at all. I feel her presence far more strongly than I have ever felt anyone else's. Even after our divorce. I exhaust myself in an endeavour to cling to her. Something, quite independent of my own will, binds me to her. I tell myself, 'Let it go. Find a new direction.' But it doesn't work. Somehow I know — this is the end. There are moments when naked despair breaks out of control and all I want to do is to die. I make a sudden decision to go to Nanga Parbat again this summer, 1977, and make another solo attempt. I *will* kill this loneliness, or let it kill me.

Women are immeasurably superior to us men. Not only can they bear children, they are more outgoing, not so wrapped up in themselves. This truth hits me when I am so hopelessly lonely, that I fear total disintegration. Death becomes the final prop for me in this state.

An awareness of my own death is in the forefront of my consciousness as it was seven years ago when, after the traverse of Nanga Parbat, I crawled semi-conscious, famished and frostbitten, down the upper Diamir Valley, my brother lost. I can leave now with no regrets; can abandon everything that was once important to me and go away for ever. I have no other designs; without dreams, without hope, I want to go far away.

Where is my self-confidence? Does it depend entirely on her, on Uschi? Is she the only one who can give me comfort? In my debilitated condition, I am once more gripped by a terrible fear. My thoughts are tangled and disjointed. Yet all at once the knot is unravelled: I know I only do it as otherwise this fear would kill me. I will pack.

My passport is in order, I have enough money, all the equipment I need for my solo climb is in the cellar. It's all ready; all I need to do is go. And that's what I intend to do, to go!

An hour later I have everything I need for my suicidal mission laid out neatly in front of me: rucksack, packframe, two cameras, a piece of rope, a small bundle of pegs and a few ice screws of course, an ice axe and

NANGA

crampons, sleeping bag, tent, altimeter and compass, the old Nanga Parbat map ...

Looking at it all in my living-room, I suddenly burst into tears. I lie on the sofa and weep. For a long time I lie there motionless, and know that I won't go. Again I am filled with deep sadness. I am not going. I know for certain that were I to go now, I would die. The idea of voluntary death is familiar enough to me, and never before has the wish to flee from everything I have known and desired, been so strong as it is now. I am tempted by the idea of exercising my last free choice, trusting my fate to a deadly game. My own death is my own business after all! But then I realize the fallacy of my argument. My own business, yes, but not hers.

Half a year goes by. I am not as single-minded as I was. Sometimes I go one way, sometimes another. With the result that I make no progress at all. It is as if I want to mark time, and I feel lost and aimless.

I let the idea of climbing Nanga Parbat on my own hang fire. Meanwhile, perhaps I would like to go to Mount Everest. Or perhaps not. Out of this uncertainty I do manage to get myself to Mount Everest in May 1978 and to concentrate on a single objective. And when the time is right, to make for this ultimate objective, to reach the summit of the world without an oxygen mask.

Returning home after the climb, I know that in six weeks I shall set off again for Nanga Parbat.

Whether in the meantime my feelings for Uschi have altered slightly, I don't know, I only know that it is now possible to live again.

Something has changed, of that I am sure. More than ever, I am determined to live as I feel I must; to do whatever it is I like doing, provided only it doesn't disturb anyone else. That is the only ethic I recognize. And I get very upset and irrational if anyone else tries to disturb me. From this point when I become more like myself again, I cease thinking in contrasts. So that I no longer divide things up into good and bad, right or wrong, but am content to simply accept what happens without wanting to understand or analyse everything. In the same way that I feel that I am only one half of a natural pair, so I feel that besides the obvious 'me', there is another side to myself. But I don't try and work out what this other side is.

Nanga Parbat towers over its surrounding summits on all sides. The Diamir side is especially impressive seen from the heights above Bunar.

I now want to prove to myself, by myself, what it means to be alone. And that's the reason I am going to Nanga Parbat. I don't tell anyone else about my plans and what I am thinking. This time I don't want to go to see if I will survive or fail, I just want to go.

It is impossible to grasp how high Nanga Parbat soars above the rocky floor of the Indus Valley, it outstrips its neighbouring summits by more than a thousand metres.

I am no different than I was — the old loneliness is still there, the terror of being on my own — they are the same, but I do feel a new sense of equilibrium.

As I make all the most important preparations, these are the sensations I feel. I know that this trip can help me rediscover my own soul, and I prepare myself for an ascent to the limits of human potential.

SOLO

What is the point of doing any more now, my father asks, as do several of my friends. Just back from Everest, it can't be necessary to set off again right away. Necessary — no, but possible, I think to myself. 'But you've done all there is to do,' people try to divert me from my purpose.

NANGA

'I haven't exhausted all the possibilities yet,' I answer, but they don't understand. Who could believe it was not a question of seeking some new mountaineering sensation, but much more one of launching myself into an unknown world. What makes me shudder is not the thought of the solo climb but the vision of spending a lifetime doing what I have had to do in the six weeks between Mount Everest and Nanga Parbat. Having to answer the same question a hundred times over, that's what I cannot bear; I feel that I will go mad if I don't quickly do what I've always wanted to do. I am not prepared to wait until the evaluation of the Everest expedition is ready.

'A solo climb of Nanga Parbat will diminish your Everest success!' How often people said this to me! And similarly, 'And then what? Once you've reached the top, you can't go any further. Or do you want to stay up there and meditate?'

No, I only want to be myself. In Europe I can't get away from the blaze of publicity any more. I am interviewed, presented and put on show.

I am called a 'Supreme Showman; a product of my time, Someone who knows what price he can exact for exceptional achievements, and how best to drum up fresh publicity.'

The friendly admonition, 'You'll burn yourself out too quickly,' bothers me only fleetingly. I shrug it off, I want to make my own decisions where they concern me. And when I experience envy and ill-will at the hands of those who like to call themselves mountain-lovers; when suspicions are peddled; or the Everest success is doubted, I treat it as a joke. My lifestyle is criticized as 'frivolous for a climber'. The 'high moral value of conquering the summit' seems to me ridiculous.

'Someday even he will conform,' I hear my 'good old friends' whisper. 'He's well off financially now after Everest.' Despite that I want to go my own way, even if it kills me. I don't want to shrivel away under this mound of how-do-you-dos and handshakes. All the eulogies and all the royalties can't satisfy my hunger for life.

In these six weeks I have not had much quiet time for reflection, otherwise I might have been off and away before this. Between interviews it is only with great difficulty that I keep a grip on reality. Everything seems so colourless and washed out.

SOLO NANGA PARBAT

I don't intend to submit to anybody in future, not even myself. I can't live my daily life like other people. It would finish me. That is why I go my own way; only when I'm doing what's right for me, can I feel strong. I don't know where this strength comes from, and I don't try to explain it; it's enough that it's there, I use it. Till now I have found my full strength only in wild gorges, high lonely valleys and high mountain country.

A year ago I worried myself, looking for a meaning to life. Now I just accept it as it is — in all its ugliness, craziness, irony — as it comes. Sometimes that way all my questions are answered, if I don't think about them. Should others come to torment me, I put them aside and go to Nanga Parbat. I have just reached the conclusion that I hold the answer, I alone.

I don't know why this idea of a solo climb has grown so strong again. A year ago I would have given it up once and for all. I felt I was too weak for it and indeed, too old. My separation from Uschi had thrown me into such a deep depression that I no longer knew at all what I should do.

In the meantime of course I haven't forgotten Uschi. That I can never do, nor would I want to. Even if softened by time, my feelings for her are still very much alive. Sometimes when I wake at night after I've been dreaming, I feel very lonely. In the beginning it was painful everytime I woke up, like the parting itself. When I came to terms with living on my own and accepting my fate without regrets, the despair and self-pity left me.

Perhaps I had been taking myself much too seriously and that is why the separation hit me so hard. Until I could put it all behind me, my life was in total chaos. No, I don't want to blot out her image altogether, nor do I cling to her as I once did, but I know that perhaps I can never again love a woman as I loved her. I don't mean in degree, but in manner. More or less is not important; it's the *how* that counts.

It is now the end of June. I am walking through Munich at midday I keep looking at the sun and it makes me almost cheerful. I blink and it seems to me as if I was looking beyond the cumulus clouds above, straight up to 8000 metres. I believe I can tell the correct altitude by the colour of the sky.

NANGA

I have ceased to dwell on the sadness of my life and reassembled its scattered pieces.

Later, as I drink a coke in the Marienplatz, I idly watch the people going by and become very enthusiastic with my idea. Then two men and a girl come and sit by me, obviously recognizing my face. It turns out that they are all climbers and well informed, and they ask a lot of questions.

'Aren't you frightened of going to Nanga Parbat alone? The very idea terrifies me,' the girl turns the conversation round to my new objective.

'Frightened? Of what?'

'Don't you ever feel uncertain and doubtful?' one of the men wants to know.

'Sure. I used to a lot. Less so in recent years.'

'You don't enjoy fear then?' asks the other.

'No — if I do feel fear, I run from it.'

'What about other people who go to eight-thousanders. How do they feel?'

'It varies. A lot of Japanese for example climb faces that are crazily dangerous — but they're prepared to take the risk. I wouldn't. If I think something is too dangerous for me, I don't go any further.'

'You like to know beforehand that you can get up?'

'I wouldn't put it like that. Even if I wasn't sure, I would always look for a way up.'

'So — uncertainty, then, it excites you?'

'Oh yes — and possibility. Of course I'm still young. When I get to sixty or so, and am not so strong physically, then perhaps the Matterhorn will be a problem. Whether it will still excite me then, of course I cannot say here and now. But I imagine it could.'

'Do you, do you think, always set yourself unrealistic goals?'

'Perhaps.'

'And what is your answer to critics who accuse you of sensationalism?'

'It's true I have been accused of having a fondness for sensation. But it's not my mainspring. If I wanted to satisfy people's needs for sensation, then I would only take on objectives that I knew I could succeed with.'

'The Diamir Flank, though it's prone to avalanches, doesn't actually appear impossible anywhere. The middle section is very steep and there

There are so many photographs of Nanga Parbat that most climbers would recognize it from a picture. But it is hard to imagine what it is really like.

are a lot of shaky seracs up there, but there are the ribs of rock, and one of them seems to offer a possible way up. It's harder than the Rakhiot side, but shorter, and there are safe camping sites on the rocks.'

The man certainly knows what he's talking about.

'It's ideal for a solo climber, the Diamir side, but so far everyone who has tried a direct line has failed.'

'You just want to be the first again!'

'If I knew someone had already soloed Nanga Parbat, then perhaps I would try a different eight-thousander. It is the uncertainty that attracts me more than anything else, that gives me the impetus. If I knew it could definitely be done, I wouldn't find it anything like as attractive.'

The girl shakes her head in bewilderment.

'If someone shows me the way to do something, that takes a lot of the mystery away. If I knew nothing about the world at all and from a small child had been allowed to explore it for myself, I wouldn't need to climb Nanga alone now. But we are all spoonfed.'

After a pause I continue.

'If a child were to dig this Coca-Cola tin out of the sand, he would be solving mysteries for himself, and that is how it is with me and Nanga Parbat.'

'But it's all so *unimportant*! Life isn't a game, and we can't spend a whole lifetime just digging up coke tins.'

Being unable to explain my actions properly, makes me feel somewhat helpless. There's no need to explain of course. I have simply made up my mind to solo Nanga Parbat because this is the sort of decision I am prone to make by my very nature, or because I have the necessary time money and inclination to do it. Not because I somehow feel it to be important. And it doesn't matter to me that it isn't important.

'It isn't of any value to humanity — to climb Everest without oxygen equipment or to solo Nanga Parbat,' one of them said.

'Who says it has to produce anything?'

'A lot of money, perhaps, for you!'

'If I went to Everest with that as a motive, I wouldn't have come back — I'd have perished for sure.'

'And what if on one of your adventures you someday lose your legs from frostbite, or lose your eyesight, what if you are crippled for life?'

'If it was unavoidable, and if I were blinded, say, in both eyes, I don't think I could go on living. I would stay up there.'

'What kicks do you get from climbing high mountains? Is it a sexual thing?' the girl asks.

'You're not serious?'

'Yes — I want to know.'

'I don't climb or write for any kind of sexual gratification. Definitely not. I don't think the question arises in any competitive or performance sport.'

'Climbing, as it's generally understood, is a dangerous activity. Is it as dangerous for you? Or do you know you won't fall?'

'I'm fairly confident I won't fall — but it's still dangerous.'

'Does your enthusiasm for mountaineering go so far that you would sacrifice a personal relationship for it?'

'That's not a question you should ask, just like that.'

'Why not?'

'Because, by asking it, you are not accepting me as I am.'

These three obviously knew of my divorce, but could have no idea, however, how helpless and alone I felt standing there. My life is not one-sided, different from theirs, perhaps, but in no way easier.

Once I made up my mind to go to Nanga Parbat, a lot of the little worries that had been niggling me in connection with the idea of a solo climb, evaporated. It was the same with my marriage. I thought a lot about it before coming to a decision, and I made it as the person I was then. And once I come to a decision, I keep it, so far as it depends on me. Uschi and I, however, were separate individuals, and it happened that our relationship became inflexible with time and it was as if we were both walled up in it. I didn't know at the time we separated that my lifestyle was really that of a single person. It's only when you live alone that you can go your own way completely, make your own decisions and take full responsibility for them.

During the five years of our marriage, I took on a lot then too. Uschi often came with me. I have never given up my way of life, not for Uschi and not for anything else. My three table-companions acted as if they felt I was evading the question. I carried on, 'No — there isn't any conflict. I wouldn't be me any more, if I wasn't able to climb mountains.'

'With Everest behind you, are you now looking for even more dangerous objectives?'

It seems like an inquisition. And I don't feel they understand me at all. For them, this town is a place to remain in, and they feel quite happy here in their inactivity, even indefinitely. But it would drive me mad. No rugged countryside, no wilderness; I have mountains in my blood — that is not enough, and at the same time, too much.

I can wander around town observing people for hours. I do it often and I enjoy it. But after a while it drives me up the wall.

To be frightened, that won't be too bad. What I find hard is when people keep telling me what I should and shouldn't do. Nor is it easy to give up a world I'm used to and find another for myself, in order to be able to carry on living. I have clung desperately to everything for too long and in the process worn myself out and those to whom I have held fast. Now I want to play my own game, without hesitation, without regret, and I want to play it, even if on Nanga Parbat I lose.

One of them brings the conversation back adroitly, 'If you look at pictures of Nanga Parbat from a climber's point of view, the north-east side appears to present relatively harmless snowfields and glaciers, the north-west face, on the other hand, is a difficult ice and rock face. You could make a comparison with Mont Blanc, the standard route from

NANGA

Chamonix on one hand, and the steep climb from the Brenva Glacier on the other. Why choose this steep, difficult face?'

'Just because,' I say and stand up. At that moment it doesn't bother me any more whether these people approve or not, or if they think I've gone mad, in a couple of days I shall be on my way.

With twenty kilos of hand-baggage I arrive at Munich–Riem Airport on 30 June, 1978.

Buhl, Diemberger, Schmuck and Wintersteller had about 2000 kilos of expedition luggage when they set off for Broad Peak in 1957. Peter Habeler and I took 200 kilos when we went as a two-man party to Hidden Peak in 1975. With one-tenth of that I am now about to set out alone.

The journalists ask all the usual questions, and yet this time I feel more can be read into their voices.

'How far are you prepared to go this time?'

'That I can't say. I shall be careful. I've got no worries at the moment.'

'Are you sure you're capable of doing what you've set yourself to do?'

'No — I have, for instance, failed on three of the eight-thousanders that I've tried so far, but I'm not unhappy with that.'

'These experiences you seek, can they only be found in climbing, or do they exist in other spheres of life?'

'They may be translated into all spheres of life.'

'But no other sphere is as risky as mountain climbing.'

'Hardly any other demands such a degree of honesty about oneself, particularly in the final stages. I might fool myself down here over some things, but not up there. If I were to over-reach myself at 8000 metres, I wouldn't survive.'

'What would you do if you couldn't climb any more?'

'At the moment all I can say is I have to go to Nanga Parbat alone.'

'Do you think that this solo climb will be the high point of your career, that it will be significant?'

'The question of significance doesn't come into it when you're up on the mountain — it's only here I can ask myself that question.'

'Do the inhabitants there, think as you do?'

'No, they wouldn't contemplate a solo climb like this. The people there live constantly in the state of mind that I perhaps only achieve close to the summit of Nanga Parbat. It would never occur to an Asian — Hindu or Buddhist — to climb such a high mountain. He seeks to elevate himself spiritually; one way and another he can "transport" himself up there. Who's to say I'm not up there now, even though I sit here?'

'Ah, now — you're talking about two different things! One way you have to physically climb the mountain, put the actual distance behind you, the other you do in your mind.'

'They seem the same to me.'

'Have you always had this sort of perception, can you remember, before you went climbing?'

'I don't think so. Except as a child. I have the feeling that these days I have gone back to reacting as I did as a child. I remember lying in the sun when I was about five years old, time seemed to slow right down and I was unable to distinguish properly between what was real and what my imagination. I found that very fascinating.'

'Most of the things people do are imitative, not original or independent, and that goes for what people are too. What is it *you* want out of life?'

'I believe that although we are the same basically, we are also very different. There is a right way of life for each one of us. Whoever finds his own way and has the courage to follow it can't go far wrong. It's just that most people get talked out of being who they really are.'

'We are always being persuaded to be what we're not,' someone remarks bitterly.

'Too true! There are a lot of people who seem to think they have a say over my life — religious and social teachers, politicians, gurus, media-men, editors . . . but despite them all, I do what *I* have to do.'

'Is your lifestyle in conflict with religion?'

'I have no religion. I am religious, sure, in my own way, but there's no conflict because all ways of life are equally valid so far as I'm concerned. Anyone who can keep hold of his religion has been very lucky — or unlucky.'

'You'll make it!' and, 'Don't give up!' are the last messages my friends call after me as I go through the passport barrier. I know, too, that there are some whisperings to the effect that this time I've bitten off more than I can hope to chew; for though no-one comes out with it directly, the

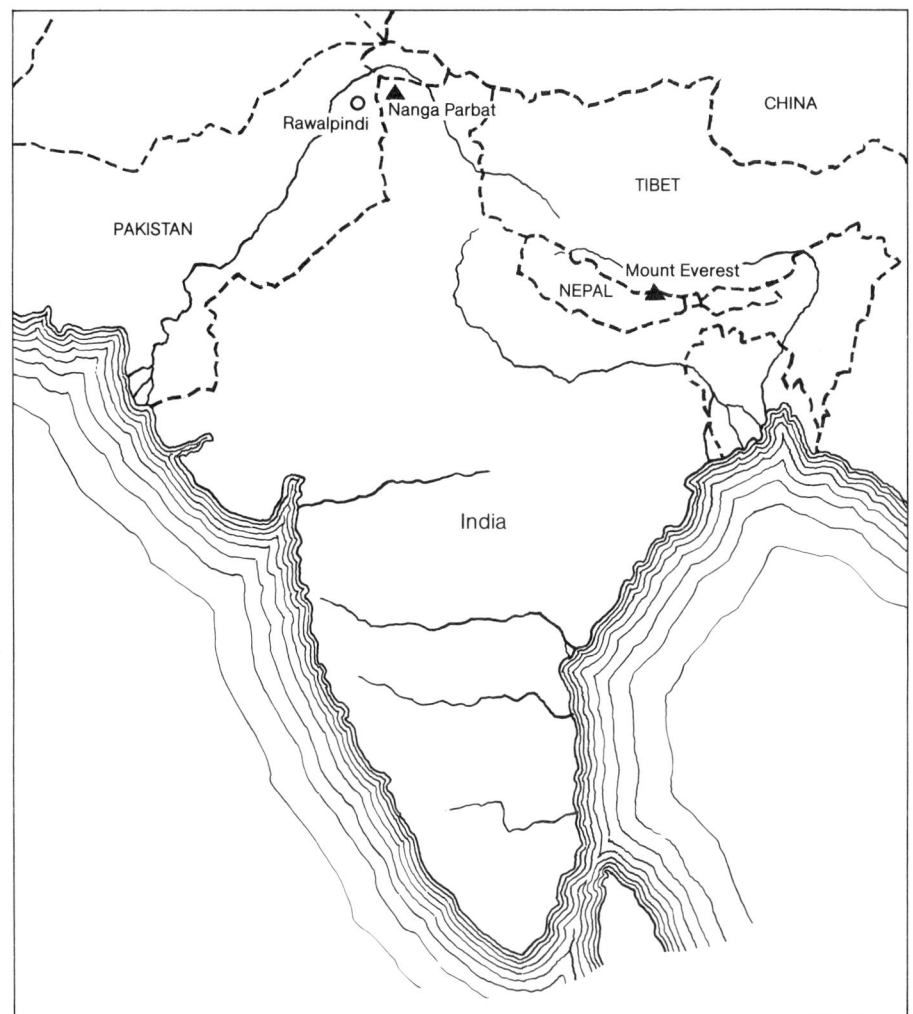

Nanga Parbat is situated exactly within the bend of the Indus.

insinuation is there that I am on some suicide mission. As if my life was no longer my own. I certainly am not planning my Waterloo, but I do want to choose my own path. That is my right.

As I fly over the Alps towards Milan, I suddenly have the feeling that my life is somehow continuing down there in the little Villnöss valley which has been my home for thirty-three years. This second life, rooted in a South Tyrol village community, is spread out below me as an alternative possibility; wooded slopes, Dolomite peaks, mountain hamlets.

Between this expedition and the last, things have not been easy for me there. And this just because I said publicly that I didn't climb Mount

SOLO NANGA PARBAT

Everest for any country — not South Tyrol, not Italy, not Austria, but only for myself. Nor was the climb for any organization and certainly not for any political party. Truly, I did it just for myself. To be motivated by personal desire obviously gives offence in a land where everyone seeks idealistic justification. There is little sympathy for my mode of life in South Tyrol. I often feel like an adventurer from olden times, an adventurer who had forsaken everything he loved for adventure, and now, after many great experiences, was coming home; everyone was joyful and forgot they had wanted to stop him from embarking on his travels. If on his return, he doesn't take the festive hullaballoo too seriously, guarding his successes like a treasure, then dubious motives are immediately attributed to him.

For those who stay behind, things haven't changed since the days of the first big expeditions. They still cling to such sentiments as expressed by Willy Merkl: 'Himalaya, Abode of Snow, Rooftop of the World, the coveted goal of all who hear the mountain's call. The depths of the sea, the desert steppes, the Arctic and the Poles, even the world of the air — all have been explored and conquered by man's restless spirit. Earth's last hidden secrets lie undisturbed on its highest pinnacles. But man will not rest till he has solved all the mysteries of the world, will thrust into the unknown, and it is this desire to know all, that gives him the astonishing impulse of his deeds.'★

Many people need to attribute a significance to everything. All too eagerly they take over the mountain they want to climb. They don't experience any sense of wonder. The many expeditions to Nanga Parbat in the thirties, set off with their instructions to conquer, swastikas emblazoned on their flags, and vows to struggle for the Fatherland inscribed in their hearts. It was the same way, a short while later, they also departed to war.

'As we once more looked up to Nanga Parbat, to the glittering crest high above us, all sense of bitterness against fate was loosed from our hearts in the presence of a deeper understanding. Splendid though it must be to victoriously return home with this mighty mountain as a prize, it is

---

★ Willy Merkl, *Ein Weg zum Nanga Parbat* (p. 209).

It is impossible to convey to the layman the scale of an eight-thousander. I could not visualize the sheer size of Nanga Parbat myself, even though I had already climbed it. Left, in the foreground, the Moor's Head; in profile the South-east Ridge.

nobler still that a man should lay down his life for such a goal, to be an inspiration for the young hearts of those following after.'*

For me, Nanga Parbat remains mysterious, inscrutable, even though by now it has been climbed six times. To me it is very important to scale it alone, and I have the greatest respect for it. But now, too, it is the long march to the foot of the mountain which attracts me – the mentally undemanding progress, being able to step right into the panorama.

I look out of the aeroplane window. In a way I am glad not to be down there at home any more. It may be my house standing down there on

---

* Fritz Bechtold, *Deutsche am Nanga Parbat* (p. 64).

SOLO NANGA PARBAT

the hill of St Magdalena, but it does not seem home to me any more. I do not know exactly when and how I came to lose my sense of belonging there, it had always been so strong till now, but sometime during this summer of 1978 I have become a gypsy. At home everywhere – and nowhere.

As soon as one ceases to cling to things or to worry about oneself and others, when one no longer strives towards progress, towards building things; if one can cut free from the past – then one doesn't need any home beyond one's own mind.

Perhaps I ought never to return to this valley, to my past, to other people's opinions.

Half-asleep, images tumble through my consciousness. Death is tacitly included as a real possibility in my plan. A measure of curiosity is there too, and the question of whether I can endure it. I am also looking for evidence about myself. And to put substance to a dream. And then again, this solo climb, it's not a real climbing problem at all, but a figment of my imagination. I want to climb a mountain as I see it in my mind, not as it is. By foreswearing technology and even a climbing partner, in my fantasies, I am making an altogether different mountain out of it.

Perhaps by escaping from the loneliness of everyday and facing the ultimate possible loneliness, there is a hope that I might lose my fear of solitude.

Twice I will have had experience of being the complete soloist, the absolute solo-traveller. Once in the summer of 1969 when I climbed the most difficult faces in the Alps on my own – the North Face of the Droites in the Montblanc area, the Philipp–Flamm–Route on the Civetta, the Solda on the North Face of the Langkofel, the direct route up the slabs of the Marmolada di Rocca – and now, in 1978, en route for Nanga Parbat.

In 1969 I worried at the prospect of bivouacking on a rockface. I possessed the ability and endurance to climb these very hard routes on my own, without technical aid. But I knew what I lacked was the psychological strength to sit in the middle of the face on a narrow ledge waiting for night to end. And this is the only reason that I did these solo routes so fast, each in a single day, until the first ascent of the South Face of the

NANGA

Marmolada di Rocca. I would mostly start climbing in the late morning in those days, which gave me a chance to get over any qualms that may have built up during the night before. By the afternoon I would be back down in the valley again. Whilst I was climbing on the face, I was concentrating completely and there would be no room for any anxiety or doubt. Solitude, which I was perhaps not mature enough to bear in the beginning, didn't therefore arise.

On Nanga Parbat it will be different. There I must be on my own on the face for one, maybe two weeks. And the higher I climb, the more conscious I shall be that a retreat is getting increasingly more difficult, if not impossible.

The art of walking lies in going the right way;
that's where your friends are and where you are strong;
let yourself go in the direction you feel able to go, if at all possible.
If you find your own way and travel by it, strength, direction and
  purpose are yours,
and nothing and no-one can hold you back.

Mohammed Tahir, Baluchi from Queta.

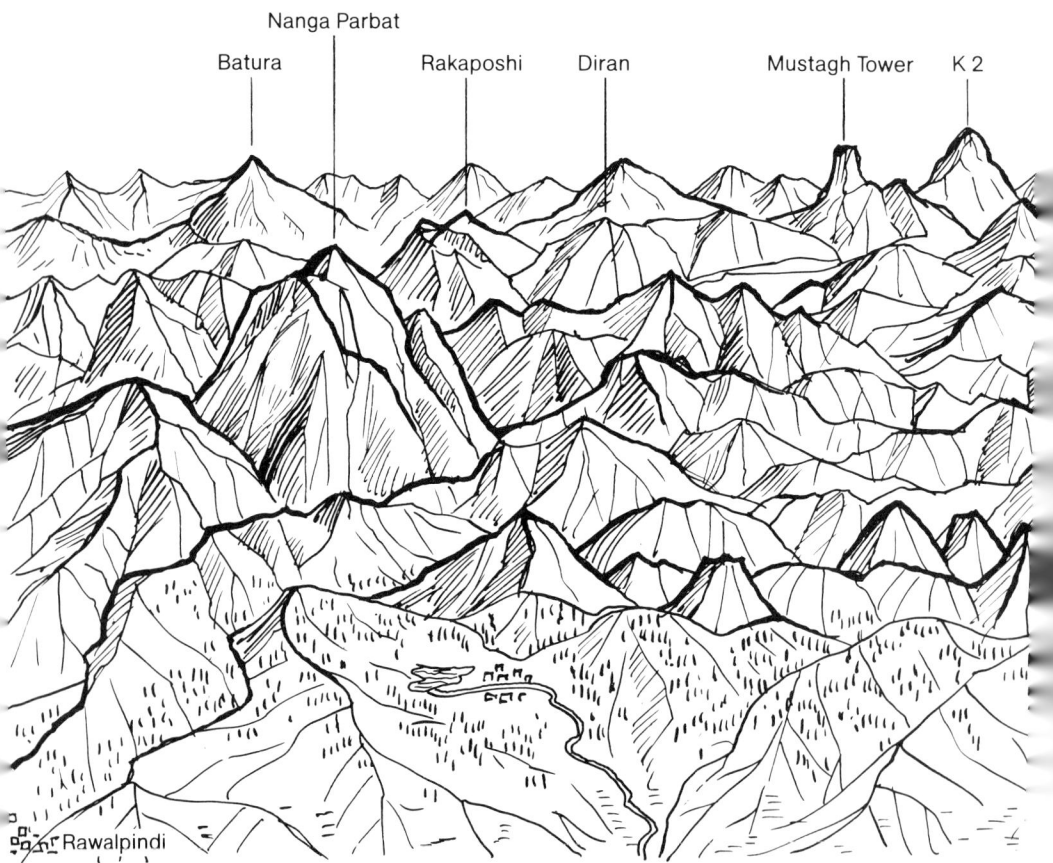

TIKE

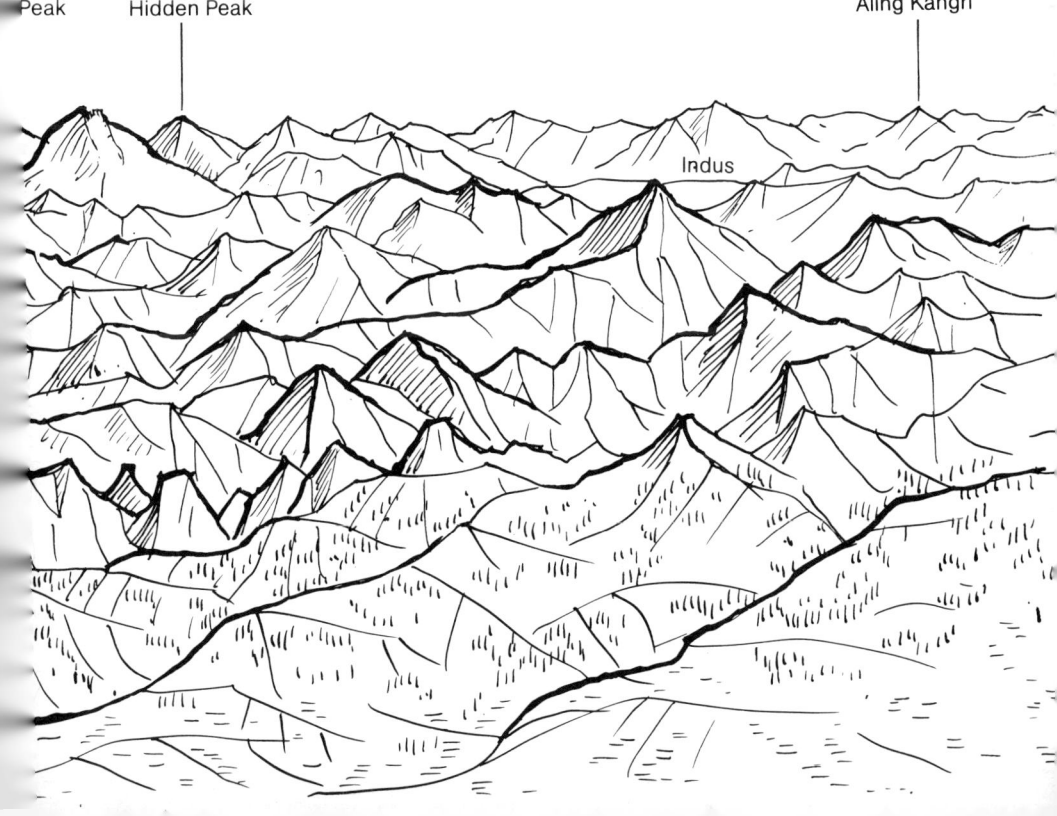

In 1978 the Karakorum Highway, the road built through the Indus Valley by the Chinese, was still closed to foreigners, and consequently I was granted permission to walk into Nanga Parbat through the Kaghan Valley. In Rawalpindi I hired a minibus and took this as far as Balakot. From there it is still another 100 miles to the Babusar Pass, and a further week to Base Camp. In Balakot I loaded our expedition boxes onto a jeep, including the rubber mats and bowl purchased in Pakistan, and we drove intermittently until we were beyond Burawai. The gravel roads were often buried in mud. Three times I had to make a detour around old cones of avalanche debris, and finally the road was completely blocked. Even though the three of us hardly knew each other beforehand, we soon became a little team. Mohammed Tahir, known as Terry, was assigned by the Government of Pakistan as Liaison Officer to accompany me; Ursula Grether was in charge of the medical side of the expedition. From Naran we made an excursion to Saiful Muluk, a mountain lake about 3000 metres above sea-level, and spent a beautiful day there (next double-page). The water is beautifully clear, herds of cattle and sheep graze all around, and the peace is exquisite. The Kaghan Valley is one of the most beautiful of all Pakistani valleys, similar to many high valleys in Switzerland.

The lower Kaghan Valley is green, wooded and rich in fruit; there are mangoes, apricots, grapes. Higher up, in Gittidas, Besal and Burawai, the valley grows wide and barren, like the mountain pastureland in the Alps. Often the villages there are only occupied in the summer, and nomads put up their tents in the valleys. One of these nomads, a huge man and very extrovert, took over our transport arrangements from his campsite to Besal. It was already getting dark when a few miles from Burawai our jeep got bogged down. We unloaded everything, the jeep went back to Battakundi, and I looked around for a place to camp. Not far from the road I came upon a nomad family. I went towards them and the old man immediately offered me a piece of chapati. We got into conversation and I asked him whether there were any horses or porters anywhere in the district. He cast a glance at our luggage and said it could all be carried on a single camel. For the two miles to Besal he wanted 100 rupees. That was too much! I tried to bargain. Had I paid fifty rupees a mile throughout the journey, the trek-in would have cost not 5000 but 10 000 Deutschmarks. The old man, however, a Baluchi, wasn't prepared to haggle. That impressed me. He then really did load all the boxes and sacks onto one camel, even sat himself on top, and that same night, by moonlight, we reached the little village of Besal.

The approach route through the Kaghan Valley to the Diamir Base Camp.

MY DREAMS REALISED

Ten years ago I was overawed by the achievements of Hermann Buhl and Walter Bonatti and daunted by such prospects as the eight-thousanders or Aconcagua South Face. Nowadays nothing seems to me more unattainable than my own dreams. I used to follow the aspirations of others, but now it is my own dreams I pursue. Before I ever imagined going myself to the Himalaya, I read the reports of Welzenbach, Merkl, Bechtold and Bauer, of their expeditions to the mountain which was nicknamed Germany's Peak of Destiny:

'Again there is a deep blue sky arching over us as we ride out next morning down the valley beside the wildly foaming Khirin River. After a long while we reach Godai, and then, around the next bend, we see it for the first time – Nanga – the mountain of our dreams! The view of the South Face is breathtaking; with a height of 5000 metres, it is truly the greatest precipice in the world. We have to crane our necks right back to take in its awesome sweep up to the snow-trimmed summit. One thing is sure – this is the grandest spectacle we have ever seen. Or put another way, never have we felt so small as now before the unique bulk of this mountain.'*

In 1970 we climbed this 'awesome' face, with a large team and many tons of equipment. Forty whole days my brother Günther and I spent on the face before we reached the summit.

During this time my conception of Himalayan climbing changed. I began to see the eight-thousanders differently than I had pictured them from expedition books. At the same time I dispensed with many of the habits I had learned from other high altitude climbs. Even then I had a presentiment that I would renounce the customary notions and practice by which these mountains had always been tackled in the past. That would be the only way I could rediscover the explored Himalaya, could fashion my own ideals and discover a purpose for my life.

* Willy Merkl, *Ein weg zum Nanga Parbat* (p. 189).

SOLO NANGA PARBAT

At this moment this solo climb is my cherished ideal and that is why I am bound for Nanga Parbat. The pleasure this gives me might be hard for a non-climber to understand. But it gives me heart, strength, a calmness of mind and a singular feeling of lightness. It makes the incomprehensibility of my life comprehensible. I am acting, doing, what I always wanted to do without having to weigh it all up; what was before and what comes after are cut away. Moreover, I am doing it because it means something to me — everything. It is not important whether I succeed or not; I am doing it. That alone suffices.

As a solo climber, I too am bound by the Pakistani Mountaineering Rules, requiring me (as far as Base Camp) to be provided with medical aid and a liaison officer. I must also pay the full fee of 1200 dollars for an expedition permit — a hefty whack out of my budget of 10 000 DM. Terry is the 'Major', Ursula the 'Doctor Sahib' of the expedition.

Ursula Grether, a medical student in her last year, has offered to accompany me to Base Camp, although she is not herself a climber, and to wait there with the liaison officer until I come back.

Ursula is one of those unusual girls who can be as at home in the Hilton as in a tent. For years she has travelled the world alone; she loves to wander through wild mountain country. She got herself to Base Camp on Everest by her own initiative, and now in Rome we have met again to fly together to Pakistan.

We are both travelling as tourists, she with her personal luggage and the most essential medicaments, I with the climbing equipment and a few kilos of food, including hard peasant bread, soup concentrates and ten cartouches of gas. All the other necessities we will buy in Rawalpindi. On the direct flight Rome–Rawalpindi we receive preferential treatment. We are allowed into the first class section and spoilt with champagne as we talk over the adventure ahead in detail for the first time.

We arrive in Rawalpindi in the middle of the night and immediately find a room in Flashman's Hotel, even though we had not booked. Rawalpindi, 170 miles north-west of Lahore, is like a Wild West town without the cowboys: wide, straight streets, overhead electricity lines, regular facades. The clamour of hooting cars, cheerful jolting carts, street traders, bustling women (veiled and unveiled), all rob the town of any sense of order. It lies at the foot of the mountains, but despite that is very hot in summer.

Islamabad is the new capital city of Pakistan, lying seven miles northeast of Rawalpindi. Here the climate is more pleasant. This satellite town has grown up in the space of a decade and is characterized by big administrative offices, beautiful parks and streets, as well as shopping centres.

We spend the next ten days travelling backwards and forwards between Rawalpindi, where we are staying, and Islamabad, where all the bureaucratic formalities have to be transacted.

We are allocated Major Mohammed Tahir — whom we call Terry — as our escorting officer. He is a warm-hearted and gentle man of twenty-eight, six feet four inches tall and weighing more than fifteen and a half stones. He comes shopping with us and to the Ministry of Tourism. Whenever there are any problems, he is there. That is the marvellous thing about expeditions to Pakistan, the authorities are so dependable. Herr Awan of Mintour has been in his job for several years and always gives good advice. The liaison officers are keen, well-educated young men. I get on well with Terry and he is proud to have been assigned to us; he appreciates my idea of a solo climb.

Ursula and I in the meantime have moved to the cheaper Miss Davis Hotel and are very comfortable. Several Japanese expeditions are staying there, as well as some French climbers. Whilst we are there we learn that a Swabian Expedition will be on the south side of Nanga Parbat at the same time, and another group from Upper Austria are hoping to repeat the Kinshofer-Route on the left-hand section of the Diamir Face. I will therefore keep to the centre of the face and that way I can guarantee that nowhere on the mountain will my route overlap with the others. In other words I want to get from base to summit and back again without any measure of assistance, as with traditional solo climbing in the Alps.

In Rawalpindi Ursula and I mostly eat local food. The Pakistanis cook in *ghee*, a kind of melted butter, or in mustard oil or vegetable fat. Meat, fish and vegetable dishes are heavily spiced. Sweets are usually very sweet, and prepared with saffron, rosewater and *kewra* (distilled from flowers), and decorated with edible silver icing.

The evening before we leave, we order *Tikka kebab*, bite-sized pieces

SOLO NANGA PARBAT

of meat, marinated and grilled. As a sweet we have *Shahi Tukray*, a pleasant-tasting bread pudding. Pieces of bread are baked, then cooked in milk or cream, sweetened with syrup, flavoured with saffron, and decorated with almonds and pistachios.

'What gave you this idea of wanting to climb Nanga alone?' Ursula asks suddenly.

'I have already dispensed with many of the aids available to climbers. On Everest we managed without oxygen as well. The next logical step is to do without a climbing partner. I want to be completely autonomous.'

'Yes — but human beings are not autonomous.'

'True — I know that. I used to miss my mother very much when I first left home. I was dependent on her for a very long time; the last time I came to Nanga, I was dependent on Uschi. Even when my eldest brother left home to go to school (I was the second eldest), I used to pine for him for a long time afterwards — despite the fact that we were nine children.'

'Is it that you can only break new ground if you do make yourself autonomous?'

'Perhaps that's it.'

We were given the Kaghan Valley and the Babusar Pass as our route for the march-in; not the easiest way to Nanga Parbat for there are a lot of passes to cross. Added to this it is a region known for its bands of brigands. The Kaghan Valley is ninety-five miles long and rises to a height of 4000 metres. The scenery changes all the time and the bracing climate attracts even Pakistani tourists. During the summer months sightseeing tours are arranged up the valley, but at the moment the upper part of the valley is still impassable.

We're off! At ten a.m. on 12 June our truck leaves Rawalpindi. The old Ford minibus looks as if it will break down before it finishes the journey. In the simmering heat we travel up hill and down dale. Midday sees us in Balakot. We transfer from the minibus to a jeep and after a short rest continue on our way. The road goes high above the river on the left-hand side of the valley. We drive along steep-sided ravines. The sun is so high in the sky that the mountains to our right throw no shadows. There are massive mounds of avalanche debris to cross shortly before we

I spent most of the journey through the Kaghan Valley lying on the roof of our jeep. That's how I got my sunstroke.

reach Naran. That makes for a tedious delay, unpleasant in this heat. The sun burns down unremittingly.

Naran is one of these typical Pakistani linear villages, half the houses are grouped around the road in urban fashion, the other half scattered amongst the fields and on the barren slopes. We stop in front of a fruit store and I leap out to buy three mangoes, as well as a melon and some pears. Numerous flies crawl over everything and at first that's all you notice. If you touch the fruit they fly in a thick swarm all around. The bazaar opposite sells chapatis. The cook fetches me two, hot from his oven in the ground. We eat them in the street. I love chapatis, I've had them every day since I've been in Pakistan. There are a lot of people in the bazaar so our jeep has to go slowly through the crowd. For a couple of hundred metres, shanty buildings, no taller than head height, line the road, bright with wares. People here are in no hurry. They gossip in the middle of the road while the traffic builds up. A young boy leading a pregnant donkey through the bazaar holds a portable radio to his ear and he is so light on his feet that it looks as if he is dancing to its music.

In the late afternoon the jeep goes on ahead and we stroll to the rest-house. There are green meadows all round it with a couple of grazing donkeys. The house itself is a fairly bleak building of stone and concrete, only the window frames and the roof timbers are made of wood and painted green. This four-cornered 'box' with its neatly-pointed walls looks out of place against the dun-coloured hand-made dwellings of the local inhabitants. The staff and the chef are lined up in the middle of the

SOLO NANGA PARBAT

enclosed area in front of the resthouse as if they had been waiting for us. The little grass plot is bathed in warm sunshine and everything looks friendly; here too the smell of chapatis wafts across to greet us. As we get closer I see a crowd of people around the entrance and to judge from their clothes they are tourists from Rawalpindi or Karachi or Lahore. Standing there stiffly in their colourful costumes in front of the hotel, the staff look very decorative compared to the Parkistani tourists. As if they had been grouped there merely to be looked at — an exhibit from an earlier age.

We go up to the people and as Terry talks to them they all become very animated. Hugs and greetings. One man comes out of the low building and calls out, 'Hallo!'

'Good morning', I reply and it's only when everyone laughs that I realize that it's evening already. Obviously we are the only foreigners here and they are pleased to see us. We are given two rooms and order an evening meal for eight o'clock.

'Mutton with chili sauce?' asks the cook politely before he disappears.

'Tike,' I reply, with chili.'

A short while later Ursula and I go out into the main street again. I glance back at the resthouse before we plunge into the dust and throng again. It certainly does look out of place, especially with its chimney smoking. The shadows have now grown longer and the men are slowly closing up their booths. One is sprinkling the street in front of his stall with water from an oil can. Ursula beams delightedly, 'What a fantastic atmosphere. Crazy.' I look briefly at the time and then at the sky. Six o'clock in the evening. Cloudless. We have put a good distance behind us today, I am very pleased. 'Tike,' I reply to Ursula. 'If it goes on like this we'll be in Base Camp within a week.'

'Tike,' she grins, expressing her pleasure.

Tike is an Urdu word that can mean almost anything — yes, or quite right, I like it, or everything's fine. Whenever one says it, one is more or less agreeing with what went before, confirming or also denying. *Tike* can also mean the right way.

We have been travelling now for fourteen days, but still we are in no particular hurry. We make a side trip to a lonely lake at Saiful Muluk, where we spend a couple of hours wandering around it, drawing solace

The trip to Saiful Muluk, a mountain lake above Naran was an adventure in itself. We often had to make up a road of stones over avalanched snow.

from its still waters and the mountains on all sides. I test the strength in my legs by making a couple of jumps up and down; then I sit down again and stare into the water which mirrors the sun. I couldn't stand it any more in Europe being torn the way I was, and that by people who believed they knew what was best for me, behaving as if my life was no longer my own. Now I have to get myself together again if I want to survive on Nanga Parbat. I feel that this, my wildest alpine dream yet, belongs to me alone. It is not a question of setting myself some deed to do that will still be talked about in days to come. I know too well that everything gets forgotten and that that is right and proper. What concerns me is the here and now. Sitting here like this, I ask myself whether I now fulfil all the necessary conditions to enable me to climb this mountain alone. Alone from the very bottom to the very top.

Since coming back from Everest I haven't done any further training, nor do I do any at all now. Life is too precious to me for such mortification, spending days on end, weeks on end, months on end practising doing something I don't like in order to be able to do something else better.

SOLO NANGA PARBAT

I jogged and climbed a little purely for fun so far as time allowed. Otherwise I was very busy working. So I wonder if I have the necessary psychological reserves for seeing this Nanga Parbat venture through?

I ask myself what it was that caused me to fail before. I don't know the answer to this day. I fled at the prospect of a loneliness I had never experienced. It was the anticipation of fear that frightened me, of not being able to make the right decisions up there. Frightened, too, of cracking up under the loneliness. My three earlier attempts failed by virtue of my mental unpreparedness; I ran away from myself. But the idea itself would not leave me, it took a firmer hold than ever the more often I failed, the greater my mountain experience became. So when, during the Mount Everest Expedition in the spring of 1978, I finally received permission from the Pakistani authorities for this solo climb, I was glad.

Loneliness is something that lurks within all of us; it is not something that attacks us from the outside. I know intuitively that only when I learn to utilize this force for my own purpose, will I be able to climb Nanga Parbat alone. The ability to reach the summit, I know I have; the instinctive climbing sense to select the right route and the necessary endurance to climb a great face alone for days on end, many days on end – that too I possess.

During the rest of the approach journey, I spend most of the time lying on the jeep roof, or running alone along the gravel road, watching the people we pass on the way. They regard us as if we came from another planet. Without having prearranged it, Terry and I have evolved a kind of catch-phrase, a motto, that we shout to each other over and again whenever difficulties arise. 'Nobody can stop us!' Nothing and nobody can stop us. This sentiment expresses our commitment. Not mine alone, although it is I who wants to go to the summit, but all three of us whom chance has brought together.

The valley grows more grandiose the higher we go, and the traces of avalanches across our path become more frequent. At Burawai, some 3000 metres high, situated at the junction of two streams, they have closed the bridge. I proffer 100 rupees and we are allowed to cross at our own risk.

When it becomes impossible for the jeep to go any further, we load

It was already evening by the time we crossed the Babusar Pass. Ursula and Terry were dead beat and I was ill.

all our expedition luggage onto a single camel, and a tall white-haired nomad escorts us to the next village where we can get horses. Very late that night we reach Besal. It lies some 3150 metres high, encircled by barren mountain ridges. We find shelter in a tiny stone house.

It is noon the next day before we get back on the road. It has taken an eternity to fetch the three horses from the pastures and saddle them up.

As I walk ahead of the baggage train along the east bank of the Lulu-Sar Lake, local people pass in the opposite direction. It rains. By the time we reach Gittidas, I am feverish. We reach the last resthouse at the foot of the Babusar Pass, standing in a meadow on the valley floor. One look and we decide to cross the pass straight away, despite my heatstroke. Although the Gittidas resthouse is so massively built that it resembles a fort, it is nevertheless uninhabitable. The upper storey has been destroyed and the outer wall bears the traces of numerous bullets. It isn't a place one approaches willingly.

The Babusar Pass presents me with fewer difficulties than the trek on to Babusar itself, when I have to stop frequently to be sick. We stumble on through the night and in the darkness the sharp black summits rise like threatening walls around us.

It is pitch dark when we do finally reach Babusar. Two dozen houses

SOLO NANGA PARBAT

in a clearing. Here and there fires burn and somewhere a dog barks. Terry, who has hurried on ahead, has found us shelter in the prison and prepares a hearty welcome for us. We sit on our mattresses for a long time celebrating the successful crossing of the pass I was quite ill first thing this morning, now I am completely kaputt.

There is an endless palaver the next morning paying off our horsemen from Burawai. They complain because they will never see half of their fee which had to be paid to the agent before setting off. It's a shame, but we cannot help that. Our expedition purse is not bottomless. They don't understand that. They are sure we wouldn't make such a long and expensive journey if a handsome reward of gold or silver didn't await us at the end. They think we must be on the trail of some sort of precious stones and inexhaustibly rich.

Near our camp in the prison is a patch of grass, fifty metres wide and 300 metres long, with a stone wall around it. It is the polo field. Every little village has one. This game, dangerous for both rider and mount, has been a traditional sport in these mountain regions for hundreds of years. It has little in common with the polo played in the posh clubs of Europe and America. There is only one rule: the game can only stop when one or other side has nine goals. The chase after the little white ball is kept up without pause by the riders on their agile little horses. Each team tries to force its opponents against the stone wall and bring them to the ground. In their enthusiasm for battle, the fanatical players often hurl their polo sticks against the skulls of their adversaries, rather than the ball. It is horsemanship straight out of the days of Genghis Khan.

We travel down-valley some way in a jeep the political agent has put at our disposal, then we continue on foot. At first we pass through a high-level wood, later across barren slopes. The bushy broad-leaved trees progressively give way to pines, and in between, hamlets surrounded by lush maize fields, apricot trees and vines. By a series of steep steps we progress deeper down into the valley until suddenly, all plant growth ceases. The surrounding slopes can only boast the occasional tuft of parched grass and the temperature betrays that the Indus itself cannot be far distant.

The porters call a halt in a gorge, an unpleasant spot, and here we are forced to camp. It is a place subject to enormous variations in temperature.

TIKE

As soon as the sun disappears behind the mountains, a cold wind rolls down, to be immediately supplanted by a warm wind up from the Indus Valley. This to-ing and fro-ing doesn't stop until late in the night when it finally balances itself out. I cannot drop off to sleep for a long time because of the constant rumble of the rocks in the riverbed.

Already, after these few days on the march, I have abandoned my usual eating habits. I often miss mealtimes altogether, just eating and drinking whatever is to be found at wayside stalls. Anything pleases me. If there is no beer available, then I don't need beer. And I walk when I feel like walking. The only thing that irks me is our dependence on the porters.

At this time of year it is hot all over Pakistan. We walk through a region where water buffalo graze beside the road, a region where it's not unusual to see rock caves used as dwellings. More frequently I have to pause to allow a herd of sheep to cross the path.

I used to suffer badly in such heat, so that I could hardly breathe and got very tired. Now it no longer affects me like that.

The valley is bordered on both sides by low weathered ridges. Everything has a desert-like appearance. And yet, here and there, by skilful irrigation, little green paradises have been created. Our luggage becomes so dusty it looks as if it has been dragged through the sand for weeks.

I think, if we had not been in the right frame of mind, we should have given up already on the journey in. It used to be possible to travel by road from Rawalpindi to within three day's march of Nanga Parbat. This route is now closed for political reasons. The Chinese, who have built a road between China and the Pakistani heartland, don't for the time being allow foreigners to use it, and so we have to approach Nanga Parbat by making a detour from the south. We are assigned porters, half a dozen wily Pakistani farmers, and they know exactly how to extract the last rupee from us!

We don't want to break into the food we had bought in Pakistan for the time being — jams, cheese, cornflakes naturally, and sugar and milk. So we live off the land.

The heat in the Indus Valley is now unpleasant. The path clings high to the steep slopes, and we travel along until suddenly one of the many terraces brings us close to another village. So it goes, up hill and down hill.

The Indus Valley was open to travellers in 1970 when we went to the Rupal Face; in 1978 foreigners were forbidden to go there. The South Face of Nanga Parbat ranks as the highest rock and ice wall in the world. To the left, above the gentle slopes (across which the Schell-Route runs), the so-called 'Direttissima' leads up the central section of the face.

The scenery here, in all its harshness, is elemental. People, like animals, live exposed lives. By our standards they are poor. But they don't see it like that. A hill-farmer is happy enough if he can rest in the shade of a rock. This terrace culture is all he knows, and he believes things are good if they are as they have always been.

The children wear hardly any clothes. Their skin is encrusted with dust and they all have fat little pot-bellies. Despite this being the dampest time of year, clouds of dust hover over the villages. This region — with the Chinese province of Sinkiang to the north, Afghanistan to the west, and to the east the wide plains of the Punjab — lies in the Monsoon's shadow.

Under a spreading broad-leaved tree I stop. This is a good camp site, I think, as I take off my boots and socks. The meadow hasn't been mown but the grass is quite short, soft, almost silky. I wash my feet in an irrigation ditch. Only when I hear something cracking and rustling above my head, do I notice a small boy sitting up in the branches picking leaves. The foliage and the grass smell damp and warm. I sit under the tree, whose roots stick up out of the ground like a little hill. The gentle breeze that earlier had driven thin banners of smoke over the village, reaches me. It brings with it the scent of the huts as well as the warmth of the rocky hillsides all around. There is a bright shimmering in the air, the light before dusk. Flies and ants crawl over my legs. The boy keeps throwing down thin leafy twigs. I lean back against the trunk of the tree and close my eyes. Overhead the leaves whisper, a blade of grass tickles the sole of my foot. I feel reborn.

After a short while I doze off. In the complete peace something remarkable happens. It is as if my thoughts had acted like a dividing wall and now, without my noticing or smelling or hearing anything, everything surrounding me has gently percolated through into me.

Whoever has found his path and follows it, keeping straight ahead and climbing up, fulfills himself. The straight line which, projected to infinity, closes into a circle, is the right way. That I know from mathematics.

A little later I dream. I see myself crossing the final pass and straying across endless snowslopes. I feel as if I am battling upwards against the

During the march-in we had to change the porters from district to district. This meant that we frequently had to find them footwear, redistribute the loads, and settle on a daily hire rate. According to the length and difficulty of the particular stretch, the porters wanted from sixty to eighty rupees per man per day. At these rates a bearer was earning ten times what a Pakistani city workers could get. After the crossing from Gushar to Muthat — over a 4000 metre high pass — I met two men in the Bunar Valley who had been with me on earlier Nanga Parbat adventures (below). I immediately took them on as porters and they came with me as far as Base Camp. But although we knew each other well and you could even say we were friends — it made no difference, everyday we would have to renegotiate terms. Bartering is part of the way of life of a Pakistani hill-farmer and if you are not prepared to do it, you are laughed at. In Gushar we had more trouble with porters. They wanted a full day's pay for the two hours to Hoe (next double-page). To show them that I meant business, I picked up my own rucksack and went ahead to the next village to hire new porters there. Terry stayed behind with the luggage and followed on in the evening with the new men.

I spent a peaceful afternoon in Hoe (previous double-page) found a campsite by an irrigation ditch and took some photographs. At first only the children came to look at us, but when word got around that a 'Doctor Sahib' was in the party, old men and women came also. They asked Ursula for advice and medicines. Mothers brought their children encrusted with grime. When Terry arrived in the evening and was able to act as interpreter (he spoke excellent English, whereas our Urdu was limited to only about fifty words), Ursula was at last able to accept patients: eye disorders amongst the elderly, malnutrition and rashes amongst the young, bronchitis, and goitres — these were the most common disorders. Though the women were at first shy of me, they approached Ursula without any inhibitions. In fact they were often quite cheeky. Although many of them were treated, their men would not let us photograph them. That is typical with Muslim wives. They went back into their little single-storied huts and peeped surreptitiously out of their dim doorways. The children, on the other hand, were much freer and uninhibited, almost unafraid. Some of them would have happily come with us to Base Camp. They brought us lassi (sour milk) which was a favourite drink for Ursula and me; Terry preferred chai (unsweetened tea).

storm, and am almost falling victim to tiredness, desperation and hallucinations, when I stumble out on to a rock pinnacle which proves to be the summit, engulfed in a wave of explosions.

When I wake up, it dawns on me that though I am searching for something, this something is not death. To look for death would be to look for nothing.

Under a clear sky, we settle down on the still warm grass for the night. Near our campsite is an irrigation channel from which rises a cool, pleasant vapour. The porters, who have been on strike, don't come until almost evening; again things become noisy and lively. They look a very rakish lot, most of them carrying some kind of shotgun – English muzzle-loaders or weapons of Russian design. But only a few have more than a couple of cartridges in the wide sash around their chest.

WALKING ALONE

It is early morning. The floor of the valley is still in shade but the sun catches the mountain tops. We walk on, down into the gorge and up the slope on the opposite side in the direction of the pass. The valley opens to the west.

The farmers have loaded our baggage onto a few donkeys but make slow progress on the steep, stony terrain. Ursula and Terry, too, have hung back. They get on very well together, these two.

At midday I scramble over barren, steep slopes where only an occasional tree can be seen. The sun beats vertically down, burning the back of my neck. I wish I had a big sunhat or a turban like the local men wear.

From where I am standing I can see far into the valleys. The deep depression of the Indus Valley must lie behind the several small mountain ridges. Far below, the stream shines in the valley bottom like a bright narrow ribbon.

I have a raging thirst. There's not a spring anywhere, nor can I find a patch of snow. It is still a good two hours to the top of the pass. My eyes

TIKE

follow the sheep tracks up the hill, and I walk on again. There are no paths here, only animal tracks. They vanish in the next hollow and can only be made out again higher up, where they run together to form a sinuous white trail.

Despite heat, tiredness and the many flies, it seems easier now to keep on climbing than to stop and rest. How nice it is to walk all day! I have only a small rucksack and nothing to carry in my hands. My attentiveness is attuned to the route and its surroundings and I experience deep contentment simply by moving upwards with no definite urgency. I do enjoy walking alone, even for hours on end. I don't like it if there's someone close behind me, or in front. When I'm walking I don't care to have to talk, and when route-finding can be left to instinct, I don't need to bother to think.

The few tufts of grass between the stones are quite parched; the air shimmers above the rocks. The flies, which were a nuisance earlier, have either gone or I have become insensitive to them. I seem to be able to feel this landscape with my eyes, my ears and my nose.

I stroll peacefully and evenly — not fast, just steadily, and I don't quicken my pace until I am within a few dozen metres of the pass. Then I run the last stretch and arrive at the top gasping for breath.

'There it is! Nanga!'

It is as if all my composure is wafted away by the first gust of wind up from the other side of the valley. I tremble with excitement. Physically I stand here on the brink of an abyss, but spiritually my whole being seems to be transported towards the east. I cannot think clearly. In a kind of hypnotic trance, all I notice is this mountain, behind a bank of clouds, towering over everything.

Then the cloud curtain lifts from the end of the valley and Nanga Parbat's North-west Face stands before me in its complete majesty. I am more than thirty kilometres from the peak and yet it seems unimaginably high. Behind the facade of dark foothills, the snowfields and hanging glaciers gleam so brightly they hurt my eyes. I scan every feature of the sweeping face. A direct route to the summit seems unthinkable.

More clouds enshroud the mountain — as if already I had glimpsed too much. Then they too drift away. I look at the chain of mountains to the

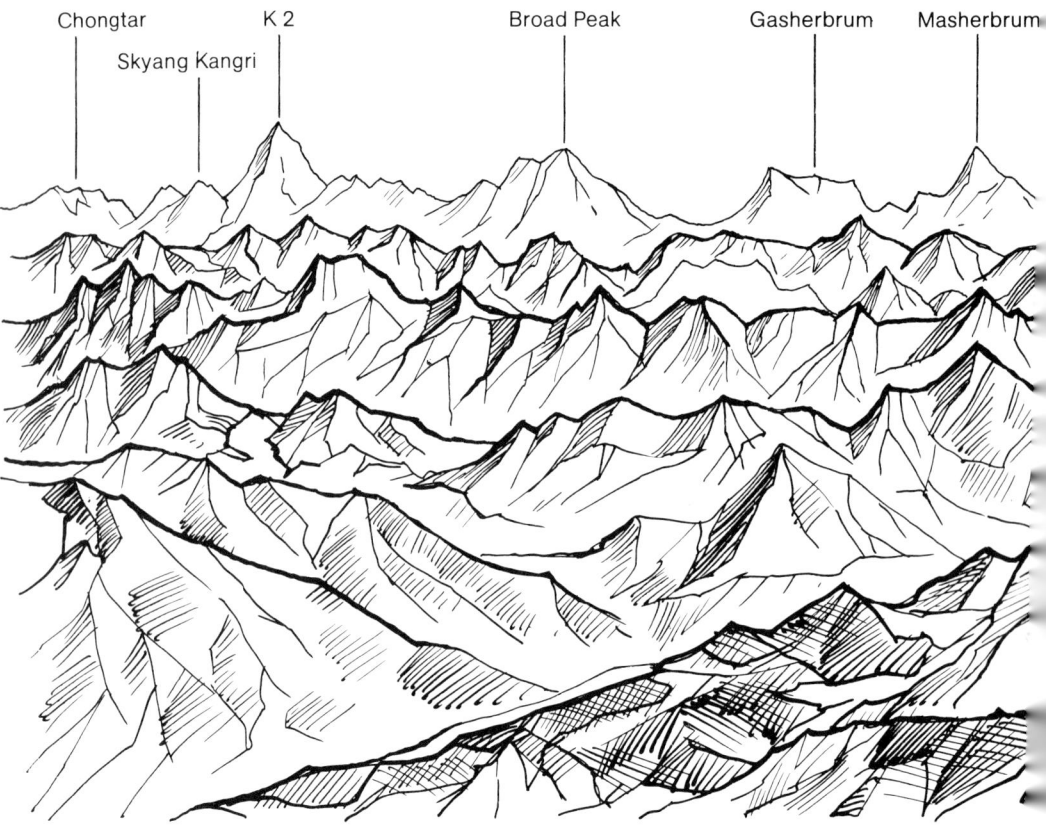

east, believing they will offer a sense of scale to the scene, yet the Diamir Face still seems steeper and higher than I remember it. It is still a long, long way off.

The country below me is grey-brown; beyond rises a range of wooded hills, and behind them, two more mountain ridges, rocky and aloof. Above them all, unreal, towers Nanga Parbat.

From the pass I can clearly distinguish which are fields and which villages, without being able to make out individual dwellings. The very layers of air seem different above the villages to those over the fields. There is a stream, curving away, and, far to the left, the deep trench that is the Indus Valley, the way I have always come in before.

'This time I'll make it!' I say to myself, not without pride, and have to laugh at the proverb that leaps to mind, 'The pitcher that goes too often to the well gets broken.' If it could only be filled in so doing!

I am sweating and the cold wind chills me, so I take shelter on the east side of the pass out of the wind. In my mind I anticipate the route to the summit. I know I will be called to make decisions that, though hazardous,

seem to me attainable. To search for possibility within impossibility, for the reality in the dream, that is something I understand. Isn't it fantastic that one can trace lines on a mountainside without setting foot on it at all?

I continue sitting alone on my hillock, no-one to disturb me, contemplating the mountain chains and ridges — the longer I watch, the more they seem to grow before my eyes. I rummage in my rucksack for the telescope and study the upper section of Nanga Parbat. How clear the air is, even though it is afternoon. In my thoughts I am already high on the mountain, having forgotten the pass on which I sit. What a crackbrained notion this solo climb is!

The arrival of the porters jolts me from my reverie, and immediately dashes my high spirits. Am I no longer to be able to walk ahead on my own and dream? It looks very like it. The porters squat silently around, looking down into the valley; the donkeys, too, flop down, breathing noisily. As Ursula and Terry come to join us, I point towards Nanga Parbat. For a while we don't exchange any words. The view from the pass exceeds all expectations. To the left of Nanga Parbat one can recog-

When I saw Nanga Parbat again in 1978, its height and steepness came as a shock.

nize Buldar Peak and Chongra Peak. In the distance Rakaposhi and Haramosh shimmer on the horizon. Ahead of us lies the descent into the Bunar Valley, already deep in shadow in the evening light. Directly opposite stands Diamirai Peak and behind it tower the steep ramparts of the Mazeno Peaks with their gigantic buttresses. The steep-sided Diamir Gorge is already dark. A cold evening wind blows on the ridge. We must find a way down into the valley before nightfall.

Everything that lies in the rain-shadow on the north-west side of Nanga Parbat is almost arid. The deeply-incised Indus Gorge below us is a gigantic canyon. Nanga Parbat with its satellites, rising beyond, is a compact massif of gneiss, isolated from, and at right angles to, the main Himalayan chain. Its main crest runs from south-west to north-east, and from it, side ridges project northwards to the Indus Valley. To the south the mountain plunges abruptly to the Rupal valley, a massive face so steep that it can only sustain a thin covering of ice interspersed by ridges of rock. This barrier marks the end of the true Himalayan arc.

The descent into the Bunar Valley proves to be very steep. I don't find any water until I reach an avalanche cone at the very bottom. Once more I am out in front, alone. I feel as if I had managed to get outside my body. Pleasurably tired, I no longer talk to myself but, passing between the high stone walls to the first village, all manner of pictures conjure themselves before my mind's eye. I am not focussing on anything in particular but seem to take in everything. Simultaneously I perceive much of what's happening around me, and it becomes part of me and I of it — and I am content to leave it at that without question. Is it the tiredness or my mental abstraction that gives me this sudden feeling of floating? A couple of times I am unable to feel my feet and it is as if they have cut themselves adrift and are continuing to walk independently. I can hear hundreds of different sounds from the fields of ripe corn to left and right of the path from the village. The crunch of my footsteps merges with the other sounds.

I approach a meadow to find my companions already there; I must have made a detour and taken a long way round. Children gather about us, offering apricots. An irrigation channel filled with clear sparkling water gurgles past. A good place to camp. Tomorrow we want to get to the start of the Diamir Valley, one of the poorest and harshest valleys of all. I remember it well from 1970 when I came down the west side of the mountain and then out by this valley.

We are living now with the valley people and they, understandably, don't really know what to make of us. When they hear we have a 'Doctor Sahib' with us, they bring their sick children, and Ursula does whatever she can to help them. She gives advice and medicines, strokes and comforts them.

Every day brings a tussle over porters for we are obliged by the 'Mountaineering Rules' of the country to change the men from district to district.

Once we are sorted out, our way leads first along the west bank of the Bunar. A side gorge coming down into the valley can only be crossed by going round higher up. Then we cross the river by a bridge. The road bends and there ahead of us lies the village of Diamiroi. We are still separated from the group of trees that surround the village, by the deep incision of another gorge. Crossing a steep, sandy patch, which is actually

I was no longer a stranger to the people of the Diamir Valley, and I knew them too apart from the few children who had been born since 1973. In this valley there are perhaps fifty families living in the four little hamlets. During the whole summer, almost the whole family with all their household belongings and their goats and sheep, move up to the higher pastures at the foot of Nanga Parbat. There they live in primitive shelters under enormous rocks (next double-page). Only once in a while will someone return to the valley to weed or clear the irrigation channels, or mend the paths if a storm silts them over yet again. In these high pastures, the local people live on unleavened bread, milk, honey and dried apricots, which they grow and dry down in the valley. Even though they own hundreds of sheep and goats, as well as a few cattle, they rarely eat meat. When we were there it was Ramadan, the Muslim period of fasting, and therefore they were not allowed to eat anything during the daylight hours. As foreign tourists we didn't have to abide by these rigid laws, and Terry, too, was not bound by them as he was travelling over a period of several weeks. Our porters, on the other hand, who were carrying loads of twenty or more kilos, didn't eat anything until after sundown.

It was essential that we had a 'Doctor Sahib' on the expedition. At that time Ursula had not completed her studies, but was experienced enough to take care of the medical needs of Terry and me, and to give the local people not only drugs, but also good advice. I don't know how I would have got on without her; even during the approach, I suffered from heatstroke and was very weak on my legs for several days. Terry, an exceptionally strong young man, had a bad attack of malaria in Base Camp as well as a stye as big as a hazelnut on his left eye. Also I may not so easily have got over the frostbite in my right thumb, suffered in my summit attempt, had not Ursula administered injections to keep my circulation going. I subsequently only lost the skin from the thumb-tip. And it turned out that the local people even visited us in Base Camp if they needed medical help. They weren't bothered by the climb up to the foot of the mountain, and often brought eggs or chapatis as payment. On the way home Ursula had the opportunity to see many of her patients again and reassure herself that they were well. As she herself said, she learned more in six weeks on the expedition than in a whole year at university!

In Pakistan a porter usually carried a load of 20 to 25 kilograms. This man took a double load.

the cemetery, we scramble up the terraced slope. Wooden pipes carry the water collected from streams higher up. Above them arch the boughs of nut and apricot trees.

There are few people to be seen. Not surprising, for most of the men are away at the high pastures and their wives have to remain out of sight. Sometimes when I turn a corner unexpectedly, I manage to catch a glimpse of a shadow in a doorway, a woman lurking to try and get a peep at us strangers.

We stop for the night at the start of the Diamir Gorge. The next morning we wait for our porters who have been staying somewhere in the village, hoping they won't refuse to climb the steep track. They arrive at daybreak.

The west side of Nanga Parbat is seldom visited and there is an air of secrecy about the almost inaccessible gorge coming down from Diamir. Our porters, to start with, have real misgivings about it, but are eventually persuaded to try. Having fervently beseeched Allah for aid, the march continues without too much difficulty.

By evening we reach Ser, a little settlement in the upper Diamir Valley. The icy ramparts of Nanga Parbat and the Mazeno Peaks glitter above a long bank of flowering sweetbriar, and as the sun goes down, the trapezium

TIKE

shape of the summit glows red over the violet-dark valley — an unforgettable sight!

Knowing that we can't go back now, the porters try and wangle more money out of us.

I know the people up here and they know me, so it is easier to come to some agreement with the porters. This is now the fourth time I have visited the valley. The first was in 1970 after what was for me a dramatic and tragic traverse of Nanga Parbat, when I lost my brother, Günther, I staggered down here at the end of my strength, already half-delirious. The following year I returned to try and find some trace of my brother, then in 1973 I was here again to make my first attempt at a solo climb. This, therefore, is my fourth visit. I know the valley almost as well as I know the Villnöss valley where I grew up.

Forty or fifty families live in the Diamir Valley. I know where they all live and to whom the children belong. I am only amazed how much the children have grown since 1973. The littlest ones, particularly, impress me. I recognize the men who helped me in 1970 when I could barely stand.

On the tenth day of our march we reach the high settlement of Nagaton. We have found a good rhythm and the porters no longer disturb me. We keep seeing Nanga Parbat towering above the other mountains, and the nearer we come, the more obvious it becomes, how simply enormous this face is. I have seen it often before but in my memory, after such a long absence, it had grown smaller.

How steep this face is! When I left Europe I was not quite sure what route I would take. I didn't want to commit myself. Even now I haven't yet taken a final decision. Nagaton, where we pitch our tents in the early afternoon, lies about 3500 metres above sea-level.

Smoke hangs in the air over the huts; sheep and goats run all over the place. Men stand about between the dwellings — holes in the rock the size of a room. Women peer out from gloomy doorways. There is a constant murmuring and rustling over the village, a conversation in which the bees and birds also take part. This place is so familiar to me. I know every cranny, every water-hole.

Our tent stands under a group of trees in the middle of the clearing.

SOLO NANGA PARBAT

Children creep up hesitantly and regard us with inquisitive eyes. They inspect the tent and what little equipment lies around it. Later, in the evening light, their eyes grow bigger. They run all round laughing. Where do we come from then, asks one teenager. 'A long way off,' I reply, 'from Europe.' 'Europe,' the children repeat and giggle because the word has no meaning for them. An old man with a sparse white beard wants to shoo the children away. They should leave us in peace, he says, and not keep hanging around.

'No, no, that's all right,' I assure him, 'they're doing no harm.' I have always liked children very much, much more, in fact, than adults.

The old man shakes his head as Terry explains that I want to climb Nanga Parbat on my own. He wrinkles his forehead.

'It can't be done,' he says, 'Americans have been here, and Japanese and Germans, often with hundreds of porters and a mass of equipment, and only once did a group get up. That was a long time ago. Three men got to the top, three sahibs, and Siegi-Sahib, he died on the way down. The other expeditions all failed before they got there.' He was trying to tell me that no-one could go that far alone, it was impossible.

'A man needs help,' he asserts, waving away the children who were again sneaking back into the tent.

'Help — and a lot of luck.'

'Tike,' I nod, agreeing with him but keeping my own counsel. Later it begins to rain and we quickly crawl into the tent. We ought to come into his house, the old man says, he has enough room. But we stay in the tent.

Half-asleep I dream of a vast landscape, interminably vast, yet there is no-one else there but me. A wooded landscape with hills, meadows, streams and now and then a shining lake. There is peace over the whole land like music, music coming from the grass, the air and the trees, the rocks and the water. I stand in the midst of it all — as if I had been set free.

The rain has stopped. Sheep and goats flock through my waking dreams. I lie like that for quite a while. From the diffused light now filtering through the tent, I see that it is evening. Is the mountain clear, I wonder.

'Come outside,' calls Ursula, 'it's beautiful!'

'Yes, yes,' I reply and shut my eyes again, hoping to prolong my dream. Outside everything is full of the pattering and bleating of sheep. The animals are coming back from their pastures and I take a look outside the tent. The herds are so thick they surge past like a thick and living mantle of fur. I wander up and down amongst the flocks of sheep and goats. Everything is so full of life and yet so peaceful. The magic that this place exudes, emanates from the trees, the sheep and the people who belong here. The valley, down below, is not so much a part of the spell. Nor the mountain — it is there, but what I see now are the living things and the beauty of this mountain pasture-land.

Later I sit myself down on the western edge of the clearing and gaze out into the valley. Out to the glacier stream where the stones roll, everything is so peaceful down there. There are just a few fires burning and a last band of light on the horizon. The lights in the valley below seem to tremble whilst the glow on the horizon remains constant — or is it fancy?

Terry cooks. He has brought two pieces of meat and he spices them with curry and chili. It tastes very good. The children watch us eating. They refuse to be shooed away again by the old man. I ask him whether it will be possible for him to bring up a sheep to Base Camp later on, if we don't go down again. We shall also need eggs and chickens. He nods and names the price: 400 rupees for a little goat or a lamb, thirty rupees for a chicken. Eggs he only gets rarely.

'One Deutschmark is equal to four rupees,' I mutter half-aloud, doing my sums. 'Tike!' Understood. He will bring whatever he can. Terry translates.

From just in front of the tents I can see the summit of Nanga Parbat looming out of the dusk. In this half-light it does not look especially big, above the sparse trees, but still a long way distant. It is windless in the evening calm, and so peaceful I fancy I see the first stars move. Before going into the tent, it occurs to me that I could check up on our height and what the weather is going to do. But then it seems unimportant and I forget to look at the altimeter.

Sparks rise from the little fires in front of the huts. I think about Uschi, who was here with me in 1971. It is the second time today that she has come into my thoughts. It's always in these quiet moments that her

SOLO NANGA PARBAT

image comes to me, but it is not at all painful. The feeling of having rediscovered myself makes the separation bearable. Certainly I still suffer from depression every now and then, but it does me good to think about her. I certainly don't want to forget her.

In this valley habitation stops a little above the pasture-land of Nagaton. This place really lies at the end of the world, and at the same time is a kind of paradise for the people of the Diamir Valley. It has fresh spring water, lush grass and wood in abundance.

In the morning the sky is overcast and Nanga Parbat has vanished. We walk up the valley where birches and scrub grow, it is a well-trodden track and we have no fear of going astray. Tiny stone huts huddle beneath a huge block of rock in the middle of a green meadow – just room enough for sheep and shepherds in bad weather.

The morning mist has cleared. Nanga Parbat now soars ahead, seemingly within touching distance, but quite unbelievable, as if it were enchanted. How a mountain like this can change overnight!

'I have never seen a mountain that exerts such an irresistible attraction,' Mummery wrote in a letter to his wife in 1895. What this man did eighty-three years ago is quite remarkable. The more I read his letters, the more I am amazed by him. 'Our first business,' he wrote, 'will be to get into condition. I expect we shall start for an 18 000 or 19 000 feet peak tomorrow; there are plenty about here, but mostly snow grinds. However that is good for the wind.

'I don't think there will be any serious mountaineering difficulties on Nanga, and the peak is much freer from hanging glaciers than I had expected. I fancy the ascent will be mainly a question of endurance. We are in excellent health, but our legs don't work so well as they should, so we shall devote three weeks to having walks. You may expect, therefore, to get a wire about a month from date (17 August) or a few days later.' And a week later: 'Crossed the Mazeno Pass (a native pass); crossed thence into the Diamarai Valley (uninhabited but beautiful in the extreme); glorious trees (mostly birch and pine); thickets of wild roses; heaps of flowers and undergrowth.'

On 4 August 1895, he wrote, 'We expect to make our serious attack on Nanga next week (seven days from now); it will require four days.'

TIKE

Mummery must have been sitting somewhere just where I am now when he wrote these words, and it seems to me that the anticipated my thoughts by almost a century. It was only later that he began to have doubts. Accompanied by a Gurkha, he forced his way up into the 6000 metre region, but was finally forced to abandon his attempt. 'Our chances of bagging the peak look badly enough. Collie is not keen on it, and old Hastings has managed to get a chill, so I am left with the Gurkhas. They are first-rate climbers and good men, but cannot afford the help of a real A.C. man. Well I shall soon be on my way home; you must not be disappointed about Nanga.

'Nanga on this side is 12 000 feet of rock and ice as steep and difficult as a series of Matterhorns and Mont Blancs piled one on the other.

'I should have got up, I fancy, if Ragabir (a Gurkha) had not got ill at the critical moment, and I had to see him down. There is no doubt the air affects us when we get beyond 18 000 feet.

'Tomorrow I cross a high pass with the Gurkhas to Bladarakoite Nullah. Hastings and Collie go round with the coolies and stores. If the north-west side of Nanga is easy, we may yet pull it off, but you will have a wire before this reaches you.'

The letter bore no date but must have been written on 23 August. After 24 August, Mummery and his two Gurkhas were never seen again.

In his last letter Mummery had remarked confidently that he would have reached the summit on 20 August, had his Gurkha not fallen ill. Was his confidence justified? General Bruce, who with his years of Himalayan experience, has a very discerning judgement took a more sceptical view. He thought that the two men, exhausted by the strenuous climbing of the previous days, would no longer have been capable of the effort of cutting steps for hours on end in completely unknown territory. They still had 1800 metres to go to the summit. He summed it up afterwards, 'I wonder whether Nanga Parbat will ever be climbed; it is probably as difficult a mountain as there is to tackle, for nothing but the lightest camps may be taken high, and even to get to one's camping places, the climbing is terrific. Even on the Diamarai side of the glacier, comparatively easy going ends at 15 000 feet, leaving 12 000 more of the hardest work.'

From Nagaton to Base Camp we only took a few porters and a couple of little donkeys for carrying the luggage. We had to cross the Diamir Glacier to get from the left to the right-hand side of the valley. The donkeys, although used to scrambling about in this region, found it hard going as the path was so steep and their mounds of luggage threw them off balance if they stumbled. It took patience and extreme caution to cross the glacier, which was covered in stones and rubble. When I was marching on ahead over the moraines directly beneath Nanga Parbat, with Ursula, Terry and the porters way behind, an avalanche poured down the centre of the face (next double-page). I was scared by its thundrous roar. I knew that the Diamir Face, dotted with seracs as it was, was constantly threatened by avalanches. Even so, the reality of such an avalanche is far more impressive that one imagines. This avalanche had broken off from the hanging glacier to the left of the Mummery Rib. It lasted for what seemed an eternity before the first blocks of ice reached the foot of the face. Clouds of powder snow hung between the rock pillars for minutes afterwards. The avalanche itself spilled out over the whole basin at the foot of the face, and it grew obvious to me that a 100 per cent safe route up the middle of the Diamir Face simply did not exist.

A little above the 4000 metre mark, a good hour from the foot of the face, we established our Base Camp in a hollow at the foot of the Ganalo Peak (previous double-page). Rocks lay scattered all round, some as big as dining-tables, some as big as rooms; in places the grass was knee-high and there were a few marmots living close by. We built up some little stone walls, levelled out space for two tents, and established ourselves in a homely fashion. We set up our food-store under a big rock so that we could see at a glance what we had in stock. Between three stones we even made a fireplace, although we were hardly ever able to use it because it rained so much. On the approach-march it had been so hot that the porters would seek shade under bushes, rocks, or their woollen blankets in the midday sun, but here it was mostly cold. So cold, indeed, that the water in the nearby spring used to freeze at night. After we had paid off the porters, they went back to their own villages and high pastures. We remained alone, left to our own devices, with no contact with the outside world. We had no mail-runners, no radio apparatus. The nearest telephone — a crank-operated machine — was a day's march away from Base Camp and functioned scarcely at all, so we were told.

SOLO NANGA PARBAT

This pertinent conclusion brings me back to reality. Already I am again doubting my own prospects of success.

Nanga rises in front of me like a massive cloud, with only the sky as background. I walk on.

I have a tremendous hunger for life. I want to be everywhere at once. I would love to be wandering about up there. Gone are the philosophical and moral ponderings. Systematic reasoning is not my way of working out my own salvation. This solo climb is the option for gaining experience that life offers to me. I would like to sing, dance, laugh.

In the early afternoon I run along the crest of the moraine, which stretches along the valley towards Nanga for two miles, as straight as a railway embankment. To my right it drops sharply to the debris-littered glacier twenty metres lower, whilst the other side is overgrown with thick brushwood.

We have crossed the Diamir Glacier and now approach the foot of the face. A moraine valley curves gently away to the left. From the tell-tale tracks of animals I can see I am not the first to discover this natural climbing line. The summit of Nanga is clear one minute, enshrouded the next. From the North Summit a series of prominent rock ribs radiate down the face. Several routes suggest themselves in the shelter of these. Unfortunately the Ganalo Peak conceals the view into the wildly fractured Diama Glacier which leads away to the east. That, too, must offer a possibility. The stillness seems to be emphasized by the creaks and rumbling of the moving masses of ice nearby. Uncanny forces of nature are at work here; it is easy to understand the farmers' fear of mountain spirits. In the west, the hills blur into the ever-deepening blue of infinity.

It is raining gently as I come upon a suitable campsite at something over 4000 metres above sea-leavel. It is a good spot. I can tell from the colour of the grass and the soft shadows in the gentle hollow.

'We'll stop here,' I say out loud. There are large rocks for shelter and fresh water; a jet of water, the thickness of a man's arm, gushes right out of the ground. While I'm waiting for the others to arrive, I construct a fireplace. The rain is getting stronger, so when they come we get the tents up right away, and as the porters struggle in, we pay them off – eighty rupees per man per day – and then creep off into the tents.

TIKE

It is 20 July. During the next ten days it rains and snows almost without ceasing. A climb is out of the question. I don't spend much time thinking about things, but read, and now and then take a look outside the tent. Often, when Nanga Parbat is clear of mist, I study the individual route possibilities with the telescope.

In Base Camp we continue to live off the land as far as possible. The farms with their cattle and sheep are only an hour away and they bring us lassi (sour milk), chickens and chapatis. Sometimes milk as well. We often let the chickens run around for a few days to fatten up before I wring their necks. Terry is a fantastic cook, particularly with Pakistani dishes. As a point of honour, he endeavours to find alternative chicken recipes, never giving us the same meal twice. Tinned food would soon get monotonous and in any case we need to be very sparing with what we brought with us. Our larder — two boxes under an overhanging rock — should last us for two or three weeks.

I wanted to study this mountain in minute detail and now I have the time to do so. The natives may look up at Nanga with different eyes, but what we see is the same.

Walking through the last pastures, I see a huge avalanche coming down the centre of the Diamir Face, plunging through a gap in the seracs in the middle of the face. I actually hear it break away; it thunders down from around 6000 metres, and spills out over the whole glacier basin below. I can see nothing but avalanche dust, the mountain is blotted out.

No safe route exists in the centre of this face. The seracs are so big that only a small fragment needs to break off and all hell breaks loose at the foot of the face. The avalanches divide into the various cracks and gulleys at the foot of the cliff and spill over everything.

The attraction of mountains for me is intuitive, naive. I am addicted to them, you might say. I often call climbing 'my weed'. I began when I was five. As I got older I climbed higher and more difficult peaks. Now I have the feeling that I am capable of finding a route on any mountain. Some routes are only 'safe' for a few hours in a day, and the art is to discover these 'safe' moments — that is what matters. The right route at the right time — taken like that even the Diamir side of Nanga Parbat is justifiable.

SOLO NANGA PARBAT

At Base Camp (4000 metres) it is lovely and green, edelweiss blooms. I often make the twenty paces from tent to waterhole barefoot. Hours, days, weeks are no longer distinguishable, all time has dissolved away. I sleep deeply — no throbbing machines, no ringing telephones. Physically I am more relaxed than I have ever been before.

NIGHT OF THE LONG SHADOWS

I crawl out of the tent and take a barefoot run across the damp grass. There is a rainbow which seems to rise straight out of the moraine that bounds the Diamir Glacier to the north. Its colours are clear and sharp against the inky cloud mass in the background. The mountains lurk somewhere behind. Individual patches of snow shimmer through gaps in the mist. Spurs of rock can be seen, and on the ledges, fresh snow. 'It must be very wet on the face,' I say to myself. This spectral display intensifies as I stare entranced; it is several minutes before I realize my feet are getting cold. Quite suddenly the sunlit crest of the Mazeno Wall lifts clear above the clouds. It is so high that I doubt its reality; it seems to swim in the air. As the mass of cloud at its base thickens, it appears to move higher. The sky is aglow with gold and the mountainsides glitter pure white. It is as if everything visual was liquefying, as if the sun was only waiting, half-hidden behind the clouds, to break through and dissolve everything there is.

'I'll set off tomorrow!' I yell, as if it wasn't just Ursula I was informing but the stones, the grass, the flowers around the tent as well. But in the same instant a strange new feeling steals over me — a mixture of apprehension, loneliness and expectation.

'Do you think the weather will hold?' asks Ursula.

'Sure, we'll get a fine weather period now after so much rain.'

She doesn't say anything more. We both stand in front of the tent and look at the mysterious cloud play in the furthest recesses of the Diamir Basin. Undecided whether I ought to pack my rucksack right away or wait another day, I take a few photographs.

Under a huge rock we kept our food depot — two boxes of tinned rations.

'Everything has changed in the space of a week,' I say, half-aloud, just for something to say.

'Will it be dangerous?'

'Everything is dangerous.'

I won't say any more, I'm not sure of myself. Ursula helps me pack and sort supplies and climbing equipment. Later, as I lie in my tent, I want to relax and get some sleep, but cannot. With my eyes closed, I lie there thinking. A strange empty feeling sweeps over me. It's always like this before a big climb, I tell myself, nothing to worry about. I try and stave off the waves of anxiety, but they won't go away.

It is dark when we sup our soup in the evening. The outline of the freshly snow-covered mountains rises against the gloomy sky. The features of Base Camp are no longer recognizable — its hollows, shapes, vegetation. We sit there silently for half an hour. I am tired. I cannot speak — and besides, there is nothing to say. There is scarcely a breath of wind and only the occasional rumble of avalanches on the face. Once some stones clatter down the raddled flanks of the Mazeno Peaks. I can

SOLO NANGA PARBAT

hear the breathing of the other two. It seems as if we are the only living things for far and wide. That disturbs me, and I keep looking in the direction of Nanga Parbat to see if anything stirs up there. But all is quiet.

Our Base Camp lies in a wild region. Below us it is green and rather balmy, like our own scenery in the Western Alps, but looking up, there are huge rivers of ice within easy reach. They have carved channels down to the valley. A branch of the glacier comes from the Mazeno Wall — a 3000 metre unclimbed barrier of rock and ice — the other straight down from the Diamir Face. That this is the spot where I spent those dreadful and intense hours after my brother disappeared, closer to death than I have ever been, no longer upsets me. I am still conscious of it all, naturally, but it is no longer an open wound. It is part of my life that I have learned to live with, I can neither change it, nor would I want to, now. It had to be.

Since I looked out of the tent earlier in the evening and saw the rainbow I have felt sure that the weather will improve. I am ready to go. Now or never, I think. There is no doubt that I am well acclimatized to the height, have sufficient red corpuscles and consequently a heightened capacity for taking in oxygen. I was two whole months on Everest and still have the reserves I built up there. Besides, the approach march took another ten days, going up and down between two and four thousand metres, an excellent height for acclimatization. Now, with ten days at Base Camp, that is surely enough.

In the tent I check over everything I want to take with me. And I keep remembering the beautiful sunset and am sure it will all go well. The weather will stay good. I know that on Nanga Parbat there is normally a rhythm of a few good days and a few bad days. I have learned that from earlier expeditions. If I want to go up, I must seize the chance now after the rainy spell.

But, the resolution made, the worries return. Sleep is out of the question. All the possible twists events might take run through my mind.

Close to the tent a cricket chirps. The sound sets my whole body on edge and I twitch and fidget. Images tumble through my brain like a torrent: snowed-up, waist-high drifts, impassable seracs, stonefalls, open

TIKE

crevasses. They all confront me at once. In my fantasies Nanga grows even higher and steeper that it really is. These imaginings soon throw me into a state of panic.

Bathed in sweat I huddle in my sleeping bag, quivering with fear, my aspirations and my composure shattered. The feeling of being alone constricts me and fear sweeps me away.

In my torment I sit up. Suddenly the vision of a body falling down the mountainside flashes before me. It comes straight at me. I duck out of its way. Fear engulfs my whole body. As it falls, this whirling body almost touches me, and I recognize its face as my own. My stomach turns over. I think I am going to be sick. It no longer makes any difference if I fall or cling on, live or die. I must have uttered a cry for Ursula wakes.

'What is it?' she asks.

At the sound of her voice there is a strong feeling of pressure inside me, then the whirling chaos of thoughts slows down, like an avalanche discharging at the foot of a mountain. The devastating panic is past. I feel as if I had woken from an anaesthetic.

I tell Ursula of my terror, how I felt I had been disembodied and strewn over the whole slope of Base Camp.

'My body fell apart. It was as if I were a jigsaw puzzle and unable to put myself together again. I was the watcher and the participant at one and the same time.'

Ursula murmurs something to me but I cannot grasp what she is saying. I keep drifting back up on the face, and sometimes I'm in the tent and on the face, in both places at once. The realization that I'm still lying in Base Camp and not shattered into a million pieces only dawns on me very slowly. Nor do I have to go up the mountain if I don't want to. I can still make up my mind one way or the other.

I look at my watch. Not yet midnight. My panic, therefore, can only have lasted a few hours. It seemed to transcend all time.

'Are you having bad dreams again?' Ursula asks as I toss restlessly back and forth.

'I don't know what it is. I am *so* frightened.' My strength, as I speak, completely ebbs away, so too do my willpower and self-control, which were once so strong. The dreams or hallucinations — I don't know what

During the first ten days it rained and snowed in Base Camp almost without stopping. During this time I spent most of the day inside my tent reading, writing, or we just talked amongst ourselves. In order to conserve gas, we cooked breakfast inside the tent, and often did without midday or evening meals altogether. We had left our old eating habits behind, but felt very well nevertheless. In between times, when the rain left off for a few hours, one of us would try and get a fire going. We took it in turns to cook; each his favourite dishes, as far as these were possible with the primitive utensils and small choice of provisions (meal, butter, jam, eggs). I don't have much skill in the culinary arts and during this time tried to remember the simple dishes my mother had shown me as a child. I cooked schmarren *(pancakes) and it was my job to slaughter the chickens sold us by the farmers in the highest pastures. My father had once managed a chicken farm, besides working as a teacher, and so I had learned not only how to pluck poultry, but also how to prepare it in a variety of ways. Although we bought nearly all our provisions in Pakistan, we suffered no ill-effects from our simple diet. Often we ate honey with cheese, cold dry corned beef, or fish soup — and they all tasted good!*

One evening, after the bad weather period, there was suddenly a rainbow above our Base Camp. A good sign. Confident that the weather would now get better, I immediately made the decision to start climbing the face the next day. I hoped I was sufficiently acclimatized and believed my condition was good enough, also. Before it got dark, I packed my rucksack: food for ten days and gas for cooking for the same period; only the most essential climbing equipment; and small bits and pieces like sunglasses, gloves, hat. Everything was ready before I settled down to sleep for the last time in Base Camp. But during the night I was suddenly beset by such dreadful dreams and anxieties that I postponed my start. I doubted my fitness, my ability, my acclimatization — and myself. There was no climbing-partner with whom to compare myself. I now realized that mentally I was not yet ready, relying on my own resources alone, to press up into the border regions of the Death Zone. I decided, first of all, to make an ascent of Ganalo Peak as a kind of test-run. Hardly a week later, with my rucksack ready outside my tent for the second time, I slept soundly. Only a break in the weather forced me back from the foot of the face that time and into Base Camp again (previous double-page).

they are – have taken over entirely. A series of images and emotions parades across my consciousness. Everything I know about this mountain, everything I have seen, all my mountain experience, stand visibly before me. Not as considered thought, but as feeling. And this feeling erodes me and casts its dark shadow upon me, over and again. At first it is a fleeting sensation, then it comes more often and more clearly. I seem to grow vertically until I am 100 metres high, or more, in any case, very tall. I have lost myself in my new dimensions. My head and the tips of my toes are separated by a vast distance. From the top down I stretch and stretch until, thin as a shadow, I crumple.

'Tell me what's the matter,' urges Ursula.

'I don't know any more how big I am.'

'I don't understand.'

'I'm disoriented spatially. Lost my sense of scale.'

'Have these dreams of yours got anything to do with experiences you had as a child? Do you dream about things that happened when you were a boy?'

'I experienced them off and on as a child, too.

'But yesterday you were fine. You'd thought about it all so rationally, and told me how logical it all was.'

'So it was. In the evening I kept my mind just on the one thing, but hundreds of others were lying in wait for me.'

'And now you don't know which has priority?'

'That's it, exactly. And it's so bad, I could go mad.

'Worse than when you set off for Everest?'

'Yes.'

'Are you more frightened than that time in 1970 when you climbed down with your brother?'

'That was quite different. In 1970 that was forced upon us. There was no other way out.'

'So you weren't frightened?'

'No – we were desperate, but at the same time strongly convinced that we had to get down, there was no other choice. It's my motivation that's being eaten away now. I say to myself I don't need to do it; then, I don't want to do it; then, if I do do it so-and-so could happen. Where all these ideas come from, I don't know. I've seen the mountain face and gone over in my mind everything that could happen to me.'

'Worked out what to do under all possible circumstances?'

'Almost all. I've seen all the crevasses I have to cross. I've imagined seracs breaking off, the big ones above the Mummery Rib. The whole of the great ice wall is formidable, true, and I have to go under it to get up to the right. I've seen bits break off that were actually as big as small villages and I've pictured how the ice would come down, whilst at the same time I've been thinking of something quite different. I don't know if you can think of lots of things at the same time, but everything seems to be going through me at once. At the end of my time at university — after I'd already decided to give up my studies, but was still working hard at my mathematical studies in Padua, I experienced something similar. Differentials and goodness-knows-what whizzed through my head side by side, one after the other, one on top of the other. Without any obvious connection. Differential equations, numbers, theories, they all poured into my head at the same time.'

'It's almost as if you've become your own observer and can see what's going on inside you.'

'I don't know about that. These fears come when I'm half-asleep. I lie there, unable to sleep properly or I suddenly wake up and am tormented by these sensations. But what is actually going on inside, I don't know.'

'You're hyperactive, you've got a raised level of excitation and can't switch off.'

'That's about it, I can't relax at all. It's dreadful.'

'Do you still want to go on?'

'If it's all in my imagination — and I do go tomorrow — what will it be like up there on the face? It can only get much worse.' I decide to bide my time and not start tomorrow as planned. Soon after, I drop off to sleep.

It's not quite daylight yet I can see through the tent that it is getting lighter. The darkness gradually dissolves. I must have slept soundly for several hours.

To take advantage of the fine weather, Ursula and I decide to make an excursion to Ganalo Peak. Terry promises to look after Base Camp.

SOLO NANGA PARBAT

Clouds still cling to the summit of Nanga Parbat, but in the far west, beyond the hills, over the horizon the sky is as clear as glass. I take a long look to see if any clouds or early-morning mists appear, but all I can see is the blue mass of the distant ranges. This is the first time the sun has broken through the clouds for days, and Nanga Parbat displays itself in all its wild beauty. Avalanches thunder down its steep, rugged face almost continuously, and I am glad not to be up there. The sight of these slopes still makes a deep impact on me, even now.

Confident that we shall have a period of fine weather, we set off. I am not tired, even though I have slept so little. I want to climb this mountain with Ursula, I just want to get going and test my fitness. Having no climbing partner I have to assess my own condition and acclimatization before I finally set off.

The weather is fabulous. We walk in a north-easterly direction for a few hours, climbing great blocks and steep rock ridges. Ursula is tenacious and agile. When we reach a shoulder on the ridge we stop and rest. The sun falls across the slope obliquely, it is no longer so warm. Without having decided upon a bivouac place, we toil on up a long cirque to the rocks above, and reach a notch behind a pinnacle on the ridge. There we call a halt. We sit down on a couple of rocks and look down at Base Camp, a good 1200 metres below. The evening sun falls directly onto the Diamir Face which looks much steeper, from our perch up here, than it does back in the valley.

Ursula's long blonde hair blows in the wind and her freckles seem to shine on her downy skin. She doesn't appear at all tired, just absorbed in thought. This mood of calm gravity suits her.

I am tired and hungry. We have hardly eaten a thing all day. In the gully behind our notch, we find a trickle of meltwater running over the rocks, and take it in turns to go and fetch some to drink.

We put our small tent on the Ganalo ridge, at a height of 5300 metres. The gently sloping snow fields under the North Summit of Nanga and the Diamir Glacier are already in shadow. The steep icefalls in the inner recesses and the steep flank below the North Summit, are jointed by spurs and pillars. The rib system followed by Mummery in 1895, which leads out of the basin of the Diamir Glacier straight up to the glacier under the

TIKE

Bazhin Notch, looks very compact in the late evening sun. By climbing Ganalo Peak we have a completely new vantage point from which to view Nanga. We see it in all its colours and nuances. Back in Base Camp I often wondered if we would ever see any fine weather. It's clear that these would have been perfect days for a summit attempt, and yet it is better that I wait. But what happens if, the next time I decide to go, I am again beset by these same fears?

'It's good that we did this climb,' I tell Ursula. I finally know which route I have to take; I see it clearly, although I cannot say how it is I know it's the right one.'

It's obvious that this is the right route for me: straight up to start with, then right, across the ice bridge, then finally, traverse diagonally left to the summit. Later I watch another avalanche coming down, an avalanche which like a moving cloud of dust, starts on the left of the face, sweeps over to the centre, and then at the bottom spills over everything. The avalanches only come down during the day, I tell myself, when the sun shines on the face; and at night when it freezes. In the mornings the first rays of the sun only brush the face and the ice holds. This is the time I must utilize to cross the lower avalanche zone and climb the serac barrier. Above that I can continue in safety.

Ursula and I squat by the tent, tucked in behind the tooth of rock, and prepare for our bivouac. Often when the mist plays around the face, it looks so unreal, so far away, that I cannot imagine ever climbing it. Now, in this clear evening light, it looks quite different. I let my eyes linger on it – Nanga Parbat, the Naked Mountain. No, Diamir is better I think, King of all the Mountains.

It's interesting that before the Second World War none of the big Himalayan giants had been climbed. Despite enormous effort and specially developed oxygen apparatus, these mountains were simply too high for that time. And even though, with the growth of Nazi fervour in the mid-thirties, one expedition after another made the pilgrimage to this 'German Peak of Destiny' to earn fame for the Fatherland, the results in mountaineering terms were minimal.

The tent fabric is motionless, like the evening outside. I put my hand out to feel my sleeping bag and discover it is covered in a thin layer of

SOLO NANGA PARBAT

ice. Until late into the night I tell Ursula about the big expeditions of the inter-war years.

'The experience was there, the equipment was primitive but solid. The climbers of the period – Merkl and Welzenbach – were too ponderous and irresolute. As climbers they were strong enough – Welzenbach, in particular, was unsurpassed above 7000 metres but he moved too slowly. In those days people expected a demon to be guarding the summit of Nanga Parbat. The Aufschnaiter Expedition of 1939, which went to the Diamir side, also failed because they were too indecisive. I am well aware that this west side of the mountain is very dangerous wherever you tackle it, but with the right tactics it ought to be possible. What I am trying to do is much more like Mummery's venture than the other Nanga Parbat expeditions. If it comes off, the story of this eight-thousander will have come full circle. Mummery's attempt failed, but now, eighty-three years later, it is perhaps possible to complete his route – and to do it alone. Even though the avalanches and crevasses, the high-level storms have not changed since the days of Mummery and Welzenbach and Buhl.'

'What was it that made Hermann Buhl so different; how was it he managed to achieve what was considered impossible?' asks Ursula.

'He had the right attitude, but also the fitness and climbing know-how. Perhaps he understood how to exploit strength, which the others weren't able to do. From a big expedition, he launched himself off alone from the highest camp and climbed the final ridge to the summit in a single day. Somewhere on the descent he bivouacked, and the next day struggled on down, plagued by phantoms, spooks and hallucinations. I am convinced of one thing, that Nanga Parbat would never have been climbed in 1953, but for this final extra effort, but for the ability and willpower of a Hermann Buhl. The expedition had him alone to thank for the summit. Disregarding the fact that Buhl could not have gone to Nanga Parbat at all had the expedition not been planned, organized and financed by other people, the first ascent is entirely thanks to him. He set off as a young man but when he stumbled back, he was wizened and old.'

'Then didn't Buhl make the first solo ascent of Nanga Parbat?'

'No, his summit climb was not an absolute solo. There had been a big team with him and they had worked for weeks to prepare the route as

I obtained a good view of the Diamir Face from the southern slopes of Ganalo Peak. From there my planned climbing route appeared logical.

far as some 6900 metres. From there, two climbers had set off together, and it was only after one dropped out that Buhl continued alone. It's not a solo climb from the last camp to the summit that interests me – that has been done several times before. This year, for instance, by Franz Oppurg on Everest; I myself reached the summit of Manaslu alone in 1972. But what I want to do now is to climb alone from the very bottom, without previously having been on the face. We had a relatively big team when we climbed the Rupal Face on the southern side in 1970; it consists of some 4500 metres of steep ice and hard rock and we spent forty days fixing ropes, setting up camps, reconnoitring and preparing the route. We had climbed up and down a dozen times before we started the serious summit attempt.

'Tell me honestly, compared to these other climbers, don't you just happen to be that much better?'

'No, not at all. Almost any young, fit person could climb Nanga alone – if he wanted to. People can do anything that they really want to do.'

'You're sure of that? Sure you're just ordinary, normal?'

SOLO NANGA PARBAT

'Who can be sure he is normal? I can't say that I'm normal and the others are abnormal, or that I'm the abnormal one and all the others are normal. It doesn't matter that much, either. I prefer to leave it open — no-one can say for sure what is normal anyway.'

'Statistically, you can.'

'That doesn't prove anything. That only gives you the "norm". If the whole world was convinced I was abnormal, it wouldn't mean a thing. I'll stick with my abnormality, so long as I'm free to go my own way.'

'You want to be completely autonomous, to ignore other people's guidelines and be yourself, unconditionally.'

'If five psychiatrists, three doctors and two wives were to say I'm off my head, I would still be convinced I wasn't. That's something I hear every day, that I'm crazy, but it doesn't bother me.'

'Nor should it.'

'It's not important.'

'And all those worn-out brain cells?'

'Nobody counted them before and after. In any case there's enough left to make me sometimes doubt my own existence and other times be amazed by it.'

The next day I climb the long corniced ridge up to the summit of the East Ganalo Peak. It is hard work because there are a lot of rock gendarmes to circumvent. Ursula stays behind and waits for me. On the way back afterwards, we have Nanga Parbat in front of us all the way down. This climb has restored my confidence. I am in really excellent form. And the view of Nanga from up there looked so inviting that I can hardly wait to get started. The phase back in Base Camp — when I said to myself that I didn't want to to do it, couldn't do it, it wasn't that important anyway — seems finally to have passed.

'Look at those lines — isn't it a fabulous mountain!' I shout in my new enthusiasm to Ursula as I climb down.

'Is that why you're climbing it, because it's beautiful?'

'Partly that, yes.'

'What kind of satisfaction can that give you?'

'There are one or two mountains that are so beautiful you simply have to climb them.'

TIKE

'Couldn't you just fly over them, or look at them?'

'Oh no, that misses the whole essence.'

Most people are not interested in personal experience. The concept that one can willingly tax one's physical and mental resources out of a pure joy of living; that one can become obsessed with a hunger to experience the world — and the mind too — to solve the puzzle for fun — such an idea does not occur to them. No. Practical work, that's different. They can recognize that, where there's an instant utility or profit. But pure thought, pure exercise, a pure thirst for knowledge without any useful end-product, that has no interest for them.

The false impression that expeditions should be financed and undertaken only by 'professional expeditioners' is an extension of the idea that climbing is all about 'exploring the last white patches on the globe' or peakbagging. The fact that it is primarily concerned with the often bitter business of discovering oneself, people seem not to grasp.

It is not surprising that many non-climbers deprecate a sport as dangerous as climbing. I understand, too, why there's such an outcry, with accusations of foolhardiness and irresponsibility, whenever there's an accident somewhere. The unspoken envy, however, which one senses in their indignation, really arises from that fact that they instinctively feel that in high mountains the desperate business of living can be transcended by sheer joy of being alive. In such moments one can discover God inside oneself. When during an interview, the pastor from Villnöss was questioned about my activities it was not without reason that he described them as blasphemous.

BREAKING LOOSE

Back in Base Camp I have a good feeling. I now know that I have enough strength even without a partner. Having someone to compare myself with is what I have been missing. Without anyone against whom one can see if one is stronger or weaker, it's often difficult to know what condition

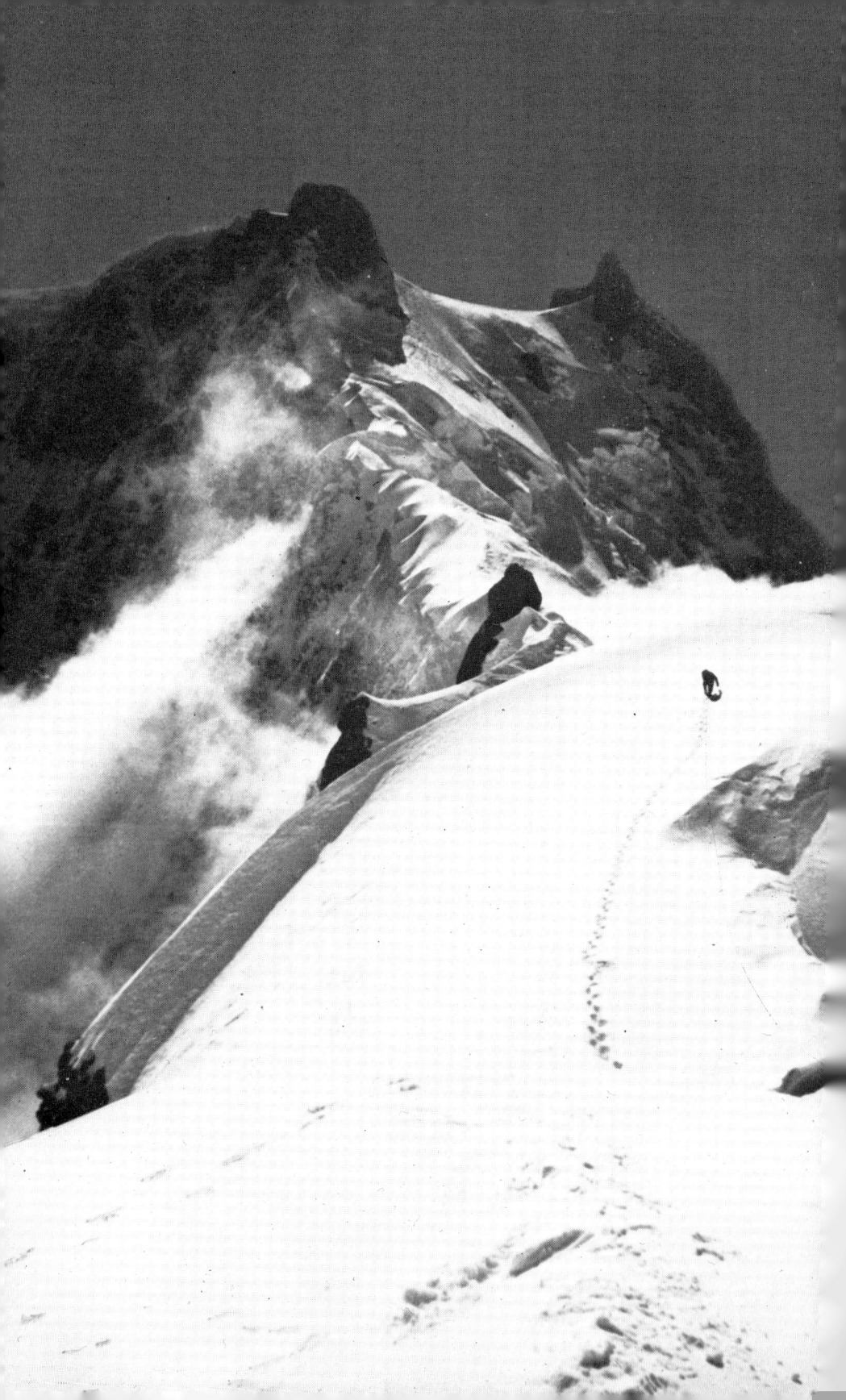

Hermann Buhl climbing the East Ridge alone in 1953. His friends, waiting below, disappeared from his view as he passed between the two black teeth of the Silberzacken. From below it is not possible to see the Silver Plateau.

one is in. This climb on Ganalo Peak, some 6600 metres high, has shown me that I am splendidly acclimatized. I was also nimble enough. From a climbing point of view there's nothing to worry about.

The face remains in shadow till late into the morning, making it look particularly steep. 3500 metres high, it has an average gradient of forty-five degrees. The lower section is less steep than that; on top is a trapezoid rock buttress about 450 metres high, almost as high in fact as the Tre Cima in the Dolomites. I lie on a thin foam mattress and study the face.

It is now the beginning of August. My permit runs till 15 August. Time presses, yet I am in no hurry. If I haven't made my attempt by the middle of the month, I will overrun my time. Somehow I know this is the right year for me.

'How are things now — better?' Ursula asks.

'Yes — as I said to you coming down off Ganalo Peak, I'm back on an even keel now. The loneliness which was a real problem over the last year, has now become an advantage. As soon as it augurs well for a longer period of fine weather, I shall be off.'

The sun is warm on my bare feet and I doze blissfully. Such peace! For almost six weeks I have been cut off from letters and news bulletins. What is important here? That the Pope has died, or a politician resigned? These are things I don't learn until weeks later. Being inaccessible to communications from outside makes way for inner communications.

Some days ago I had been irresolute, but suddenly something in me — it could hardly be called common-sense — hankered to leave everything behind and get started. Only for a moment did the prospect of being completely on my own for one or two weeks worry me, then I was glad about it. The decision is soothing even though it triggers a series of strong emotions. Curiosity, respect and near-suicidal nonchalance all overlap in me.

As I lie there looking across the green meadows to the face, my attention focusses on the huge icefall in the centre. It gnashes away under pressure from the glacier above. The ice is the colour of splintered glass.

'Reinhold,' Ursula rouses me from my reverie, 'what will happen if a bit of your equipment breaks while you're up there?'

SOLO NANGA PARBAT

'Luckily I won't be taking many bits of equipment — axe, crampons, cooker, tent — they are all so simple that practically nothing can break. I know they're as good as they can be, and if they go wrong I'll just have to patch them up.'

'What with?'

'My penknife. I'll manage.'

Terry asks, 'What do you mean when you say "by fair means"?'

'By fair means — I mean to climb without the boost of technical devices. Clothes, goggles, rope, cooker, tent — they're technical too, in a way, but they don't count, they don't have the effect of making the mountain smaller, as it were.'

'But you reduce even these to a minimum?'

'Yes.'

'And what are the things you are rejecting?'

'Expansion bolts, for one. If I put these into the rock I could climb anything at all, even things that are basically too difficult for me. So were I to put in 1000 of these bolts, one after the other, I could climb an "unclimbable" 1000 metre face, no trouble. So by means of a trick I would manage to do something that was impossible for me. Take oxygen apparatus — that would allow me to climb to a height where I might otherwise die. People used to say Everest couldn't be climbed without it. And believing that, it became an acceptable aid. A technical device makes things possible that were previously really, or apparently, impossible. It takes away all the suspense, too. So, I don't want these kinds of tricks. What other people do is their own affair.'

'By putting these technical aids aside, like crutches, you achieve a high degree of autonomy,' Ursula puts in.

'Yes. If I made use of all the forms of technology that exist today, I could climb anything. But I would be dependent on the technology, and the success, too, would not be because of me, but because of the technology. Taking it to extremes, I could say: why wrestle with this dreadful panic such as I experienced in 1973 and again a week ago; I could have a helicopter built and fly over the top of Nanga Parbat. But that doesn't interest me at all! I want to be independent of technology — and in this particular experiment, independent of other people as well. I've often been

TIKE

aware of being dependent on other people, of someone or other across the way; the climbing partner is the very last thing I could give up. If I can make myself independent of partners also, I have achieved autonomy. I would like to be self-sufficient, at least for a short while; to have the strength to do everything for myself; to see if I can cope alone.'

'Does your decision to go it alone have anything to do with the fact that you haven't got a partner any more?'

'No. That's an easy question to answer. I have been endeavouring to climb an eight-thousander on my own right from the time of my marriage to Uschi. It's interesting that I didn't succeed then even though at the time I was mentally very well adjusted. Besides, it's easier to find good climbing partners today than it's ever been.'

'Perhaps you failed just because you were well adjusted, and by definition, dependent.'

'Yes, that might be true. I realize that well enough.'

'This close relationship with someone — is it an advantage or a disadvantage?'

'I can't say categorically, but I do believe I can now sense how far a relationship is an advantage and how far a hindrance. That was something I didn't know in 1976.'

'So you avoid its happening again.'

'Perhaps before my divorce I made the mistake — which incidentally almost everybody does make — of supposing the meaning of existence to lie in one's partner. That's a question of feeling. I'm not one for rational reasons. For instance, when I'm at home I can say to myself, Nanga Parbat solo, that is the ultimate. That is the outer limit of alpinism, the last frontier. It will make the whole climbing world sit up and think. But here everything is quite different. As soon as I'm on my own after the ten-day trek through Pakistan, it goes — all that. Then there used to be my personal attachments and somewhere along the line the idea of a solo climb crumbled. So the meaning of life is not really Nanga Parbat, you say to yourself then, and it's not in the nonsense I talk either. And then I projected a lot on to Uschi and clung to her, thus I lacked the strength to come out of myself — to accept what I am and to go my own way.'

'So now you need not be dependent on anyone.'

SOLO NANGA PARBAT

'Not if I'm to rediscover myself. Get myself back together.'

'And what sort of reason is that for climbing a mountain?'

'I don't know. The climb is an unknown factor and so too is the sense of it to me.'

'You're changing the subject again.'

'Really I can't be bothered about the meaning of things.'

'So you're completely indifferent — what you do, how it turns out, even whether you come back?'

'No! In no way am I indifferent to what I do. Whether I come back again or not isn't important, though.'

'You're crazy! What are you studying the face so intently for, then? If it doesn't matter, you might just as logically jump into the first crevasse.'

'I don't want to fall into a crevasse or be buried under an avalanche, and yet I have to take these possibilities into account. The art is to reduce the unpredictable to a minimum, yet still maintain an element of mystery. I know what's in store for me, and yet things are still wide open.'

'And if you're too slow, or you get in the way of falling stones?'

'I'm not going to be climbing where the stones come down. That's my strategy. And I have to be quick. That's why I'm not taking any more luggage than I can cope with. Speed equals safety up there.'

'You can say whatever you like — it has to be more dangerous on your own.'

'It's not advisable to climb mountains on your own before you know all about them. Why do you think I've waited so long?'

'And yet you're still frightened?'

'Fear is something that I've never completely overcome, but I've nearly always had it under control. I never start a big enterprise if I don't feel right, or if I'm not ready for it. You've seen for yourself how I called everything off the first time, a couple of days ago.'

'What time are we setting off in the morning?' asks Ursula.

'Early afternoon will be soon enough. It's only two hours at most to the start of the face.'

Again everything is packed. Tomorrow Ursula and I want to bivouac at the spot where the Diama and Diamir Glaciers join, and from there I

In Base Camp we lived off the land as far as possible. My favourite drink was lassi (sour milk).

will begin the actual climb the following day. It's easy enough, up to there and Ursula can find her own way back to Base Camp.

For the umpteenth time I pick up the heavy rucksack trying to gauge its weight. 'A good fifteen kilos,' (thirty-three lbs) I estimate. The way to the start of the climb lies first over the moraine, then across scree and between snow *penitentes*.* I look along the top of the face but the summit itself is not visible. It is a cloudy day and it looks like rain over the west. Not bad weather, but one or two hours of hail and rain seem on the cards. Higher up I'm sure it means snow. Low cloud congests the inner Diamir Basin and cloud sits on the glaciers of the Mazeno Peaks. Despite the icy draught from the glacier, the air is sticky, sultry. I pay attention to the changes of wind-direction and the colour of the sky. Before it starts to rain, I feel the dampness in my lungs and urge that we hurry. Ursula is following behind on the dead glacier.

'Come on!' I shout to her, 'It's going to rain in a minute.'

'How can you tell?'

'Some things I just know, that's all.'

A little later the first drops fall. The loose stones on the surface of the ice are wet and shiny, and skid under my feet if I take too big a stride. I don't want to get wet. How shall I get my clothes dry again on the mountain?

* Ice formations that resemble monks at prayer.

Ursula came with me on the climb from Base Camp to Ganalo Peak, and we camped in a narrow notch behind a rock pillar as high as a church steeple. From there, we could see straight down to the little green patches on the right-hand side of the glacier where our Base Camp stood. The glacier itself was completely strewn with stones and appeared a dirty grey colour. Up here we couldn't hear the usual glacier sounds which had become so much a feature of camp life, even at night. The ice creaked and moaned, while chunks of rock slid into crevasses and underground waters gurgled. From our bivouac, we climbed the next day through a loose gully until it became too difficult and dangerous for Ursula. At about 6000 metres she sat and waited while I climbed on alone to the summit. From the top of the Ganalo Peak I got a good view of the whole lower section of the Diamir Face. I could see down into each crevasse in the wildly-tossed hanging glacier (next double-page) and was thus able to picture in detail the exact route I should take. A few days later I would be climbing alone, without any form of roped protection, over this crevassed area. I didn't want to disappear down any of these ice holes in the process. The picture on the next double-page was taken with a telephoto lens from Base Camp and shows me — a tiny speck in the foreground, left of centre — climbing over the dirty seracs.

On the first attempt I only got to the foot of the face before foul weather sent me scuttling back to Base Camp. Then — as for the final climb — I put on all my gear for the climb at the bottom. That first time I carried a heavy pack frame to the foot of the wall full of extra bivouac equipment I wanted to leave there. On 6 August I set off again across the dead glacier to the foot of the face. The weather was now good and this time I was quite confident. Once I had overcome the short crevassed zone immediately above the moraine, I climbed without appreciable difficulty first over the debris-strewn ice, and then through a strenuous and loose gully between the Diamir and Diama Glaciers, up to around 4800 metres above sea-level, where I bivouacked under an enormous rock. Even though I had only set off in the afternoon, I was in no hurry, for the route from Base Camp to this first bivouac site only took two hours. In an emergency I could have been back in camp within an hour. From the bivouac (just out of sight on the previous double-page, to the left of the lower ice seracs) I got this worm's eye view of the lower half of the face, foreshortened and flattened.

SOLO NANGA PARBAT

We have crossed the glacier and will bivouac here at the foot of the face. My plan is to sleep here under an overhanging rock — or, at least, rest, if not sleep. It would be a tiring business crossing this rubble between the edge of the moraine and the foot of the face early in the morning, hence the bivouac. By dawn I have to be on the face if I want to make good use of the first morning hours. Before the sun comes on to the face, I must have the most dangerous passages behind me.

Again the weather is not good. At the moment that's no bother. I know I can run back to Base Camp in an hour. I don't have a torch with me, indeed I only have the barest essentials: besides axe and crampons, one metre of rope which I could use in emergency to secure myself to the face, some small bits and pieces such as altimeter, glacier goggles, a single ice screw and a piton. I have also food and gas for ten days. It is important that I can cook something warm. A tent which weighs scarcely more than a kilo, sleeping bag (filled with fine down) — all stuffed into my rucksack. I have kept my clothes to a minimum. If it gets cold, I'll snuggle into my sleeping bag and wait. Every extra kilo costs time, and I would be slower if I took them. And the slower I am, the longer I would take and the more food I would need to carry. If I reckoned on twenty days, I would never even get high, because I should need thirty kilos of gear, and to lug that lot up would take not twenty, but thirty days. Somewhere around fifteen kilos is the limit for this altitude. I'm not one of those people who are as strong as an ox; I used to be very slight, now I weigh a little more than sixty kilos (133 lbs). With fifteen kilos in my rucksack, I can still climb freely; if I couldn't, I couldn't contemplate soloing Nanga Parbat.

Close to the foot of the face I clear a space under an overhanging rock and level out the platform with flat stones. The tent will stand straight and protected. One never knows where avalanches may come at night, nor do we want to be hit by falling stones. Meanwhile Ursula appears. She is soaked through and a bit tired. It takes another hour to get the bivouac ready. I fetch some meltwater from a nearby stream that sparkles between the ice and stones.

'Is this rock safe? Will it move?'

'It'll still be here in ten years' time.'

TIKE

Ursula has yet more questions.

'And what if there's an earthquake?'

I merely look at her and laugh inwardly. If there was a strong earthquake, then of course the rock would go and our tent with it. We should be crushed.

'There won't be any earthquakes.'

'But suppose ...'

I don't say any more but unpack the rucksack. I can't concentrate on two things at once, any more than I can talk when I'm climbing. Inside the tent we get warm in no time. My wet shirt therefore dries on me.

'Do you think the weather will get better?'

'Don't know.'

Ursula makes some coffee. We don't eat much. It's steamy inside the tent. When we look outside an hour later, the sky has brightened and it's not raining any more. The cloud now hangs level with the great icefall. The view is fantastic. We have kept dry in our niche. The air above the glacier is now blue-green; like an opaque curtain it hangs over the entrance to the valley. Everything now looks much larger. A constant rumble from the face warns us of stonefall.

There is something improbable about this valley and the mountain above, especially in this dusky light. The crumbling ice pinnacles of the Diama Glacier clutch at the evening mists. Where the Diama Glacier thrusts into the Diamir Glacier it piles up like storm billows. The energy behind that!

The icy facets around the base of the mountain have lost their shining whiteness and appear grey and greenish by turns. The ice avalanches and stonefalls grow stronger towards evening. Ursula, too, is impressed by the steepness of the ice and by the falling stones that sound so close. The rocks around the foot of the face bear strong witness to the continual ice and stonefall bombardment. This really is no route for a big expedition.

We both sleep well. However, early next morning we decide to go back to Base Camp because the continuing bad weather and the attendant stonefall render further waiting useless. The many open crevasses and the loose scree make the descent very unpleasant. Yet another attempt abandoned. Failed. On the way back a massive ice avalanche roars over the edge of the moraine bank and fills the wide glacier basin at the foot of the face with its powder. From down here it is an incredible spectacle as the glistening dust silently whirls and settles; only later do we hear the growl, like thunder.

Terry, supposing me already high on the mountain, comes towards us to meet Ursula. From his gestures and sympathetic questions, I can tell he understands my feelings. He identifies with me and my intention completely.

'Is the weather too bad?' he acknowledges our greeting.

'Yes,' I reply, 'too much snow up there and too many stonefalls.'

'Nanga is the biggest mountain I've ever seen,' enthuses Ursula. 'Those little towers that look tiny from here, they're like individual massifs when you get closer. I wasn't anywhere near as impressed by Mount Everest.'

'Does Nanga have the same impact on you?' Terry wants to know.

'No. I still have the feeling that the Geisler mountains, which I first saw close up at the age of five, are the biggest mountains I ever saw. They made such a strong impression on me then that I still have their image in my mind.'

'Did you climb those Geisler, then, when you were small?'

'Yes — right to the top of the Sass Rigais, the highest of them. And the next day I couldn't believe I had really been there. And there was nobody who could give me any idea of their real scale.'

'Why not?'

'I was completely confused in my conceptions of size.'

'But you did go up it? Were you frightened? Was it dangerous?'

'Hardly any fear in those days. I can still remember so many little details about it. I remember my father hiding his cigarettes in the last tree — that's very clear. I can't think why he did it. I've never asked him about it. There was a hole in the tree and he put the packet inside with a stone on top. Then we went on.'

'Only you and your father?'

'My brother and mother were there too. The four of us. My father leading. I couldn't have said at the time which way we ought to go, why this way and not that. Now and then he helped us, told us what to do.

My first bivouac site lay at the foot of the face; in the upper corner where the Diamir and Diama Glaciers joined. As a precautionary measure I tucked the tent under an overhanging block of rock.

Up on the summit ridge it was quite exposed, it fell steeply away on both sides. I didn't trust myself there and a couple of strangers helped me.'

'Is this your summer holiday?' Terry wants to know.

'If I had to work for eleven months in a year and only had one month off, I couldn't begin to think about soloing Nanga Parbat, ever. I'm independent now, but it wasn't always like that. Of course, it didn't just happen, this situation I'm in now. I worked towards it.'

'Reinhold has plenty of room for manoeuvre,' says Ursula.

'How old were you when you started properly?'

'Climbing independently? That's what I've always liked best; that I started when I was ten or twelve. That was the first time I had to make my own decisions in the mountains. I think in those days I had the balance between intellect and instinct just about right, probably better than today.'

'So your supremacy dates back to that time?'

'You could say that. It's not any kind of physical superiority. And I don't train any more. I haven't got an iron will, nor can I cope with fear any better than the next man.'

'Do you think you would be here today if you had not been on your twenty other expeditions?'

'Those early years were the only ones that were not really crucial. In

SOLO NANGA PARBAT

1970 I wouldn't have believed anyone could solo an eight-thousander, but since 1973 I have believed in it strongly.'

We haven't been back in Base Camp more than an hour before I start getting ready for the next attempt. Being mentally ready at last to go, all I need now is the good weather, a week of good weather. My determination grows with every task I perform. I recognize this well enough. I have only to file my crampons and fit them to my boots and it gives me momentum. If I didn't keep myself busy I would be a prey to all sorts of fears. This is a basic need of mine and it goes very deep. Once more I can look up at the mountain and wink silently to myself. It's something I've always done, wink the left eye, whenever I'm about to test one of my bold ideas. Only if I'm sick or tired is it any different; I can't feel it, but I know.

Now I rummage in the boxes for provisions. Two tins of tuna fish, I'll have those; soup – eight packets, two boxes of cheese, the hard bread, and crackers, too, of course. There's no reason why I select this particular food against any other, and I don't think much about it. All that's in my mind is how many days I'll be away, could be ten. It's good to pack like this, testing the weight, shaping the rucksack. I'm always like this before one of my major climbs; the activity offsets any feeling of senselessness. Some things I do so carefully, no-one could do them any better, and these last few manoeuvres before setting out are like that. I enjoy doing them. Ursula comes and stands in front of me while I'm collecting things together, and hands me a tin of dried milk and another with a mixture of sugar, powdered milk and coffee. She watches me and says something, but I don't hear what it is. I stuff the two tins into the rucksack and fasten it up. She wants to know if I'm sure I've got all I need. I nod. As I glance up, I see she doesn't really believe me. She nods, but goes into the tent. I can hear her busy with the pots and pans, and I test the rucksack out for weight. 'About fifteen kilos again,' I say to myself. Not too much, not too little.

On 6 August, shortly after midday, I leave Base Camp. It is very warm. I turn round once more when I reach a large rock some 200 metres above camp and say, 'Tike', as if this word described my determination. Now, all things considered, I am perfectly ready to go. No hesitations, no ifs and buts, ready. My whole being is concentrated on survival, to fight

TIKE

through in the best way I can. I know that this climb is very dangerous and will push me to the limit of my capabilities. And there are many unavoidable dangers. And yet I leave nothing to chance.

There are five requirements for a lonely bird:
The first that he flies to the highest point;
the second that he doesn't yearn for company,
   even of his own kind;
the third, that he points his beak towards heaven;
the fourth, that he has no specific colour of his own;
the fifth, that he sings very softly.

                              San Juan de la Cruz.

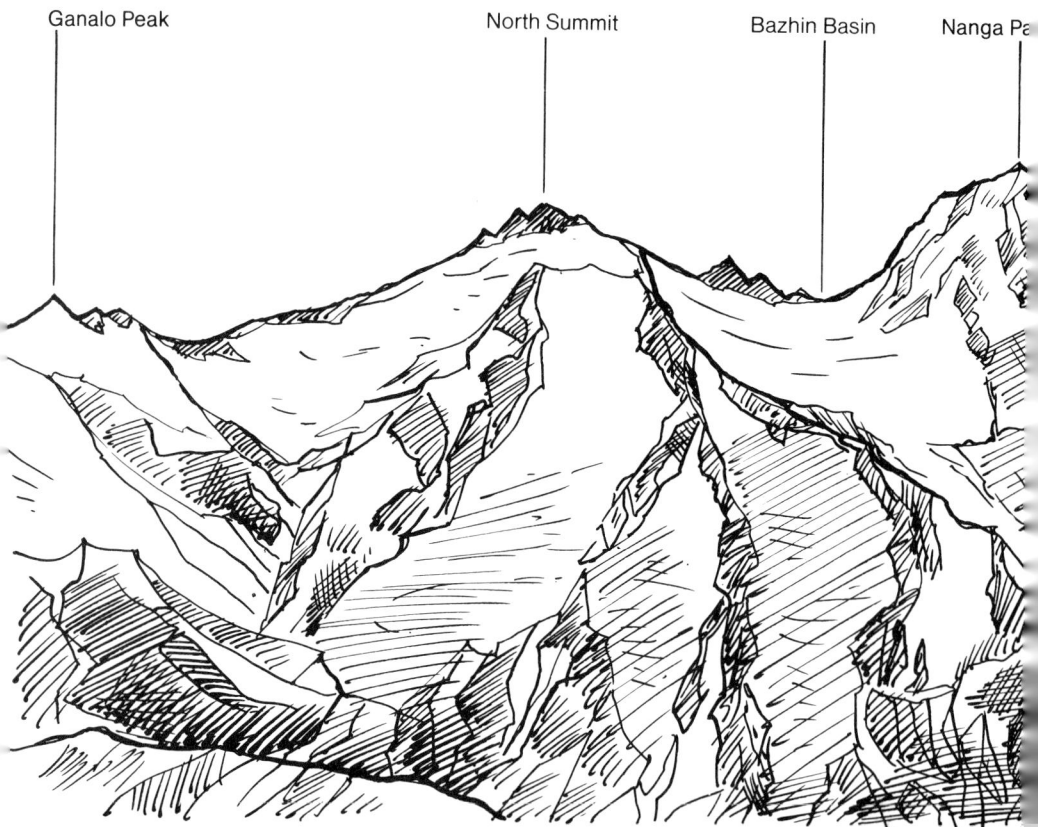

DIAMIR

WHITE LONELINESS

I have been climbing steep ice for two hours. I am not going particularly fast, but steadily and without stopping to rest. It is a little after seven o'clock. I must keep to the right to reach the narrow ice ramp which runs between the great icefall and the Mazeno Wall. I have already put one ice cliff behind me. Without using any protective means, just climbing with crampons and axe, I surmounted a fifteen metre near-vertical slope which skirts the central avalanche channel in the ice hose. 'How am I going to get down that again?' I mutter to myself absent-mindedly. There is another ice cliff in front of me. It is at least 100 metres long and overhangs in places. It forms a barrier across the face like a castle wall. I cannot see beyond it. It gets higher to the right. I don't know what it's like above.

I've been on my own now for a couple of hours.

'Go left,' a voice says.

'Really?' I'm startled by my own answer. Was there anyone there? It certainly does seem better to the left. So I take the advice and go left. It's as if I knew the other voice was right.

It's not easy that way either, but it serves. There's a recess which will take me up the steep buttress, as if in a chimney. With my legs spread-eagled across the gaping sides of this ice chimney, my hands deep into the back of the groove-like crack, I inch my way up cautiously. Frightened? The climbing demands so much concentration that there's no room for fear. There is time to do it, but not to think about it.

Suddenly the icefield around me is flushed with a strong, warm light. It lasts a moment only, but the sky above is radiant. The first sun strokes the face. I can't see the source of the beams, but it makes the great icefall sparkle. High above me the sun's rays fill every corner of the Diamir Face. My body too warms and responds. Everything in me comes alive.

Sunrise! Splendid and arousing moments. Like wind-blown sand the

Ursula photographed me with a telephoto lens from the foot of the face.

air hangs under the heavens, and Nanga Parbat traces its shadow on the clear horizon. I could still go up or down, but let myself be driven upwards, into a world which seems to me both private and uncomplicated.

'Come back safe,' Terry had called as I left.

'We'll wait for you, whatever happens,' Ursula said.

I look back down towards Base Camp and try to make out the tents but cannot recognize anything.

Suddenly, there's someone there again, speaking to me. At first this empty world of silence is broken only by the sounds of a second presence, then I see a man standing at the edge of my field of vision. I experience the feeling of my early home. My father is there. I am following him. I feel his presence and it is as if my feelings towards him had not changed since my childhood.

When the sun finally climbs over the horizon, I am alone again. My father was the age that I am now when he first took me to the mountains, I think as I climb the forty-five degrees ice slope with the front points of my crampons. I thrust the toes of my crampons alternately into the brittle surface beneath me. Three short steps, legs straddled, then a glance up

SOLO NANGA PARBAT

from my feet. I position the short axe some eighty centimetres above me, then take three more short steps. I have found my rhythm.

I can hardly remember my childhood. A few incidents only. I fell in a ditch, I remember, and banged my forehead. And I can remember a small clearing in the woods. There were just my elder brother and I there, and we were helpless. My parents had left us together there. We both cried. First my brother, then I too.

'What a wilful child you were,'
'Not only wilful, perverse.'
'You're very similar to your father.'
'Possibly.'
'Same old-fashioned ideas.'
'No, you only think that because I gave most of the orders.'
'What do you mean most? You were always the boss.'
'As far back as I can remember, I always lorded it over my brothers. I'm not proud of it, but not unhappy about it either. That's the way it was, that's all.'
'In our family of eleven children, there were always age groupings. There were the Big Ones and the Little Ones, then as more came, they became the Little Ones.'
'Later we went to school and our own father was teacher.'
'I don't want to remember anything about school.'

Suddenly a crampon slips. 'Watch out!' I say aloud. Am I talking to myself?

I have already reached the height of the Great Icefall. The weather is not good, but not bad either. Three hours ago I set off from the first bivouac. Yesterday I took another look at the first page of the Gutenberg Bible, which a friend had given me to take to the summit. He had made a little aluminium case for it and I had placed the precious page inside. I want to leave it on the summit. I don't know of course whether my photos will come out, whether indeed I'll be able to take photographs up there. Nor do I know if I'll get there, of course, but in case I do, I have this page of script with me.

I must have slept very well – no fears – for I am quite rested. Still quite confident. In a sudden renewed wave of determination, I have to

From my first bivouac I climbed up 1600 meters on 7 August 1978, through the glacier and serac zones, making a sharp angle between the Diamir and Mazeno Faces.

press on. I look up at the great wall of the Mazeno Peaks and then traverse left above the seracs. What a gigantic scale everything is. It's never easy to get your bearings on this face. To the right of the Mummery Rib, which rises almost 1500 metres and is bathed in warm, morning light, glitters smooth ice. The great serac beside me is more than half a kilometre wide and up to 200 metres high. I am now on fairly safe ground – one can never be totally safe here. This is the decisive day for me, I know that. I must get to at least 6000 metres. Lower than that, there is nowhere to

Early on the morning of 6 August, I left Base Camp. First it was necessary to cross the crevasse-riven dirty glacier. There was no-one to pull me out if I fell into one of the crevasses. Without protection, I balanced over the narrow ice bridges, often doing the same move three times in order to get shots of myself, using the self-release button. Franz Steiner, our local smith in Villnöss, had made me a screw gadget, welded to the head of my axe, to which I could fix my camera — then I only had to step a few metres away and — click! This is the only way I could photograph myself. The ice was so hard lower down, and there were so many rocks strewn about, that I could put the camera, with its 15mm wide-angle lens, onto a flat stone or ice ledge. Higher up, I kept up my little game, using the ice axe device. So my axe was useful on several counts: it was an intrinsic part of my climbing apparatus, a photographic tripod, a balancing aid; I could use it for levelling out bivouac sites, and I could secure my tent to it. Making a single piece of equipment fulfil all these functions, was an important factor of success in this solo venture.

It was still cold when I climbed the ice hose to the right of the two lower Mummery Ribs and it was frozen hard as iron; and the Great Icefall (above, left) was bathed in blue-grey light. Whenever I paused to rest, I looked up and was amazed by the huge seracs which seemed to bar all progress in the middle of the face. I knew that these morning hours were the safest for climbing. Even the first rays of the sun stroked the seracs (previous double-page), I remained unruffled for now the ice would become slightly softer and easier to get a grip on. It was not always easy to steer a course through all the crevasses, icefalls and avalanche runs, and to have to climb each stretch twice over would have cost me too much effort. The dark rock rib to the left of the picture is the top of the second Mummery Rib. In 1895, Mummery – the first man to attempt this face – bivouacked behind it. On my own 1973 attempt I spent the night at the foot of the Upper Rib, which is illuminated by the sun in this picture and stands out clearly as a distinct spur; that is where I abandoned that attempt. My brother and I climbed down this spur in 1970. Through the gully, to its right, was where I would find the last exit through to the valley, four days later. My climb ran from the middle of the picture, diagonally right and above the big Icefall again moving left, where I placed my second bivouac directly underneath the Mazeno Ridge (below).

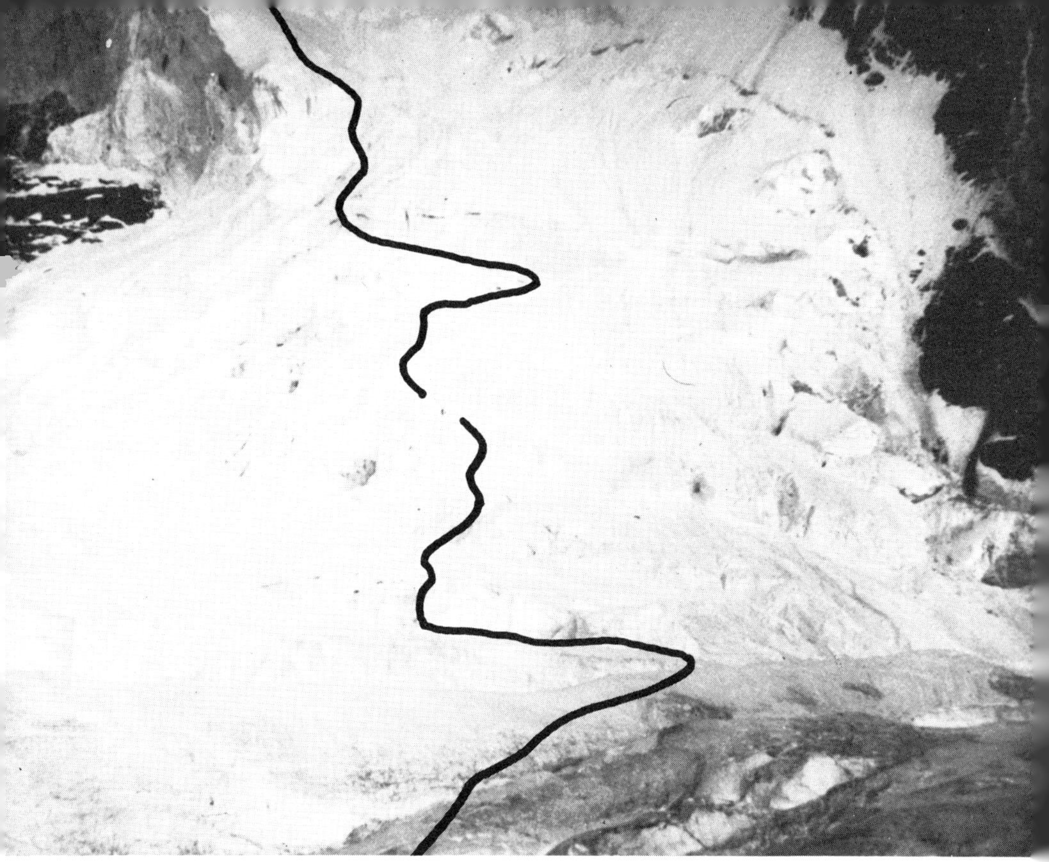

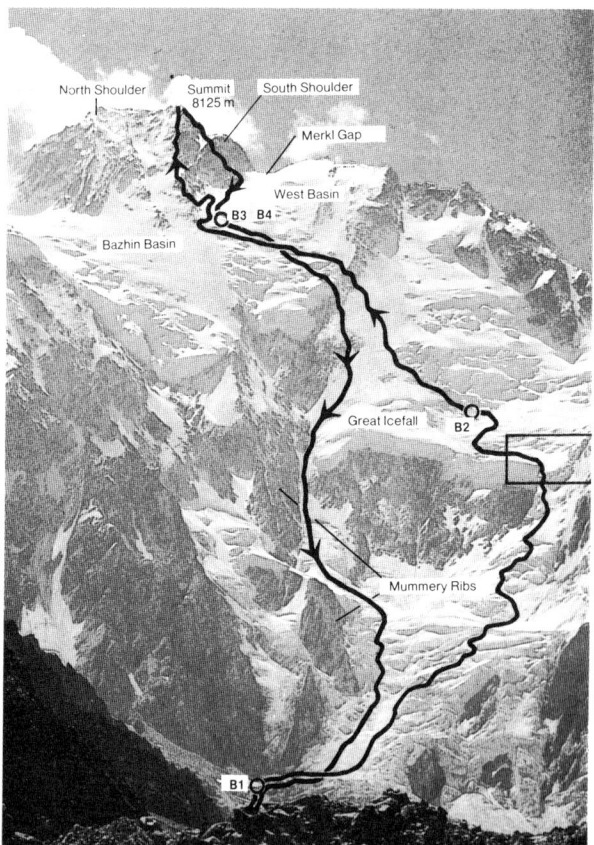

From Base Camp Ursula and Terry followed my progress through the telescope. They kept the 'little black dot' continually in sight. Ursula also shot these pictures.

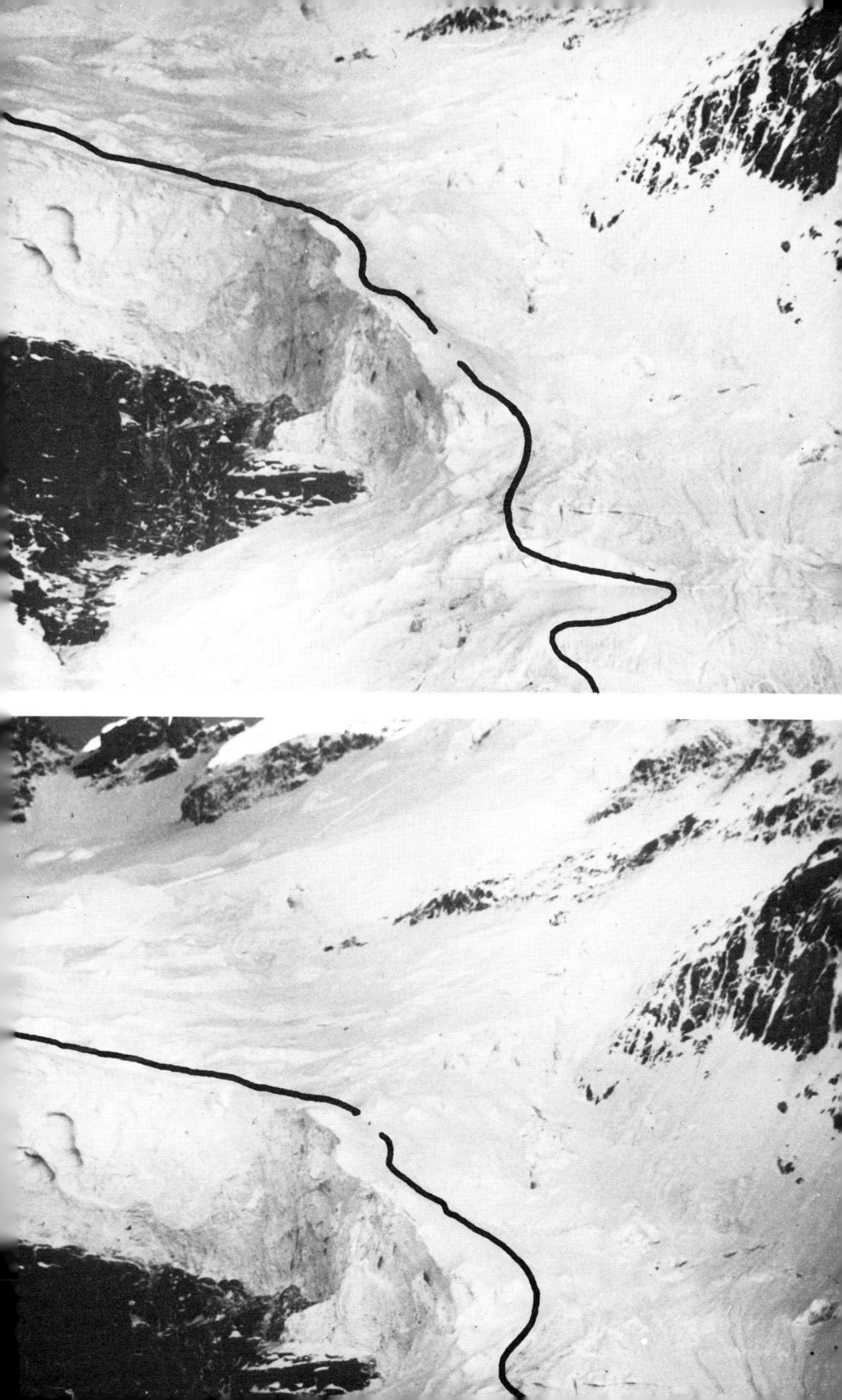

SOLO NANGA PARBAT

bivouac. That would be too risky. Above the Great Icefall is the first relatively safe zone; somewhere there I must put my tent.

A little after eight o'clock I am out of the danger zone. I feel like shouting for joy. I made 500 metres of height in an hour at the start. Being so quick, I have been able to surmount the ice bulge easily, and now I'm in very high spirits. I did not take many photographs. It's not easy to take pictures of oneself. I have had a screw welded to my ice axe on which I can fasten my camera. With the axe thrust firmly in the snow and a delayed-action release button, I can photograph myself.

I wonder how Ursula is feeling. She won't know how I'm getting on. Perhaps she can see me through the telescope. But just watching and not knowing is very hard to bear. I told her and Terry, before I left, to wait ten days.

'If I'm not back in ten days, twelve at the outside, you can go back home!'

I don't want anyone to come looking for me if I don't get back down. That would be pointless. I don't want anyone to hazard their life bringing me down from the face. I put my affairs in order before coming on this expedition.

The 'bridge' or ramp section below me, which rises a vertical height of 600 metres, is as high as a classic East Alpine face. Far above me the summit — in the cold light of morning it looks infinitely far away — is the glass mountain of the fairy stories. All the same I have a feeling that it is attainable. I only experience momentary surges of fear, of being perhaps engulfed by loneliness on my own up there; no fear at all of not coming back.

Even in the steepest ice passages I photograph myself from eye-level. I have deliberately fitted the wide-angle fish-eye lens to my miniature 35mm camera. This way I can take myself at close range without having to retreat too far. The snow is still holding well and I leave no footprints. I am at 6200 metres. I have not had to belay myself at all today, nor used either the ice screw or the rock piton. The glacier lies far below me. When I hear loud cracks on the Diamir Face, they don't ruffle me unduly. The danger zone is passed. For another good hour I climb up over the firm snow. The sun grows warm. It casts a yellow flush on the blue snow

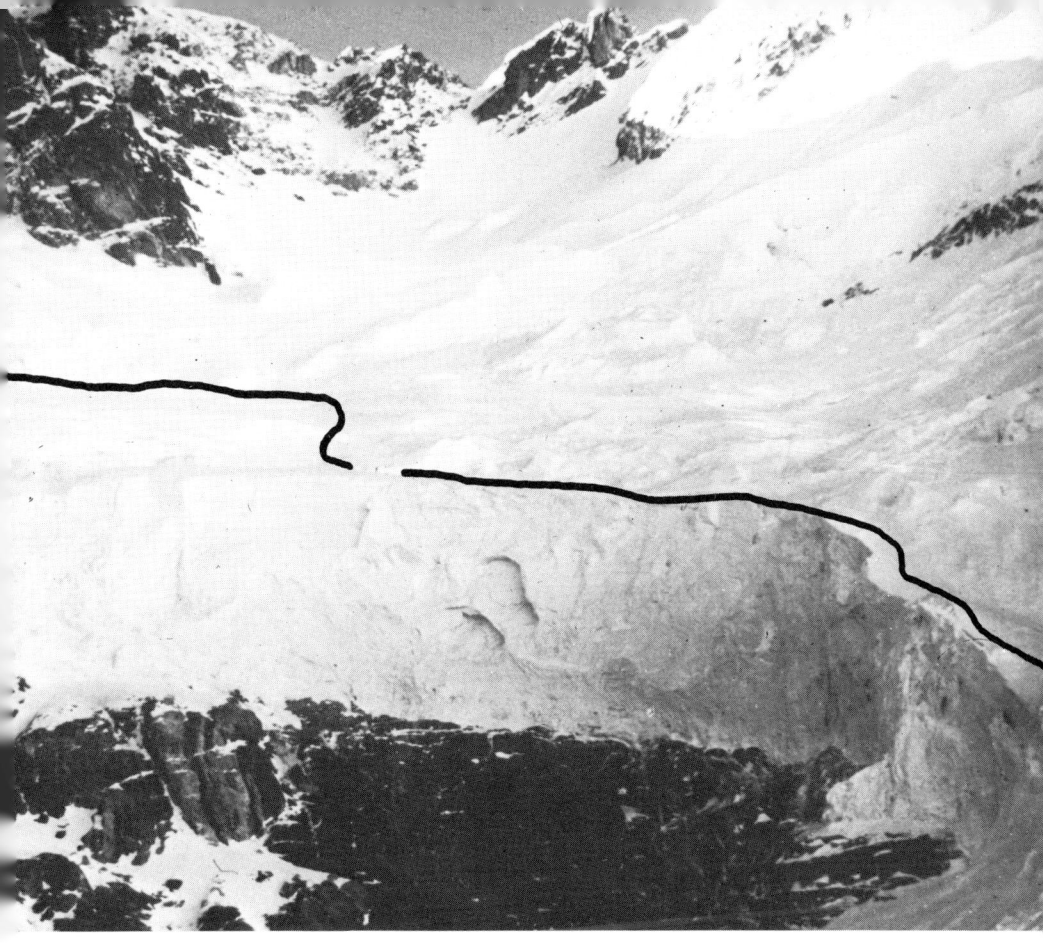

I traversed to the left above the Great Icefall. The overhanging seracs below me were as much as 200 metres high.

flanks. In one corner under a vertically poised ice tower, the blue is particularly intense. I will stop there.

I sit down on my rucksack. This is the ideal spot for a bivouac. A good place to be, where one feels secure and strong. A sense of well-being at having reached it flows through my whole body. I stretch out comfortably and gaze over the clouds to the horizon. I feel that the weather will hold.

It is not that I am pitting myself against the rest of the world. Nor have I allied with nature against everything else. I sit here as if I were a constituent part of this mountain. Every little move, I make with the utmost respect. I daren't slip, daren't trigger an avalanche nor tumble into a crevasse. I am like the snow on the mountainside, and perfectly in tune with the rocks, the ice, the clouds. No more need for philosophy. I am in concord with everything — including death.

SOLO NANGA PARBAT

I did not set off with the object of conquering a peak, nor indeed of returning home a hero. What I want is to come to know the fears of the world. I have to be able to feel new again. However the fear of being alone is not with me now, has not once entered my imagination. And the certain knowledge that I won't meet anybody up here is even a comfort — loneliness is no longer a catastrophe! Obviously in all this peace I have been able to attain a new self-awareness. How different loneliness can be: sometimes frustrating separation, then the growing consciousness of freedom. The experience, for the first time in my life, of White Loneliness, loneliness which is no longer a handicap but a strength.

Under the overhanging ice I tread out a place for the tent. If I want to sleep I have no choice but to tuck myself in under some projection. The Diamir Face is so interpersed with seracs that there is nowhere one could be safe in the open. An avalanche could suck me instantly off the face.

The world below seems more distant than the summit. Do I feel more drawn to one than the other? At the moment I am completely withdrawn into myself. And there are thick mists and clouds spreading in the valley but I remain calm. I turn the ice screw in the wall above the tent and anchor the guy line to it. When the sun reaches its highest point, I am lying inside. There is just enough room for me, my rucksack and the stove. I melt snow in the bag the tent was in. I hang it close to the wall of the tent full of snow so that as it gets warm, water drips out and I catch this in a small billycan. Whenever there's enough for a cupful, I warm it to make tea or soup. I have to drink a lot.

Having a partner is not so important after all. At first I believed that without a human counterpart, without someone as a mirror image, without a known face I should never manage. It wasn't for the conversation, but just to see someone else — he might say nothing, I say nothing, yet we would each know what the other was thinking. Have I now found a partner in myself? Images are continually emerging in front of me, imaginary friends. I am holding a conversation with someone who is sitting at my side. Is it human? It seems there is another presence besides my own. That is all I can say. It isn't just voices I hear, I actually sense a physical presence ... not palpable, but there all the same and it moves. I can practically see it. I wasn't looking for such a manifestation, nor do I avoid it. Sometimes I say to myself, 'You are a fool, of course there's no-one there at all.' Then I get a strong sensation that this intangible vitality around me is the reality. I am talking to someone. Someone answers me. There is something there that I cannot explain rationally, but whose whole presence affects me. An existence comparable to my own.

This was the site of my second bivouac.

STRANGE VOICES

I am sipping hot soup from a cooking pan no bigger than a cup. My throat feels as sore and rough as if someone had been at it with a rasp. I force myself to swallow a piece of cold cornbeef straight from the tin.

That is a mistake. Immediately I have to be sick, and stick my head out of the tiny tent. I spew into the snow half the liquid I have so painstakingly drunk during the course of the day. Without enough fluid in the body, I am lost from the word go.

I have been crouching in the tent now for six hours, at a height of 6400 metres, in the middle of this West Face of Nanga Parbat almost four kilometres high. It is fearfully hot, but I don't want to put a cover over the tent because with the sun's energy I can melt snow inside the tent. This way I am conserving fuel and can survive that much longer. The tent-bag, forty centimetres long and as thick as a man's leg, still hangs on the ridge of the tent like a great fat sausage. It keeps dripping steadily. Just before the sun goes down, the pot is full for the third time. Again I cook soup. I have to keep drinking and force myself to swallow it all. Eating is out of the question for the time being.

I overdid it coming up this morning; 1600 metres of altitude in six hours with a fifteen kilo pack. It was too much. And all unprotected. Who could have held me if I had fallen? This time I am climbing 'without a safety net or trapdoor in the stage'. That was brought home to me three times during the morning's climb. Three times I was confronted with vertical ice passages and had no choice but to get up. Each time I trembled with apprehension. I wavered; I dare not let myself make one false step. With a partner it wouldn't have been easy, but it would have been easier. We would have been able to belay one another with the rope. But on my own this possibility didn't exist. And so each time I chanced it, telling myself, 'I must make absolutely sure I don't lose my balance.'

This is the sort of climb you only do once in a lifetime. Not just because

DIAMIR

of the sheer effort, but also because of the continual hazard of climbing without protection in such a vast, vertical ice wilderness. I don't think about what would happen to me if I failed, but when I think of the descent, I do worry about these difficult passages. That's a bad sign. I'm not even up yet. Perhaps I won't get right to the top. If it's as hard as this tomorrow I don't know if my strength and skill will be up to it. With every metre I climb, I grow heavier and weaker.

Can I still get down, even from here? I don't want to think about it any more. Whatever the end might be, I push it from my mind. All I must do is melt snow and rest. So while the meltwater drips steadily and plops into the billy, I massage my legs and my right forearm which have become tight with cramp after cutting steps continuously all morning. I have been hacking out holds with my axe, pulling myself up overhangs. Every move had to be right. A single pull-up that didn't work could have meant failure all round.

My socks are dry. The double-boots I put outside the tent, they're dry too. I fetch them in. The fireball in the west dips into a mass of clouds like atomic mushrooms, and sets. The temperature drops right away. The tent-bag had dripped away monotonously so long as it was warm — stiflingly hot in the sun, in fact — now before the meltwater can refreeze in this sharp cold, I carefully pour it into a small pan and balance it over the gas flame. I must keep drinking to replace my lost liquid and prevent my blood from thickening. So as night falls and the temperature goes down to minus fifteen degrees, I drink. I dare not be sick again. Vomit once more and I shall have to turn back if I hope to survive.

Solo: there have only been a few people who have seriously tried to climb an eight-thousander solo before me. Maurice Wilson was one; he sought to climb Everest alone in 1934, but didn't come back. The following year his body was found at a height of 6400 metres. A Canadian, Earl Denman, also attempted Everest and he reached no further than just below the North Col.

Solo: the nearest people are 2400 metres below me in our tiny Base Camp. Terry, who volunteered to be here out of pure curiosity, has no mountain experience at all, nor could Ursula give me any help if there were a mountain emergency. Perhaps she could fetch help were I to signal

SOLO NANGA PARBAT

by distress flares, or over the walkie-talkie, that I was in danger. But I don't have radio, or rocket, or any other kind of emergency signal. There would be no point. Babusar, the nearest place, is four day's march away and that has only intermittent contact with the outside world. They have a hand-cranked telephone that sometimes works. To save weight, I have not even brought a torch with me. The flame of the cooker is my only source of light, and when I have drunk enough I curl up and go to sleep. I don't expect anything to happen to me at night. My mini-tent is protected by the ice overhang and I have anchored it with a piece of rope tied to an ice screw. It ought to withstand even the suction blast of an avalanche. Ought to.

I am quite exhausted and let my head sink back into my anorak which serves as a pillow. Only now does it occur to me to look at my watch. It is only a few minutes after six p.m.

Suddenly I have the sensation of floating. It is as if I were weightless. No fear of falling, just floating. My perceptions, my thinking and feeling, seem to have shifted from their normal dimension. Then just as suddenly, here I am again, lying exhausted on my back. How close the link is between tiredness and liberation from one's physical state. I accept it as quite logical. I alternate between my everyday awareness and this extraordinary enlightenment, and after a while, both feelings merge and I have the sense of hovering up by the roof of the tent, gazing down at myself below. Then it all changes again. It is more than a mere sensation, I see everything like a picture in front of me – now from above, now from below. The feelings are similar to ones I sometimes experience when I wake up. I cannot explain or describe them. The image is blurred, but its impact, so clear.

Again I find myself conversing with someone, and it really is not just me talking to myself. I am convinced there are people there, beings, who I believe I can see out of the corner of my eye. It is not like hallucinations. I experienced those in 1970 when I came down from Nanga Parbat. Then I saw people coming towards me, who suddenly were not there. Some I even recognized. They sat on horses, rode towards me, gesticulated. But then I made them out to be rocks, what I had thought was a grey horse was just a patch of snow on the dead glacier.

DIAMIR

This time I am sure there are people here but I cannot see them. I am conversing with them but couldn't say if I'm talking out loud or not. I am not trying to discover, prove anything; I am just there watching – I just am, that's all. Rationally, I don't believe in these companions myself, but then, when I don't think of anything in particular, there they are again. It is clear to me that these voices come from outside. At intervals I say to myself again, 'There's nobody there. I'm not talking to anyone. I am alone.' But the presence of voices dispels this feeling again. I am not sure that I rationalize these experiences or not, but I communicate my thoughts in the strong conviction that these other beings are there.

When I shut my eyes I can hear my friends better. I feel their presence more strongly than when I glimpse them out of the corner of my eye. It doesn't strike me as odd that there are people here helping me with the cooking, talking to me. I am glad of their company, and I talk to them as much as possible, about my childhood, the state of my personal life . . .

When I take a last look out of the tent, the ridge of hills in the west is bathed in a brown-grey light. It is a long while since the sun disappeared. Rain clouds are building up quickly on the mountain slopes. I must wait here and see if the weather gets better or worse. So long as the clouds cling to the ridges, it's too dangerous to continue further.

The stillness on this face is uncanny. Only a light wind, driving the clouds into the valley, whispers around the tent poles. I can smell snow on the breeze.

'It will rain lower down for sure,' I state.

'It's raining already.' Whoever said that has no definite form, he is just there.

The cloud and the damp air make me sleepy. How thick and heavy these banks of cloud are! They stand out, almost black, against the bright, starry sky.

It's only in the bivouac that the problems really start. When it's just distance separating me from the nearest living people, that's alright, I know I can get back. But up here on such a dangerous face, that's by no means so sure. It accentuates the time and distance between me and other people immeasurably. The solitude one experiences when voluntarily locked in a room, and the kind of solitude I am experiencing now are totally different. Here it is not just waiting for things to change; with every upward step I am putting two steps between me and the nearest human habitation. And every step becomes more strenuous the higher I get. Ultimate solitude is a problem which man is not equipped to cope with.

It is possibly easier, for the single-handed yachtsmen sailing round the world, to let the currents take them when the storms rage. True, even sailors must struggle against the forces of nature; but I would never get high on an eight-thousander if I didn't also struggle against my own body, if I didn't force it upwards against its will, left to its own volition it would go the other way.

I wriggle deeper into my sleeping bag and put the half-filled billy on the gas flame. The melted water must not turn back into ice, yet I am using too much fuel. It is difficult doing everything on one's own. With the left-hand I hold the pot so it doesn't spill over, with the right I pour the soup concentrate out of the aluminium foil into the steaming water. There's no-one to stir it. It occurs to me that my left crampon is broken. With a broken crampon I won't get up or down. I must fix it. I repair the binding with my penknife and am reassured when I test it on my boot and it fits.

What is the matter with me? My fingers went numb the minute the sun went down and now my arms and legs have gone to sleep. Shall I be able to reach the summit in two days? I've only got to be sick once more and I won't make it. I would just have to get down as fast as I could. And I would never have the strength, mental or physical, to make a new attempt. For safety's sake, I don't take any sleeping pills.

SAVED FROM THE ICE

On the morning of 8 August there is great consternation in Base Camp. Ursula tells me days later how it was; at five-fifteen she hears Terry cry out loudly. She is only half-asleep in her tent and Terry's breathless,

DIAMIR

agitated voice drags her instantly to consciousness — Nanga Parbat, Base Camp, Reinhold away three days.

'Ursula, an earthquake, and an avalanche right on the wall!' Avalanche! Earthquake! 'Here? Where?' She is wide-awake — no, she must be still asleep. Her eyes won't stay open. She gets tangled up in her sleeping bag, throws the dish with the cooker and food towards the door of the tent, but there's something caught up on the tentpole and she can't find the knot. She has never heard Terry so excited. Whilst she fumbles with the knot on the tent door, she shouts out, 'Can you see him?' Meanwhile Terry arrives in front of Ursula's tent with our telescope in his hand. With her legs still inside her sleeping bag, Ursula crawls far enough out of the tent to see the Nanga wall beyond the small canopy. The avalanche has already reached the bottom. Quickly she pulls on her jeans, runs across to Terry barefoot and takes the telescope. She is looking for the 'black dot' which she has been following for more than sixty hours. Suddenly a strong wind blows up. It whirls her hair around her head, a squall of snowflakes catches her in the face. Putting her arm up to protect herself, she swings round, and crouches down. After a short look at the blue sky, she believes she is going crazy.

Ursula has often experienced difficulty in distinguishing between dreams and reality, so she demands time and plenty of proof when deciding what is real or not. Even now she cannot say for sure that what went before was a dream and this is where the reality starts. Looking up at the blue sky again, and at the same time being blown over by the wind-blast, she knows she is awake. The ice crystals hurt her eyes and face, and she turns away from the mountain and the avalanche. She gets momentary relief. Again she thinks, with luck it's only a bad dream.

Terry explains that this snow squall is a consequence of the avalanche and not in contradiction to the blue sky. His explanation puts an end to all her illusions. It's no fantasy, no nightmare. This reality-dream-reality phase lasted at most a couple of seconds, but it was enough to terrify her with thoughts of a falling body.

'He is there!' Terry whoops. He has made out the 'black dot' on the face, a moving dot. Ursula breathes a sigh of relief but a lingering doubt remains. Since yesterday she felt they must have been mistaken about the

SOLO NANGA PARBAT

moving dot, she cannot imagine I could have got so high on my first day.

She is sure the dot is much too high. But if that is the case, then his bivouac site would have been far lower and so would definitely have been carried away by the avalanche, she thinks. Suppressing her feelings, she accepts Terry's assurance. Like a straw she clutches to his insistence that the avalanche went down below the bivouac site. [Could he but see, I am cheerfully sitting up here watching the progress of the snow and dust clouds.] But when Ursula considerd that had I put off my climb by a day, as I did before, then I should have inevitably been in the path of the avalanche, it sends cold shivers running up and down her spine. When she finally saw for herself the black dot moving off towards the summit from the spot where yesterday my tent stood she would dearly have loved to fling her arms around Terry's neck.

Terry told Ursula of an earthquake more than a hundred years before which brought down so much ice and debris from Nanga Parbat that it caused an unprecedented catastrophe. Between the years 1840 and 1841, the west side of the Lichar Ridge of the Nanga Parbat massif, opposite Gor, collapsed as a result of an earthquake and dammed the Indus Valley at the narrows, where later the Rakhiot Bridge was to be built. It caused an obstruction some 300 metres deep. The main river was completely choked. In April 1841 Jabbar Khan, the chief of Astor, warned the Government of Kashmir that the river could probably only be held back for another month or so, the dammed lake was already sixty kilometres long. At about the same time, Raja Karim Khan of Gilgit, also sent warnings, written on birch bark, down the main valley of the Indus. But little notice seems to have been taken of either of these warnings. The dam burst. Every dry channel filled with water and the river was racing furiously, like a wall of mud; it hadn't in the least the colour of water. It was a fearful torrent of foul water, carcasses, camels, tents, mules, donkeys, trees and household furniture. Those who didn't see it coming were inevitably lost. Many clambered onto rocks, only to be speedily swallowed by the waters. Only those who took to the mountainside escaped. The toll was immense. Hundreds of acres of arable land were licked up and carried away by the water. All the trees fringing the banks, and the men

Sitting on a plastic container with the telescope propped on a pack-frame, Terry maintained continual surveillance of the face for almost five days.

in the trees, and the horses and mules tied to the trees, all were swirled away and lost forever. Just as a woman with a wet towel can sweep away a legion of ants, so the river had swept away a whole army!

While Ursula and Terry prepare their breakfast at Base Camp, I am on my way, high on Nanga. A Pakistani farmer brings them a report of the earthquake; he has heard it on his radio. The epicentre was exactly in the knee-bend of the Indus, it was force eight. I know nothing of this, of course, all I know is what I have seen – how the ice face beneath me broke off in a massive sheath.

I woke at five in the morning on this Tuesday, 8 August. My altimeter registered fifty metres higher than the evening before. It wasn't that I had been spirited up the mountain in my sleep, the air pressure had fallen. Not a good sign.

I melted some hard-frozen snow in the cooking pot, warmed the water and suspended a teabag in it. After the tea, I made soup with water and a stock cube. In the icy stillness of dawn, I suddenly heard a noise like some huge, distant waterfall. I tore open the iced-up entrance and stuck my head outside the tent. Half the ice face beneath me must have broken away. Everything seemed to be on the move. To my left ice avalanches roared down like torrents. Beneath me a wide avalanche swept like a tidal wave down the mountain. It was made up of the ice that I had climbed yesterday. It swept right over the spot where I was bivouacing yesterday at this time. Spellbound, I could see what would have happened to me had I set off twenty-four hours later. No panic, although the blood was pounding in my temples. I merely said to myself, 'There goes your

At about 7400 metres above sea level, that is just 800 metres below the summit, I installed my third bivouac. On a flat snow patch between two crevasses, I erected my igloo tent, which was specially made (for this Nanga Parbat climb) of Gore-tex fabric and with duralumin poles. In the afternoon it was so hot that I hung my sleeping bag over the tent to protect me from the heat of the sun. I filled the tent-bag with mushy snow, which then with the help of the sun, produced water. During this time I would lie in the tent, sleeping off and on, and experiencing strange encounters with invisible companions. The tent was just big enough to allow me to lie down. At the foot end I stowed my rucksack, my cooker was to my left, bits and pieces like altimeter, scarf, watch, I hung to the sides of the tent. Gloves and socks I left outside until the sun went down, so that they could dry out. I fixed crampons to my axe, which I drove firmly into the snow within reach of the tent entrance. During the afternoon its shadow fell across the tent, and only in the late evening (next double-page) was its silhouette no longer visible through the fabric. The weather seemed to be holding, and so I awaited the approach of night on 8–9 August. I had now been fifty-four hours alone, bound for the Death Zone.

Just before sunset, I stepped outside the tent for the last time. I now stood precisely on the border between day and night (the third bivouac site is about a centimetre to the right of the summit fall-line, where the cold blue and dark rose meet below the summit trapezium). For the summit bid the following day, there were two possibilities open to me: I could climb the flat basin to the right of the ridge and follow this to the South Shoulder and thence to the summit (this was the way I descended in 1970), or from the bivouac site, keep left, directly up the poorly-defined spur edge — rock, interspersed with snow — and follow this to the summit. This route was certainly intrinsically more difficult, but perhaps less strenuous, than the climb through the wind-blown and avalanche snow which fills the Western Basin. On 9 August I was fairly tired and consequently set off relatively late. I kept my crampons on, even on the rock passages. My tent to the left of the rocks, was soon hidden from sight, as it was screened by a crevasse above it (bottom picture). I was already much higher than the Mazeno Peaks and Ganalo Peak which border the upper Diamir Valley to left and right. The face now fell away for more than 3000 metres, down to the Diamir Basin, and the glacier, from this height, looked no bigger than a snake. Despite their bright colours, I could not see the Base Camp tents from here, lying to the right of the serpentine moraine.

way down. You won't get back that way — you'll need to find something else for the way down.'

In the chill blue shadows of the early morning I folded up my tent and packed everything back into my rucksack. Everything I'd need for the next few days went in; two tins of corned beef, tin of liver sausage, a pound of cheese, two hard loaves of peasant bread, soup, tea, coffee.

I don't feel as if I shall ever warm up. The snow is uneven — sometimes sheer ice, sometimes crusty and sometimes powdery. I only feel secure on my feet if my crampons crunch well in to give a firm hold. There is a cold wind blowing from the summit straight into my face; the rucksack weighs heavily. I had intended to leave a small cache of food behind at the campsite for the descent, but now that I shan't be able to go back the same way, I have to carry everything with me. Perhaps I will climb down the south side.

I climb diagonally left towards a jagged serac where I have spotted what looks like a weak spot in the defences. If I can find a way through, I shall be on the gentler slopes of the summit region, safe for the time being. I'm not happy about the weather, I think it will snow. There are cirrus clouds in the west and the summit of Nanga Parbat wears a rainbow-tinted cloud, like a hat.

It takes me longer to climb the first 100 metres this morning than it took to climb 500 metres yesterday. This won't do at all! At this rate I shall never get to the summit!

When the avalanches poured down out of every corner of the Diamir Face — below me, to my left, to my right — I thought, at first, avalanches so early in the day, I've never come across that before. Then I reconciled myself to it. Like a nightmare the spectacle has remained with me. When I saw the masses of ice pouring down towards our Base Camp, I was terrified they could overwhelm it.

I am not saying luck had anything to do with my deliverance — I was just high enough to be out of trouble. I don't know what chance led me through the dangerous lower slopes at just the right moment, but it is the same chance that could just as easily take me right into the path of an avalanche another time.

Looking down between my legs to the foot of the face, it strikes me

On the morning of 8 August I climbed diagonally left from my bivouac (bottom centre of picture). The Mazeno Gap is on the right; it was following this connecting South-west Ridge that Hanns Schell and his Graz climbers reached the summit in 1976.

that the glacier which was rather dirty-looking, now appears covered in fresh snow. Otherwise little has changed.

I am now level with the highest of the Mazeno Peaks and can see out beyond the walls of the Diamir Valley to left and right. From up here it seems as if I could see the features of the whole world. I could spend hours just looking. But I must go on. I continue upwards, propelled by something I cannot understand but feel well enough.

This icy flank is a wonderful world! I find it very attractive. When I look up to the summit, a wave of very positive emotion sweeps over me. It gives me strength. Now, poised here between the summit and the dubious descent, I can divine who I really am. I have only to look at the clouds and the mountains all around to know that I belong to this place.

Between nine and ten the sun catches me for the first time. It grows warmer, and later, unpleasantly hot. I have passed the 7000 metre mark and approach the trapezoid summit block beneath which I hope to find a safe campsite. At times sinking up to my thighs in snow, I draw near to

I found a place for my third bivouac under the steep concave summit wall above the West Basin. Below me was a huge hanging glacier.

the rocks, step by step. Five steps, pause, another five steps. In the glittering light and with my strongly-absorbent sunglasses, it is difficult to make out a suitable campsite. Added to which, the heat and the heavy rucksack are wearing me down. There doesn't seem to be an overhanging rock anywhere, under which I can place my next bivouac. And this powder snow is bottomless! If only I had a partner now who could take turns breaking the trail! But there is no-one but me and I must scout, struggle on, take the lead, with no-one to help me, no word of encouragement.

The rocks are all buried deep. There's not a square metre of flat ground anywhere. I trudge back to the right. Finally, between two fissures in the ice, I find a site that will do. I am completely dehydrated, not an ounce of strength left, and I collapse in the snow. I simply can't manage anything more, can't put up the tent.

Today I have climbed a few steep passages, and haven't taken many photographs. The fact that the weather seems to have changed for the better, hardly interests me at all at the moment, although I do know that there is no way anybody could rescue me from up here if I couldn't make

DIAMIR

it by myself. Not even a helicopter could reach me. I only hope that Terry and Ursula are not worrying too much.

Whatever could have possessed me to get myself into this misery. As if climbing Everest without oxygen equipment wasn't enough of a 'first' for one year. I lie in the snow, sucking in the thin air and exhaling it in such a way that I hold it again briefly in my lungs. The afternoon sun burns down. I've got to drink, got to start melting snow again in the tent-bag. In this scorched pitiable state, I suddenly start thinking about things that I have never really consciously considered before. Perhaps my infinitely lonely position is only bearable because of this.

Lying there exhausted, drained of thought and energy, I suddenly have the feeling that there is a girl sitting next to me. I say to myself, why should I put up the tent alone when we can both do it together. My tent is a very simple construction — an igloo-shaped bag which is suspended on two semicircular, criss-crossed hoops of duralumin. The only difficulty in putting it up is in keeping the poles taut.

The girl watches me as I stamp down the snow, and I think, she'll get too hot if she moves about. But although I have to do it all myself, it's still good to have her there. After half an hour the tent is up. I spread out the sleeping bag on the top of it to shade the inside. I put in the mat and rucksack, and hang up the snow-bag, which doesn't start dripping for a couple of hours. I feel more confident today than yesterday although a sea of mist fills the valleys below, enshrouding everything below 6500 metres. But on the western horizon a thin bank of red haze promises fine weather. It looks as if the world ends there. And for the present I am not at all interested in what goes on beyond that. All around me I see children, men and women. I don't know them and don't want anything from them. It's just that they are there, on and off. And I talk to them. We discuss everything I do. For instance, when I look at the altimeter, I tell them what it reads.

The sun burns fiercely through the cloud, particularly onto the tent. I lie almost naked inside. I take the occasional mouthful from a half-open tin of corned beef. My ice axe in the snow outside casts its shadow across the tent. From time to time I fetch in some snow or take a look at the weather. The huge banks of cloud on the horizon form their own ranges of mountains. Such fascinating shapes, vague, like objects underwater!

As I cook and drink, and practise storing air in my lungs, my confidence gradually seeps back. I am now settled in, safe in this forsaken spot. The feeling of absolute solitude only occasionally washes over me. I crawl out of the tent awkwardly. The girl is there again. 'We're a good way up already,' I say.

'You'll reach the summit tomorrow,' she says.

'Only if the weather holds.'

'It will.'

I stand for a while outside the tent and look out westwards. All around there is nothing but banks of cloud. The harsh light on the snow, the air — still warm — and occasional glimpses of stars in the sky. The girl only laughs when I tell her. Out of the corner of my right eye, I fancy I see her get up and move about.

Again I look up through a gap in the clouds at the afternoon sky and notice the stars. 'You know I've never seen that before,' I remark.

'Really, haven't you?'

More gaps appear in the clouds and the sky above is blue-black.

'Take enough snow into the tent,' the girl says, and I imagine I see her duck and go inside. She has a nice voice. She stays in my memory a long time. She doesn't tell me anything, we just converse. Mundane things. But we talk.

'Sure,' she says, 'the weather will stay fine . . . until you get back down again.' She might well be right I think, the wind has almost dropped and despite the cloud it is still warm.

Four o'clock in the afternoon. 'I'm glad I came alone,' I say.

'Glad?'

'Yes. I feel better than on other expeditions. I don't get on anyone's nerves and no-one disturbs me. I climb as fast as I want to, pitch the tent when I want to; I feel much freer, up here on my own.'

As the sun's rays pierce the grey cloud, everything around me seems to come alive. The clouds themselves start to move and I hear strange sounds all around, a hissing and then a whistling. Is it hallucinations? I am fully aware that I am speaking to myself, or to my shadow, that everything else is unreal. But then my friend comes back and we talk some more. How strange such encounters are; I can only sense this person opposite me, not touch her nor look directly at her. Sometimes she is so close she almost brushes against me, but when I look round, I don't see her.

It is a truly crazy feeling, being quite alone and yet able to call friends at any time. Often before I have carried on some inner dialogue unconsciously to prove to myself that I was not alone. But now here I am and not alone.

In the evening I go outside the tent one last time. My glance falls on my own shadow. Standing in front of the tent, I see how the light changes from a warm yellow to a cool red. Later it grows greenish and then violet-black. Above, on the summit of Nanga, the last glimmer dies away. I watch for a while from inside the tent, like an animal peering out of his lair. I squint beyond the sparkling snow and the setting sun, and am at peace.

LOST FOR WORDS

When I wake the next morning, 9 August, something weighs heavy on my senses. I am awake without wanting to be awake. I experience an oppressive transition stage between half-sleep and grim reality; all my old anxieties return. I am frightened of being in this place, frightened of being me, frightened of being. Sleeping, I had forgotten that I am alone, but this sudden confrontation with such utter loneliness immediately envelops me in deep depression. In the months after my break-up with Uschi, it was often like this when I woke up. The sudden pressure which threatens to dash me to pieces, a well of despair bubbling up from deep sources and taking possession of my whole being. It is so strong that I have to cry. I open the tent and look out. Immediately I feel better. It is as if this really is a good spot for me. The ordeal to test my breaking point is over. My contradictory apprehensions about facing loneliness and the hankering

NANGA PARBAT
9.8.1978

Reinhold Messner

1o absolute Alleinbesteigung
(neue Route in der Diamir-
Wand)

Incipit liber bresich qué nos genesim
In principio creauit deus celú dicim⁹
et terram. Terra autem erat inanis et
uacua: et tenebre erāt sup facię abissi.
et sps dūi ferebať sup aquas. Dixitq;
deus. ffiat lux. Et facta ē lux. Et uidit
deus lucem ȹ esset bona: ⁊ diuisit lucē
a tenebris. appellauitq; lucem diem ⁊
tenebras noctem. ffactūq; est uespe et
mane dies unus. Dixit ñ; deus. ffiat
firmamentū in medio aquaȝ: ⁊ diui-
dat aquas ab aquis. Et fecit deus firmamentū: diuisitq; aquas que erāt
sub firmamento ab hijs ƭ erant sup

My 'Summit Book', the first page of the Gutenberg Bible.

DIAMIR

after solitude have been reconciled. A friendship with myself is yet possible.

Morning has not properly broken. It is lighter, true, but then it was never completely dark during the night. The air is very cold. The realization of being alone yet having resources to spare has given me a strong feeling of identity. I and my dreams are one.

The play of the dark clouds below me both worry and fascinate me. Now and then between the surging clouds a mountain top emerges. It is like being witness to the Creation. Like seeing everything from the outside. It doesn't occur to me to be surprised at the threatening bad weather. It is a weird sensation, 'Tike,' I say, just that, a word that slips into my mind unbidden. I could blow soap bubbles and suspend the tent on them. For a tiny moment something warm passes through my dog-tired body.

I go back to sleep and only emerge from the tent at seven o'clock. The sky is overcast but I can still see the summit. If the snow and ice between here and the summit is firm, I could be up in two hours, three at most. But it turns out that I have to plough through bottomless drifts, treacherous as quicksand. I wade on, infinitely weary.

My invisible companions are not there. I am on my own again. I can't seem to move from the spot, it feels like being hobbled. It is impossible to thrust aside the snow which is hip-high, I have to tread it down and burrow a way forwards, leaving a wide, deep trail behind me. At ten o'clock after three hours of gruelling drudgery, I know I will never reach the summit like this. Nor will I get down if I continue to wear myself in this way.

When it becomes a matter of life and death, then the summit becomes of no importance, that summit which yesterday had so much allure that it presented the only justification for this last alpine adventure. Either I turn back here and now . . . or? Or I chance the last option I have — to climb the steep rock barrier in a direct line with the summit.

This helplessness! This being cut off from every living soul would drive anyone to madness in time! No-one to balance oneself against! No other face as a mirror image; no friend to assist or lean on. The full consciousness of it all doesn't penetrate completely, but is there subliminally all the time, and with it an inhibiting worry about going on.

I twice changed films on the summit. With my small camera I shot a whole film of black and white, positioning myself so that I had the summit against every possible background.

The borderline between giving up and going ahead has grown very narrow. I want to allow myself one last attempt. If the rocks are feasible and the snow on them not too ready to avalanche, I have a slight chance.

From my boyhood, rock-climbing has been my speciality. I climb carefully, giving it all I have got, as one has to on a vertical Dolomite face if one is to get up at all. But Dolomite faces are blithe, practice cliffs compared to this. I shall never know how I managed not to slip here at 8000 metres with my big clumsy double-boots and poor vision through the snow-goggles. Obviously my natural instincts are assisting me. Perhaps now that the summit is within reach, my soul is already up there. I balance along narrow ledges, no wider than the palm of my hand, and wallow through snow-choked gulleys. All my senses are wide-awake. Inner reserves are tapped, reserves that I no longer believed I had.

One minute I am in the light, then in shade. Clouds drift across the sun. Everything is vague, blurred. It snows intermittently. The valleys are hidden in mist; only occasionally does a transitory view of pastureland reveal itself out of the gloom. It is all incomprehensible, beyond description. One moment all seems clear to me, then it is as if madness is gaining sway. I no longer completely belong here.

The western horizon seems unutterably far away and unreal. I can no longer imagine people living down there. Nor do I feel any kind of sympathy with or pride in myself. My terror first thing this morning and the wonderful discovery of being here have left their mark. No more proud satisfaction at being so exposed as on earlier expeditions. I'm not trying to flee from the industrial age back into the stone age, nor am I fleeing from other people, I am merely in passage. As if I wanted, by climbing this vertical ice wilderness for no reason, to shake myself from the loneliness that has beset me for several months. Already I have left the

well-ordered world far behind. For days I have been living in this chaotic emptiness of ice, and everything streaming through my body leads to new cognition; and so I rediscover the world.

The images surrounding me are unreal. The emptiness calls me louder than billboards or advertisement-fringed boulevards. The more desolate the ice slope, the more I seem to see, the more the images grow inside me. During this climb my human side is awakened and at the same time stifled. And again my exhaustion is so great that I can no longer think. Yet in my tiredness everything appears crystal clear. In this state, elevation and banality lie very close together. The simplest physiological needs are as important as the most high-flown philosophical doctrines.

I make slow progress climbing the summit block. Here and there I can make use of rock passages but often I have to toil over snow bands and gulleys. When I stop to rest I now see large desert areas to the west. They lie under a transparent film of haze and cloud. The world around me is so empty and ghostly, it is uplifting and beautiful to see. I think how high I have climbed already. One would imagine there is something presumptuous about the sensation of thrusting into regions which are barely accessible. All I experience is a kind of floating above all the things I have left behind me and perhaps which never were.

The climbing goes without incident. Only in places where the snow lies hard-packed in narrow fissures, do I have trouble finding safe holds for my feet. I don't use any pegs to secure myself. Fear of falling doesn't worry me but now and then it occurs to me that my strength might give out.

I am enjoying the physical contact with the ice, the rocks and snow, especially on steep passages when I take my hands out of my gloves and feel the raw rock under my fingertips. Despite a slight numbness in my fingers, I can feel its texture, rough like emery paper. My boots can't slip off it.

I have to stop and rest immediately if I go faster than my strength allows. I consciously breathe faster — hyperventilate — in order to pump my blood full of extra oxygen. Looking up at the summit is painful

because I know how much exertion lies between me and it, its silhouette touching the heavens.

I keep noticing little indentations which would take a peg, but I don't use them. The one and only peg I have with me is in my anorak, just for emergency. When the cracks are wide enough for me to insert a finger to steady myself, I feel safe. I endeavour to position my boots so that the leverage is not too great and my calf-muscles not over-exerted. My crampons grate against the rock, and apart from my heavy breathing, this is often the only sound I hear.

Having put one 80 metre buttress behind me, I come to little snowfields, which I have to plough my way across. It is obvious that the exertion is far from over yet. I much prefer rock passages to these flatter snow sections. From here it would be possible to swing out right across the near-vertical face to reach a direct line with the summit, and then climb up on dry rock, but without a rope, such a traverse is unthinkable. So I have to keep going despite the strenuous trail-breaking work.

I have already made the decision between doing a solo climb with self-belaying tactics and a solo climb without any direct aid or self-protection. To climb a face like this using pegs or expansion bolts would never have tempted me.

I am not making such smooth progress anymore. Sometimes I have the feeling that my legs are no longer properly co-ordinated, one with the other. I push myself as far forward as I can manage, and then I have to cower in the snow, resting. Only after I have recovered a bit, do I look upwards, and then go on again. Even on the last few snowfields, I still have the feeling that perhaps it is not possible, but at the same time with each step success becomes more likely. Every metre exacts an effort of will.

For a body, drained and desiccated, it is agony to struggle against gravity in the thin air. The whole body is involved in making every step. This interplay or co-ordination I am more aware of now, although I have known it from many earlier climbs. It is fuller and stronger than it was. I am fully aware of the danger of the climb, but this awareness doesn't have the effect of cramping my muscles or movements in any way.

A leaden tiredness causes me to go slower and slower. But after a few minutes rest when I look up again, I feel fine. The rock is icy cold, but when the sun catches it, it seems warm and less exposed. It's harder to get a grip in the shade.

The air above the summit ridge is still clear, the sky deep-blue to black. Does the world come to an end up there? Although I'm not perspiring, there is a salty taste on my tongue and my lips feel sticky. Another half an hour brings me to a rock projection, big enough to take my whole foot. I ponder for a short while whether I should not after all put in a peg and secure myself there for a quarter of an hour. But I decide against it and sit down as best I can. I dangle my legs over the edge, trying to relax, and lean back against the rock behind me. I can feel its pressure on my back and the damp cold underneath me, creeping up through the seat of my pants.

I take a shorter rest than necessary, then stand awkwardly and look upwards again. It is as if the distance between me and the summit had altered while I was resting. Even the sweeping plunge below seems to have become steeper, more exposed. Were I to let go, I should fall into emptiness. I struggle with my camera and take a couple of eye-level shots of myself, then pull a bit of hard bread out of my trouser pocket and gnaw at it slowly.

Then I nestle back against the curve of the rock, both feet on the tiny perch, my trunk leaning against the face. I stuff my gloved hand between my left cheek and the rock so that I can doze standing up. Well satisfied, I poke the bread in my mouth and chew it thoughtfully. At most it can now only be fifty metres to the summit; the last fifty metres of this 400 metre rock spur on the summit trapezium.

'It's going well,' I mutter to myself.

'That's right,' says someone else, 'you're climbing slowly, it's true, but you'll be faster going down.'

'Ah, yes — I've still to get down.' I must make myself move on for I know these last fifty metres are the most strenuous of all and I cannot afford to hang about.

I straighten up, then lean out to look down the mountainside. I don't feel like thinking about the descent yet. I must get on. I'm horribly thirsty, but know I won't be able to drink again until evening. I keep getting a queasy feeling in my stomach when my vision slips beyond my chunky plastic boots to the shimmering grey tongue of glacier at the foot of the face. Instinctively I cling more tightly to the rock. Looking down into sheer endless depths allows an element of uncertainty to creep in which I don't feel when I'm actually climbing. So long as I'm on the move, weighing every step, this butterfly-feeling vanishes, even if I look down through my legs. It only gets me if I'm not concentrating, resting. It's not an altogether unpleasant sensation, it is as if my centre of gravity had momentarily shifted – it comes back once I'm involved again. I used to experience this feeling in the Dolomites as a child; it happens when I'm on narrow ridges, ledges or exposed pitches.

This long rest has done me good. I climb more easily now, more naturally. At one and the same time I get myself under control and yet let myself go. It's not a conscious final spurt, I am climbing more naturally than before. There's no longer any question of failure even though my strength is nearly spent. Momentarily I think that there won't be enough time for the descent, but this worry quickly evaporates. I am lighthearted again.

I no longer have to battle against gravity; I drag myself along in an all-consuming weariness. Panting like a dog, spittle trickles from the corners of my mouth to freeze in my beard. My brow, resting on the axe-head, is hot. With contorted features I crouch there oblivious of myself. How my lungs roar in my ears! How my heart hammers! These two sounds, superimposed in my head, are painful.

I straddle up a small gash. Suddenly there's a tinkling sound – the lens hood has fallen off my camera and now lies ten metres lower down. I haven't the strength to go back for it – besides I'm only programmed to climb upwards. I photograph myself less often now; on the difficult passages I need both hands for climbing, and to use the self-release button would mean climbing the relevant section three times over, which I don't

want to do. I haven't the strength for that; I'm only glad to get up once without falling.

When I finally reach the summit it is about four o'clock on this 9 August. I plunge my axe into the granular snow on the highest point of all and gaze around: the Silbersattel, below which Willo Welzenbach and Willy Merkl died all those years ago, seems almost close enough to touch. To the right of that, the Rupal Valley, and in between, a vast, sky-scraping precipice. I have stood on this spot once before, eight years ago, at about the same time of day. Günther was with me then — only to be killed shortly afterwards by an avalanche on the way down.

I wander around in a circle, repeatedly looking at the view, as if I can hardly believe I'm really here. There is no great outrush of emotion such as I experienced on Everest; I am quite calm, calmer than I have ever been on any eight-thousander. I often thought about that, later, and wondered why these swelling emotions, which on Everest wracked me with sobs and tears, should have been absent on Nanga Parbat. I have come to the conclusion that being alone, as I was on top of Nanga, I could not have borne such a strong surge of feeling. I would have been unable to leave. Our bodies know more than we understand with our minds.

Having come full circle around the limit of the snow, I have absorbed everything. Yet I can not say what. There are no feelings of ecstasy, but not of anticlimax either, nor yet am I indifferent. Just relieved and a little proud. I give myself a little shake, then sit down facing west on some rocks sticking out of the snow a few metres below the pointed summit pyramid. It is four thirty p.m. Sitting here like this I suddenly remember the page of text, and fish the aluminium container and the peg out of my anorak. I hammer the peg into the nearest crack and fasten the container to it. Gently I remove the parchment once more and scribble name, date and route on it.

Even looking at the cornices, through which Günther and I emerged after our climb of the Rupal Face in 1970, I remain calm.

I spend ten minutes taking photographs of myself, first in colour, then

It was already four in the afternoon before I reached the highest point of Nanga Parbat on 9 August (next double-page). I screwed my camera onto the ice axe, positioned myself in front of the lens and waited for the click of the self-release. Axe and camera cast a shadow on the snow. Cumulus clouds hung all around; in the valleys and above the sky was overcast with ragged cirrus. The Rupal Peak, a five-thousander south of Nanga Parbat gives the impression from this height of being built from a set of child's bricks. The shadows were already long, and gusts of wind at intervals whirled up the powder snow. On the upper picture opposite, a prominent pyramid is visible; this is the South Shoulder, 8042 metres high. The sunlit cornice to the left of that marks the upper end of the South-east Ridge. That is exactly where Günther and I emerged from the Rupal Face in 1970. On the extreme right of the picture is a dark, vertical rockface, under which Felix Kuen and Peter Scholz bivouacked after the second ascent of the Rupal Face in 1970. I climbed back between the South Shoulder and this rockface to my tent which I'd left standing on the upper Diamir Face on the evening of 9 August. I was fairly worn out by the time I got there. And on top of this had a premonition that the weather was about to turn bad. A dark band of cloud was advancing from the west and the sun disappeared earlier than usual. The lower picture shows my return to the bivouac. When the camera clicked, the ice axe must have been crooked in the snow.

After thirty-six hours of blizzard conditions at 7400 metres, the first opportunity to descend came on 11 August. I decided to abandon practically everything up there, to toss all my superfluous equipment into a crevasse, and at five fifteen a.m. I left the last safe camp in the knowledge that I had to get down to Base Camp that same day. A further bivouac, and without tent and sleeping bag, would be out of the question in my condition. I would not survive. I had to put behind me more than 3000 vertical metres to reach Base Camp, comprising ice cascades, passages of rock, and in places — steep blank ice. Not until I was far below the big serac barrier did the first rays of sun slant down on me. Then the surface layer of the ice began to thaw slightly and I could get a better grip with my crampons. I concentrated to the best of my ability putting every ounce of effort into it. Face to the mountain, the axe in my right hand, I climbed steadily down on the front points of my crampons for thousands of feet until I reached the ice hose, which — like a wide chute — formed a sort of outlet to the foot of the face. That morning on my own I made many thousands of individual climbing moves — identical and yet each one different. It was not yet midday when I reached the lower slopes. By this time I had to keep stopping to sit down. I wanted to do nothing but rest; I had ceased to think long ago.

black and white, and then some more colour. The snow on the summit is now quite trodden down. I photograph myself looking east towards the Silbersattel, to the south, to the west, and again to the east. The mountains of the Karakoram are hardly visible. A massive bank of cloud has risen from the Indus valley and blots out most of the landscape. To the south, the Rupal Peak becomes clear; it looks so small I can hardly believe that it is a 5000 metre mountain. The Mazeno Wall, too, looks steep but small, and the Ganalo Peak, viewed from here, similarly makes no special impression.

My concept and I are an integrated whole. The world stands still. How far away everything is from here. To the south, immensely far below, I can see through a window in the clouds, a shining speck of water, and carpets of fields. Already the first mists are whipping across the ridge. It is only a short cloud-play but it makes the view into the Diamir Valley even more mysterious. I point along the Silver Plateau towards the northeast, as if I were indicating something. The wind has grown stronger and is whirling snow in my footprints.

The summit throws its grey-blue shadow into the Rupal Valley, where it lingers until the sun disappears behind clouds. It is now five o'clock.

I won't be able to get down the rocks again, they are too steep, and the detour around by the West Basin is very strenuous.

'You ought to go down before it's too late.'

'There'll be a moon.'

I am still fascinated by the huge cloud banks which fill the valleys and sail over the crests of mountains, 1000 metres below me.

Night creeps slowly into the valleys. It is like a vague dew-cool layer of mist, blurring all detail. Only in the higher clouds is the warm sunlight still trapped. I still can't bring myself to leave the summit. I suddenly notice ice crystals shimmering in the slanted rays of the sun. Now you really must go, I tell myself. Will I be able to find the tent again in the dark? When it comes to survival, how strange some decisions seem. The summit seems so peaceful and the descent so unnecessary. It is as if I had no further meaning at all; as if I had crawled out of a sea of loneliness into

the safety of the cosmos. As far as the eye can see there are clouds, snow peaks — no trace of life. This mountain, the very epitome of hostility, cold and remoteness, conveys to me a strong sense of total empathy.

The horizon is like a circle around me. My footprints in the snow are the only visible disturbance. It grieves me that there is no-one here with whom to communicate these profound impressions, but then, I could never put into words what I feel. I have finally reached a point where I have ceased to be able to think. The blurred horizon, the furrows in the sky are beyond language. I don't arrive at these discoveries by conscious intellect, I simply sit there and let the feelings permeate me. Straightaway, I know everything beyond any doubt. I would like to lose myself for ever in this twilight over the horizon.

'I,' I say, but already this single utterance from my very core threatens to tear me apart. As I sit there, I too become a cloud, a vapour. This infinite tranquility touches a spring of happiness within me. And the silence urges me to treat the summit very gently. 'I and the summit are one, yet we are different . . .' When I want to say more, the silence bids me be silent too. The story of my life stretches out before me like the wind. With it the clear consciousness that it won't go on for ever. That doesn't make me sad. The world enfolds me and spits me out, I can feel it seething and whirling.

When I stood here eight years ago, my feelings were more intense — different, anyway; perhaps also the same. Günther was with me then, he came over the last snow crest to the summit. For a moment now I have the feeling of floating on one of these clouds and looking down as we embrace each other. Then I see despair surrounding us as it becomes clear that it is impossible for us to go down the same way we came up. It hangs like a rebuke between us. I can recall the events from that time on as if I had two separate memories.

Today I am not so moved as I was then. In those days Nanga was my first eight-thousander and I was still inexperienced.

After an hour I start down from the summit, at first coming down the South Ridge and then across the snow of the Western Basin. The shadows

are long. The track behind me shows dark against the rose-coloured snow. I let step after step fall in the uneven snow. How tired I am, I notice. Often it is only with the greatest effort that I can lift my feet from the deep tracks. By the time I notice that the ramp I am following loses itself amongst steep rocky slabs, it is too late. I can't go back, I am much too tired for that. A direct descent is also out of the question because there are vertical bluffs between me and the West Basin. Trusting to instinct I look for a route amongst the outcrops and snow patches. Sometimes I have to focus all my strength on a single point in order not to slip.

Arriving at the bivouac site, I come back to reality. The tent is small and covered in ice; all its walls are sloping, its entrance so narrow that I can only squeeze in with difficulty. Sitting inside, with my feet out in the snow, I remove my boots and wallop them together to clear them of snow before bringing them inside. It is still light. I lie on my sleeping bag on the narrow mattress and try to sort myself out. I shut my eyes to try and get some rest, and think of the descent. Cut-off – that's a familiar enough situation to me!

AN ENCOUNTER WITH DEATH

Before I go to sleep I know the weather is worsening. During the night I can sense the mist pressing against the tent. There is an uncanny stillness and I have a foreboding that the storm will pin me down.

Suddenly the wind gets up and a piping and whistling emanates from every ridge and cranny. In the morning I take a look outside the tent as I do my cooking, but I can't see how hard it is snowing as it's still quite dark. Everything is overcast and I can make out fresh flakes amongst the trodden snow at the entrance to the tent. There seems to be only one light patch of sky up to the left of the tent, but even that may be a delusion.

Towards six o'clock in the morning I crawl outside and look at the cloud. The snow oozes from the tent roof. My bare hands immediately feel cold and wet. I can hear a woman talking to me again close-by, but I cannot make out what she is saying. I rub my face with a handful of snow to wake myself up. The altimeter has gone up twenty-seven points. Visibility is practically nil; descent is out of the question; I shall have to wait. It's a question of survival.

I have enough food to last for five days, but on Nanga Parbat spells of bad weather can go on for ten days, so I must ration my gas and food. I don't want to die.

If I went on now, I would almost certainly lose my way like my two friends, Franz Jäger and Andi Schlick, who disappeared in a snowstorm as we came down from Manaslu in 1972.

And so I wait. I crouch in the tent, dehydrated and very, very tired. I am also getting very clumsy. Twice I upset a full pan, burning part of my sleeping bag in the process. Yet my instinct for survival remains undiminished. 'If I go easy on the gas,' I tell myself, 'I can hold out here for five days. Just so long as I drink something every day.'

Already the first avalanches whistle down the face, pushing the wind out of their path. For a long time I stare at the drops of water running down the inside of the tent. I am fortunate to have discovered something. Then I start chatting again; with my invisible companions I discuss what it would be like in a land where it was possible to communicate with everyone one met, just as we talk to each other, and where one is taken seriously by everyone and in turn, takes everyone else seriously.

It is still snowing. I try and create a little more order inside the tent, but to no avail. All the time I keep picturing the severed descent route, huge seracs over which I cannot abseil because I have no rope; blank ice down which avalanches now thunder. I hadn't reckoned on bad weather overtaking me without warning. Now I haven't the slightest idea how long it will continue. Although I know the Diamir Face intimately, in this mist it could become a booby trap.

I spend the next hours until it is properly light, day-dreaming. Strange

SOLO NANGA PARBAT

that I can occupy myself with dreams in such a hopeless predicament. I can imagine how my tent will get buried by snow in this little recess.

From thoughts of the future I turn to memories of the past; life's opportunities give way to the possibility of death. Later I feel thirsty and recall an instant when as a little boy with an empty bottle, I went trotting off to the spring to get water for my grandfather haymaking in a nearby meadow. It's something I often did, and I can still remember how the cresses grew around the spot where the water bubbled out of the earth.

I cleared a pool and let the sand settle before laying the bottle flat in the water and waiting for it to fill.

If I spend any longer with my shoulders out of the sleeping bag, I will freeze. Even though I keep doing little exercises against the cold, I still can't seem to warm up. The first warm water I heat, I sip reverently. Mentally I recap the situation, to traverse out to the Mazeno Gap on the Rupal Face is out of the question because of the new snow, the avalanche danger is too great. Descent by the 'bridge' has been rendered impossible by the earthquake. The Upper Mummery Rib is coated in ice. The only way remaining is a steep ice channel to the right of the Mummery Rib. If I don't manage to find a way down there, I'm lost.

Doubtless there will be a lot of water-ice in the lower section of the channel, too, but there are no exceptionally big cliffs there and my crampons are still quite sharp.

The cloud deck over Nanga Parbat settles lower and lower. Terry is unable to see me through the telescope all day. Nevertheless he trains it at every gap in the mist, stubbornly trying to focus on a small section of summit wall. He gets so cramped, he has to keep standing up to straighten his back.

Up here the storm rages, there is new snow and it is icy cold. All the rocks below me must be covered in a thick sheath of ice. If every chimney, every groove, every fissure is iced up, then there is no retreat route for me, as a soloist. I know, of course, that there is no possible site for a bivouac the way I want to go. If I tire halfway, that will be the end of it.

When I stick my head outside the tent again, the first star shines in the dark sky. It is evening already then. Or am I seeing stars between the

The Silver Plateau lies tucked between the two Silberzacken to the east, and the summit ridge and the North Summit to the west. It was up here that one of the worst ever Himalayan tragedies started in 1934. Nine men lost their lives as a result.

clouds at midday again? Below, to the west, the valleys lie enshrouded in thick cloud. I have no idea what the forecast is, no idea that outriders of the monsoon are approaching Nanga Parbat from the south.

On the little gas cooker, standing unsteadily between my bag and the side of the tent, I brew another cup of tea. Then I try to sleep. Occasionally I prop myself up, my right arm supported on my sleeping bag, to take another mouthful of drink. I mustn't let my blood thicken. Food — a bit of cheese followed by hard bread — tastes tacky and insipid, and clings to my dry palate.

I force myself to relax despite the nagging doubts about the descent. But as I am so cold, I have very little control over myself. This enforced inactivity is getting on my nerves. A day spent lying doing nothing also costs energy. Cut off like this, at this height, everything is an effort.

There is no spot on the ice face beneath me where I could rest, so I know I won't be able to recover my strength during the descent.

In my drowsiness I notice how the ragged clouds chase across the sum-

SOLO NANGA PARBAT

mit. 'It will soon pass,' I say to myself — recalling a favourite phrase of my mother's. Just saying something out loud breaks the silence. Perhaps I only want to cheer myself up. By a slight change in the intensity of light through the tent, I can tell it is now night. The moon rides clear, then veiled, by turns. It is an uncanny atmosphere.

The stars seem suddenly to have been extinguished. The weather is worsening again. The dramatic effect of this changing light is heightened further by the fact that on the whole face, there is now not one breath of wind. For the first time I have been on the mountain, the air is totally still. There is not a whisper to be heard among the snow crystals. And what is more ominous, it has become quite warm. Or do I only imagine that because I have crawled right into my sleeping bag and pulled it over my head in order to warm myself up with my own breath. For a long while I lie there with my ears pricked, listening into the silence. Nothing and nobody interrupts it. The softness and warmth of the atmosphere makes me think of bad weather, of snowstorms. I remember the story of those dramatic days of July 1934 when Merkl and Welzenbach perished. I have read that so often. I am now at exactly the same height that their expedition was — in a snowstorm just like this. They were already high above the Silbersattel, within reach of the summit. But in the night before their final assault, the storm overtook them. Even inside the tent they barely survived. The bitter cold affected them badly. Their clothes were stiff with ice and began to thaw inside their sleeping bags from the heat of their bodies. The storm blew great banners of snow from the ridge above the camp. Merkl and Welzenbach had survived many dangers in the Alps without ill effect. They and their comrades knew well enough, however, the difference between a storm in the Alps at three or four thousand metres, and a Himalayan hurricane at eight thousand metres.

The next day, 7 July, the blizzard continued. Sunlight was obscured by the whirling eddies of snow. Merkl, Schneider, Welzenbach and Wieland made their preparations inside the main tent. But what should they do? Sit it out? Sahibs and porters lay apathetically in their sleeping sacks. The hurricane rendered all cooking impossible. So came the second night. A night of ebbing hopes. Tent poles snapped, and fine snow dust penetrated every crack and seam. The hurricane grew in strength from hour to hour.

DIAMIR

By the morning of 8 July, they were all convinced that an immediate retreat was essential. The lives of five climbers and a dozen porters were at risk. Merkl gave the order for Aschenbrenner and Schneider to go ahead with three porters and forge a trail. The others got ready to follow. The advance group struggled doggedly down. When they reached the Silbersattel, the blizzard grew so violent that it was only with the utmost caution that they were able to descend the steep slope. About 100 metres below the gap, Nima Dorje, one of the Sherpas, was blown off his feet by the storm. They succeeded in holding him. In the raging blizzard they could not see more than ten metres ahead. Only once, as the clouds tore apart for a moment, did they see the second party following, climbing down from the Silbersattel. At about seven in the evening Aschenbrenner and Schneider arrived, completely frozen, in Camp 4. Throughout that evening and the whole night following, they waited in vain for the others. Willy Merkl and his men never came. They had made a bivouac below the Silbersattel. Welzenbach slept in the snow without a sleeping bag. Again nothing to eat. One Sherpa died. Merkl had his right hand frostbitten, Wieland both hands. Later three Sherpas collapsed. They were hanging in the ropes or lying in the tent, dead. On 9 July the heavy snow clouds tore apart once more and for a few minutes the ridge above was visible. Beneath the Silbersattel a large party could be seen descending. But why were they only as far as that? A long way behind them a solitary figure was wandering. This was Uli Wieland, who a little later fell asleep from exhaustion and died in the snow. In the night another half a metre of fresh snow fell. Snow-flurries were blown from the Silbersattel horizontally, a hundred metres out over the Rakhiot side. Four men were wading down, leaving an open furrow behind them as deep as a man. It was four porters, utterly exhausted, at the very end of their strength. Their hands were frostbitten, one was snowblind.

Welzenbach wrote his last message:

'Camp 7, 10 July. To the Sahibs between Camps 6 and 4. We have been lying here since yesterday, after losing Uli on the way down. Both sick. An attempt to press down to 6 failed through general weakness. I, Willo, have probably got bronchitis, angina and influenza. Bara Sahib is generally weak with frostbitten hands and feet. For six days we have had nothing warm to eat and practically nothing to drink. Please help us soon here in Camp 7. Willo and Willy.'

During the night of 13 Welzenbach died in the camp. In the morning Merkl mustered his strength. Supported on two axes he began to go down the ridge. When the mist parted he saw tents below. Rescue from there was out of the question. The snow lay too deep. Merkl couldn't manage the uphill stretch to the Moor's Head, he was so weak. He tried repeatedly but finally collapsed. Two Sherpas were still with him. The three dug an ice hole. With his Sherpa, Gay-Lay, Merkl wrapped himself in a blanket; as a groundsheet they had a rubberized mat, but it was only big enough for two and Angtsering had to make do with just a blanket. So they spent the night in the inexorable rage of the storm.

On 13 July from Camp 7, three people could be seen descending. Halfway to Camp 6 in the saddle before the Moor's Head, one went ahead and waved. Again the three collected their strength to go on, but Merkl and Gay-Lay could only manage another three metres and no more, so they wearily slipped back to the cave. Angtsering still had the strength to breast the last rise.

It was not until the next evening that he stumbled, exhausted and badly frostbitten, into Camp 4. Schneider and Aschenbrenner tried again to reach Camp 5 on 15 and 16 July. Useless! They were repulsed by bottomless snowdrifts. In the morning they clearly heard a distant cry, but there was no signal from the man on the col.

When, four years later, the bodies of Merkl and Gay-Lay were found, they lay perfectly preserved in the snow. From the position in which Merkl was found, it looked as if when he laid down he had not done with life, but merely wanted to rest for a while; he had slipped his hands out of his gloves which he then spread out on his thighs. There seemed no doubt that Willy had died before Gay-Lay . . .

I feel as if I was there. The thought of death only serves to make me aware that nothing is really important.

The question of what happens after death doesn't concern me. To me, both possibilities seem conceivable – a life after death, or equally, complete annihilation.

Angtsering was the last of the 1934 summit party who managed to struggle back to Base Camp alive. He was totally exhausted and told of the deaths of Willo Welzenbach, Merkl and Gay-Lay, who had been unable to complete the descent.

I haven't got a mirror, yet I run my fingers through my hair. I wonder what I look like at the moment — barely human?

Later, gently at first but intensifying, progressively there comes a humming and whistling around the tent. I don't know if I've been to sleep or simply been lying here. Nor do I know how much time has passed since I was straining my ears into the silence. Now it is windy outside. There is something tense, something tingly in the air. I feel like opening the tent, but I don't. I catch myself staring through the tent, trying through the fabric, to make out the outline of my axe and crampons which are stuck in the snow not half a metre away. But I cannot make them out at all. If the storm has carried them off, then I am lost. A descent without them is impossible. Although I know well enough that another outburst of bad weather is approaching, I put it out of my mind. I don't want to succumb that quickly. I doze off, but in the same instant hear the first growl of thunder. This growling stifles my last hope for better weather.

At some time in the night I start up out of my bag, gasping for air. I feel confined, like someone suffocating in his own unconscious mind. The

SOLO NANGA PARBAT

snow is still falling, but only gently. I hear the sounds of snowslides but cannot work out if they are coming down beside the tent, or from the roof, or down the face. The background sound of avalanches form a bridge between my restless sleep and the icy wastes outside. I open my eyes and try and get my bearings. If I'm not mistaken it's three a.m. My shoulders and back are cramped. Perhaps only because the cold has penetrated through the insulating mat and sleeping bag into my bones. There are repeated sounds of thunder in the distance. And these eerie noises outside. Merkl's fate flashes again into my mind. During the night I frequently awake to a sense of total unreality. Moments in which desperation intermingles with amazement at still being alive.

The tent fabric is stiff with a brittle coating of ice, inside and out. My sleeping bag, too, has gathered a crust of ice. It will soon be day. Darkness has begun to fade except in the east where the summit of Nanga Parbat looms. Through the opaque tent wall I can now make out the fuzzy outline of my ice-encrusted axe and crampons. Still there then. Instinctively I grope for my boots and bring them, half-frozen as they are, into my sleeping bag. I must have slept for a few hours, or have just been lying there inert. The wind is now dropping.

Despite the biting cold which has descended upon the entire mountain, my feet are still warm. The ice-covered tent obviously makes a perfect igloo. During the next half hour I endeavour to warm a cupful of drink before opening the tent. I couldn't possibly eat anything. Already I know that I want to press on today. It is clear outside, only the sky is overcast, I will climb down, throw my tent into a crevasse and simply descend in one push to Base Camp. I'll only change my mind if the mist comes up, or it starts to snow, so that I can't see the way. How good it is to be able to make one's own decisions! I'm not responsible for anybody except myself. Despite that, my thoughts wander and I redirect my attention to something outside myself. (Sometimes without knowing exactly what.)

The descent will be tricky and strenuous. The thought of the seracs alone makes me shiver.

It was a mistake to drink so little. I feel that my blood has already become too thick, it shows in my every movement.

I worry about Ursula and Terry waiting below. Perhaps they think I

DIAMIR

am already lost. I have no idea what they might be doing. I do hope they are not too anxious.

On the morning of 11 August, Ursula writes in her diary:

Not very often and then only briefly, I sometimes try and imagine what would happen if Nanga were to seize its chance — perhaps its last chance — having let Reinhold slip through its fingers once before. I catch myself thinking that perhaps the world would turn to me for a short while, were I to report on the last hours of the 'great Reinhold Messner'. I can play this scene very dramatically and pathetically, and with impunity because nobody is there to see!

But apart from that — I'm having a lousy time. For the first time in twenty-seven years I'm swallowing Valium, without success. Stuffing myself with cheese and honey (supposed to be good for you, especially for the nerves) I have read, written, done some thinking, made my eyes sore peering through the telescope, chucked the bloody thing away because it only makes me more mad, only to pick it up again after a little while and stare compulsively through it once more. And once I flew right off the handle — what right had he to be climbing up there anyway? Chasing his 'Natural High'. Looking for gratification through the mountain — *and* probably also getting it — while all the time I, and probably Terry too, are going crazy here at the bottom of Nanga, unable to sleep, fingers crossed, and praying. Has he ever prayed for anyone at all? I mean prayed in the widest sense?

And I have cried. Not really on his account, but only because it helps me to bear the physical and emotional stress. Best of all, I would like to get him by the ears and drag him down from his accursed mountain. Later on some Austrians arrive, coming to climb a different route, and they are very nice to me, really nice. They console me with all sorts of strange explanations for the disappearance of the 'black dot'. One of them gave me a piece of crystal. I loved it, but more than that I was amazed. I say to myself, 'The climbing world is so close, it always sticks together.' And that was the last straw!

I flew into another rage. But then I said to myself, 'Just imagine Reinhold's done it!' There's no other possibility. And then I stopped worrying altogether, and convinced myself entirely. He is having a rich and intensive experience up there. He will wear himself out but return safely. I envy him his experiences and am happy for him. How could I have doubted his safe return for a moment? What could happen to him anyway? I have boundless faith in his climbing ability, and anyway what's he got to lose? If it doesn't go, then he comes back without the summit. At least his dream will still be intact! And if he doesn't come back, but remains forever on the summit — or lower? Who could have wanted a more uplifting 'high' just before death? My God! When I think of

SOLO NANGA PARBAT

our German intensive care units! Then really I ought to be praying that he won't be grudged the one and will be spared the other. Any way you look at it, he's a lucky man. So why this Angst? This dumb Angst? I madly envy him his situation, without in any way begrudging it him. I am happy for him. And I can easily imagine that even I, a non-climber, would willingly endure hardship and privation to experience what he is experiencing.

Upon the mountain, this 11 August, I notice that the weather, though not good, does seem to be improving slightly. I make my decision, without wasting too much time debating it, abandon everything and go. The equipment — tent, sleeping bag, cooker — I throw into a crevasse; I keep the rucksack and carry in it only a few films, the camera, the little bits and pieces like altimeter, sunglasses, etc.

Nothing stops me now. By five o'clock I'm out of the tent, my mind made up to stake everything on this one last chance. I leave all my rations along with the cooker, soups, everything. I have to reach Base Camp today in one single mammoth stage. Three thousand metres height loss in the steepest direct line. If I don't succeed, then I won't survive the ensuing night.

With this knowledge I set off for the one last, great thrust. I go diagonally down across the slope and suddenly slip. Desperately I try to regain my balance, convinced I am falling. Only my crampons can save me as my whole weight is upon them, and I make a few jumps, anxiously hoping the crampons will get a grip once more. If I could only get into balance! After ten or fifteen metres, jumping down the steep slope in great bounds, I regain my footing. I am trembling all over. All the blood has drained from my head. This carelessness could have ended in disaster! With my axe I chip out a large step on which to rest. Lucky again. A sprained ankle, a broken shinbone would have finished my chances. The shock of this near-miss forces me to concentrate all my efforts. I am all awareness.

The ice runnel down which I want to climb is the most dangerous spot on Nanga Parbat. But all I say to myself is: if it can be done anywhere, then it'll be here.

I know I shall die if I haven't enough strength to make it in one day, but all the same I haven't written myself off yet. I am very dehydrated after the bivouac, and wobbly on my feet, but I am still in business! I

DIAMIR

know what to expect when one has to climb down through poor snow. The mountain is not so steep here and so all the snow has collected and compacted, like the dreaded *Bruckharsh*, deep, crusted snow. I dare not make any mistakes and all my experience comes into play. The upper surface is so hard that only my crampons will penetrate it. Underneath is often just blank ice. My feet keep caving into pockets under the crust, and each time I risk losing my balance. Climbing down ice is much harder than climbing up it. At first I try it facing downhill, hunched, slowly making my way, fashioning steps. I can't afford to cut steps down the whole face. There's only one possible alternative. To climb it free, facing inwards, axe in the right hand and punching my left hand into the crust to support me, crampons on my boots. That's better. I climb down in exactly the same manner as I climbed up. No need to cut steps. But nor must I lean out or turn my body at all. This form of descent is the most dangerous. One slip and you're away. The wall plunges away beneath me for some 3000 metres. If I look down I have trouble readjusting myself to the face when I look back. I puff with exhaustion after every 100 steps — or is it only ninety — and have to lean my chest against the ice to rest. I get a piercing pain in my lungs as I breathe. My arms are so heavy from constantly wielding the axe, they are practically disabled. When I rest I exchange one brand of agony for another. Nothing here is achieved without effort. Standing still, little snowslides build up on my feet and arms and the wind blows powder snow all over me; soon I am plastered from head to foot in an icy coat of mail. The valley still lies discouragingly far below; it doesn't pay to look at it. So I channel my thoughts to more immediate matters. The next time I pause I fashion a step in the ice so that I might stand more easily. My progress gets slower and slower, my rest pauses more frequent. One time, when I'm able to sit down, I find it particularly difficult getting up again. I have to make myself false promises to get myself onto my feet. Just one more step, I say to myself, just down this last steep bit, then it get's easier. It'll be alright! The fine scratches made by the front points of my crampons, a few seconds later come sparkling into my field of vision. Once I get between the giant seracs, I dare not rest any more. Each minute I save here is a gift of life.

I take no more photographs today. But I still talk to my voices, more

SOLO NANGA PARBAT

than before. Sometimes even in French, and this, although I have never learned French!

Terry keeps his telescope trained on the dark ice hose. Tucked in between the seracs and the Mummery Rib, this runnel is the steepest section of the whole Diamir Face. Terry stays by his telescope the whole morning. It is sheer discomfort to peer into it all the time. His eyes burn. At intervals he stands up and walks about, but the telescope is like an addictive drug, he has to get back to it, has to look.

The lower I get, the slower I become. The face is no longer as steep and sometimes I can descend facing outwards. The ice is so hard here that I don't sink in to it at all as I did earlier on. For a whole hour I climb down without registering much detail; then I approach the place of my first bivouac and know I should make it. The sense of security and finding the first meltwater, which I sip from a crack, chases my tiredness away.

Thick banks of cloud rise up in the Diamir Valley. I know I have to go on as I could not survive a night in the open. Everytime I breathe out, it is like a sigh of relief. A sign perhaps that I'm on the brink of total collapse? I'm still not sure I can make it down to the grass. My calves, the muscles in my arms, my whole body is knotted up, stiff. I hold my axe as if it were welded to my hand. Another two whole hours yet to Base Camp. I don't say much to my invisible companions. Nor do I pay much attention to them. On one occasion I have to leap over a crevasse. The leap, a wide jump, calls for concentration. It's getting warm now, almost hot. Little watercourses trickle all over the ice. I grit my teeth together and resolve not to think about them. Drinking will only make me more tired. Step by step I make my way down the ice. The crevasses shimmer turquoise beneath me. The world around is scattered with pinnacles of ice, avalanche slopes to right and left. At least there's no longer a gaping void below me. My neck aches. Everytime I position my crampons on the smooth ice I take a quick glance down, then to left, then right, left, right. I get confused by my slow movements and the size of the glacier. Distances seem eternal. And yet, being alone and trusting to my own capabilities only, gives me a strong sense of identity.

The rest of the descent follows like a trance. Often I see myself tottering over the mirror-smooth surface of the ice. Sometimes, if my crampons skid beneath me, it is hard to stop, but always before I am thrown off balance completely, they get a firm grip. It is as if they had an instinct of their own.

In Base Camp they have been watching me for a long time. Over the vast scree slopes, Ursula comes to meet me. She is carrying my training shoes.

We meet. I take off my old club-footed boots and throw them away. I don't want to see them again.

BEING ALONE

Just above Base Camp Terry comes towards me. He hadn't believed I could make the descent in a single day. We both have tears in our eyes as we embrace each other.

Ursula has the feeling of not belonging and this exclusion makes her start thinking. She doesn't say anything but I can tell from her manner that she feels excluded from our men's world. Even though she can explain it away with a thousand rational reasons and feels embarrassed by it, the feeling doesn't go away.

'I always knew you would do it. You are great!' Terry congratulates me.

'Stronger than ever after this!'

'My God, I'm glad you came out of it alright!'

'The only thing that mattered up there was to survive. That's why I'm still here.'

'How was it?' Terry wants to know.

'I was in the right frame of mind,' is all I will say.

I wonder myself how I managed to pull out all the stops, and it was the being alone that put me in the right frame of mind. Knowing that now, I feel stronger than ever before. I am always at my best when I have my

I reached the bottom of the face on 11 August 1978; only then did I allow myself a proper rest there where the glacier flattened out and the danger of icefall was slight.

back up against the wall. Up there on the Diamir Face I had no time for dumb thoughts. It was so dramatic, I was in wonderful shape.

Now looking up and thinking back over the six days on the face. It is strange to remember that there were hours during that time when I didn't want anything any more. Either to go up or to come down. Just to sit and rest. I wasn't frightened, and the being alone was agreeable.

Suddenly I feel someone standing behind me and turn round. An old white-haired man has come up from the valley and offers me a little posy of flowers, brightly-coloured little daisies. I am very moved. It is the same old man who, on the march-in, shook his head and announced that I was a halfwit. 'Expeditions with twelve, fifteen, twenty men have come,' he said, 'and they haven't been able to climb it. Alone you don't stand a chance.'

Back in Base Camp I am at first euphoric, not especially tired. Ursula decides to give me an injection to aid circulation because of frostbite to my right thumb. As the needle goes in, I fall asleep.

The next two days pass between sleeping and waking. Short periods of being awake and then falling asleep again. And in between, drinking a

DIAMIR

lot. We are going to have to take a different route home, I know, the earthquake and storms have done a lot of damage in the Diamir Valley; the road is blocked.

Under the ridge of the tent hangs a drip, an altitude metre and a little garland of flowers that Terry has plaited.

I spend most of the daytime lying in front of the tent.

'I can't really believe I was there on top of Nanga Parbat,' I say to Ursula.

'You're talking a lot of nonsense, she answers.

'Perhaps this climb was only what I imagined when I was up there on my own.'

'What?'

'You don't understand.'

'Are you glad to be leaving?' Terry asks me on 13 August, which is when we have ordered the porters for the return journey.

'It is time to go, I think.'

'Would you swop this solo climb for anything?'

'Nothing.'

'Why not?'

'I wouldn't swop any climb for anything else.'

'And if you could have your life over again — would you plan it just the same?'

'I don't plan my life at all. I live it in the here and now.'

'Do you expect it to go on like that?'

'I can't visualize what lies ahead.'

'And suppose you hadn't reached the summit?'

'I don't know if I would have been more or less fortunate not to have been up there.'

'Was this solo climb your physical limit?'

'Physically — I would say, yes. I was practically done for up there.'

I find conversation difficult at the moment. And that's not just the result of my weariness. There are some things I really want to talk about but it's plain that the other two do not understand what I'm trying to say.

'To what degree, then, do you plan your future?' Terry wants to know.

'Mine? What comes next, you mean? Only what's absolutely necessary.'

Ursula was very shocked when she saw me. She confided in her diary, 'He looked completely done-in, dried out, his lips cracked and coated in green slime.'

'That's risky.'

'I believe in being independent – and that means I don't want to be dependent on my future either.'

'You can only live like that when you're on your own.'

'Even two people together, they can both be alone.'

'Human beings can't manage alone. I'm convinced of that. Man is not a solitary being.'

'Maybe not. But for myself, I believe that I have to be alone sometimes if I'm to make any progress.'

The feeling of being sufficient in myself was without doubt one of the most important factors for my solo climb of Nanga Parbat. Whether this experience will remain with me or not, I don't know. I am now in much better shape than I was a year ago. I have just had to re-learn to live alone. Neither my Everest climb nor this solo trip to Nanga Parbat had anything to do with my divorce – we had the permit for Everest before I was even married, and I had dreamed about Nanga Parbat for five years – but that doesn't mean that these two expeditions were not influenced by my divorce. I don't really think that as I was before, I could have either climbed Everest without oxygen, or yet Nanga Parbat alone.

Ursula warns, 'You know there's going to be climbers who criticize you after this climb.'

After my solo climb I presented Terry with the ice axe I had used for those five long days, climbing, levelling out bivouac sites, and for hammering in the summit piton.

'There are always those people,' Terry puts in, 'they don't aspire to any illusions of their own, haven't got anything to offer except their boring know-all theories. It's the idea, the conception, that's the important thing, and no-one can take that away from Reinhold.'

'Do you think other people will repeat it?'

'Of course they will. And the next generation will do such solo climbs even more easily and with even more style. An eight-thousander by a difficult face, in a single day, and with even less technology. It's bound to happen in time. I have only made the start.'

It's true, they will all be climbed more elegantly. Things will no longer progress by simply employing more and more gadgetry, but by individual ability. And what we have considered the upper limit of human possibility, won't feature in their book. And, given the right brand of self-criticism, whatever they want to achieve, they will achieve.

And should they be able to successfully accomplish every climb 'by fair means', there can be little sympathy for the person who out of personal vanity doesn't restrict his use of technology but still shouts loudly about his accomplishments. It was only the preconception that eight-thousanders *had* to be climbed exclusively by teams, that prevented the success of a one-man expedition before this. Himalayan climbing was governed by a mythical concept of heights and the suggestion that one might climb them alone was considered heresy. But that's the way it has always been; what today is laughed out of court as lunacy, tomorrow

Ursula came towards me across the moraine, and before we reached Base Camp, Terry too met me. He placed a garland of flowers round my neck. And the old holy man from the Diamir Valley, a Muslim priest who had told me on the way in that no single man could ever reach the summit of Nanga Parbat on his own, brought a little posy from the last high pasture. I lay down in the tent and Ursula gave me an infusion. My right thumb had been frostbitten during the descent and required vaso-dilation. Despite my dehydration, my badly-cracked lips and the terrible pain in my blue finger, I slept for several days and nights on end. We stayed in our little Base Camp for three more days. Then we ordered a few porters and prepared for the return march. The weather had turned bad again and Nanga Parbat was enshrouded in cloud most of the time. On 13 August, two farmers and two donkeys arrived (next double-page). We took down the tent, burnt our garbage and buried our empty tin cans. An hour later the place looked almost the same as when we had found it barely four weeks before. Only the grass had in the meantime taken on its autumn colours. Young boys came up from the high meadows and bartered eggs and lassi for cooking utensils, plastic containers, foam mattresses. We didn't need to hang on to very much and were glad to dispose of this exta ballast.

Whilst we had been up on the mountain, bad storms had ravaged the Gunar and Diamir valleys. An earthquake that shook North-west Pakistan on the morning of 8 August destroyed houses and bridges. The farmers told us we could no longer get out down the Diamir Valley, and consequently we crossed over the high right-hand moraine to Zangot, about level with the glacier outlet, then climbed steeply up the Kachal Gali, a 4000 metre pass between the Diamir and Gunar valleys. From there it would have been possible to continue over the Prato Pass on the north side of Nanga Parbat, but we went out in the direction of Bunar in the Indus Valley. From the top of the pass we could see back along the entire length of the Diamir Valley. Ser, Nagaton, the sparse woods and the cave at the snout of the Diamir Glacier from which now in high summer, a wild coffee-brown river flowed. Opposite, the steep walls of the Mazeno Peaks, rising some 3000 metres from the valley floor, an impressive rock and ice wall, and beyond that, filling the head of the valley, lay the now distant Diamir Face.

SOLO NANGA PARBAT

becomes orthodox. One has only to think of the Seventh Grade, and Everest without oxygen; so it will be with this solo climb.

Three days after my return, having somewhat recovered, we pack our few personal belongings and burn the rubbish. My ice axe I present to Terry and he is as delighted as a child on his birthday. With the smoke still rising from our fire, we load everything that is left onto two donkeys and head down the valley. The Base Camp is again restored to its natural state. Almost. Traces of people can never be erased completely.

The next day we cross the Ganalo Ridge from the Diamir Valley into the Gunar Valley. From the top of the pass I look back into the quiet fairytale valley under the Diamir Flank, in which storm clouds are now gathering. With mixed feelings I set off down into the valley the other side. Immediately above us rises the prominent rock fortress of the Gunar Peak. The descent over endless scree is very wearisome; though I am well acclimatized after weeks of training at altitude, I am still very tired.

Despite the height, there are only scattered patches of residual snow up here. Horses and goats graze on the lower slopes; the shepherds give us fresh buttermilk. We cross a steep ridge with storm-stunted birches and dwarf pines, and come down into a wooded valley. In the next village we are welcomed by men with the first grapes. They are the best grapes we have ever tasted.

The landscape becomes increasingly charmless as the green gives way to a monotonous grey.

I often think on this return journey that I wish I had a child. I could show him everything. I know, of course, I can't have a child on my own, and I wouldn't want one that I had to share with a woman. I don't want a child that's dependent on two people — my own individual child! It is a concept, merely; rationally I know it's not a tangible proposition.

My desire to do everything alone is stronger now after Nanga Parbat than ever it was before; I need to bring things to fruition on my own, draw on my own resources. It is not so much a need to be all-powerful, able to do anything and everything, as much as a strong desire for self-sufficiency and personal freedom. I want to rely upon myself, be sufficient in myself.

Despite my tiredness and introspectiveness, I am aware of a deep consciousness, all the enigmas of this baffling world are contained within me — the questions and the answers; I have in me the strength of life, the power to give life, death and the beginning and the end.

It is now raining torrentially, but I keep going. The water plunges down the slopes opposite in a wild torrent over rocks and through a wooded valley. Laden with silt and mud it snatches rocks and logs from its path, like a raging monster.

I have come a fair way from the last village, and now take shelter in a dilapidated hut. How beautiful and transparent the curtain of rain looks as it sluices from the roof before my eyes! I imagine it is a window with living raindrops for curtains. Terry and Ursula crawl in to join me under the roof. There is no-one apart from us. We sit on dry beams and look out at the rain. No barking dogs, no animals in the fields, utter peace. The rain, the torrent, everything seems just right to me. My spirit goes out to the water and splashes in the waterfall. The sky is grey, empty but for the driving storm clouds, but it is neither gloomy nor oppressive.

The countryside through which we descend an hour later is wildly romantic. Our route takes us through narrow, precipitous gorges, along airy tracks, past deep chasms. One false step could spell disaster.

We reach the wide, sandy valley of the Indus. The sun again burns fiercely. It is a barren desert where all plants wither, yet not unwelcoming — like the landscape of a gangster film. The few broad-leaved trees that grow sporadically on the steep rocky slopes already bear signs of autumn. There are no real villages. Here and there we pass a couple of ramshackle huts. They cling, like balconies, to the valley slopes.

Far ahead in the valley, patches of green can be seen. When the sun breaks through the grey cloudbank, it lights up this green. That is where we find the first real villages. Like fjordwater, the green meadows stretch across the floor of the sombre Indus valley to its barren, rocky sides.

Our village still lies a good way ahead and I don't know whether we shall be able to reach it before evening. I don't worry about it but simply keep going. It doesn't bother me not to know where we will sleep. Ursula is some way behind me, she too prefers to travel alone. Nor have I seen anything of Terry for several hours. How happy this solitary walking makes me!

As we were marching out to the Indus Valley, an expedition from Upper Austria began its climb of the Kinshofer-Route. Alois Indrich photographed Alfred Imitzer on the ice slope below the Bazhin Basin.

I absorb everything, stop, go round rocks and trees. It is still warm when the sun comes out. A spider sails in front of me and I pause to look at it, as I go on past, I see the white gossamer thread on which it is lowering itself from the tree. I wander on, attentive, in harmony with everything. Even myself. Here and there green patches of foliage, the stream rushing below, in the air the hum of flies. It is all there, more than I could wish for. What is lacking, I invent. So the world goes round and round within me, and at the same time radiates from me. Harmony rules between the images, a consonance between the sounds of the earth and those in my head. I don't know how far it is yet to the village, but I go.

It is not curiosity that urges me on, nor force of habit; perhaps a kind of mechanicalness. Why should I stop anyway? We march through the day and half the night. It is dark before we stand above the desolate Indus Valley. The last long scree slopes stretch on interminably and half-asleep we stagger towards Gunar. This nocturnal travelling is a primitive form of meditation.

Borderline situations are not the essentials in my life. They only open my eyes to a wider truth. They are a kind of key to unlock a condition of awareness that previously lay fallow. Like certain potent drugs, climbing too is a drug, a 'weed', my weed. It is not too important to me whether I understand or not, so long as my body knows. The sort of knowledge one acquires with one's head is for me often superficial; the other sort of knowledge fills me completely, even if it slips away again immediately.

It is a wonderful feeling to travel across this land without thinking, withdrawn into my body. Measuring it with my feet and eyes — rather than actual measurements. Simply to keep myself going to the end. I even feel as if I belong here, as if I had no ties and no past life any more.

It is fascinating to be at home everywhere, everywhere and nowhere at the same time. How did I come to this? Always till now I have had a place, a spot I dreamed of when I thought of 'Home'. Now it is impossible for me to think of any place like that. There is no 'Home' for me any more. How quickly it went! I was so sad in the beginning at having lost my feeling of home, and now I am glad.

SOLO NANGA PARBAT

Somehow I have overstepped my limitations; my strength, the loneliness. A year ago feeling I was alone, was my weakness. I am not saying that now I have got over it, no, I was only totally alone for a few days. But it was beautiful. I don't know everything about alone-ness yet — that, too, is reassuring.

Again I am filled with enthusiasm for this rugged landscape. I am again instinctively identifying what I do with what is around me. I am set on a course that never quite ends, which I must always seek out even if it appears to be clearly defined. Death points the direction. Voyaging, being in transit, is the only way I can cope with life, and alone. It is my personal alternative to a permanent condition of everyday hassle, conventional love and loyalty and a secure social status.

We are invited to sleep on the roof of a house belonging to one of our porters. It is midnight before we unroll our sleeping bags on three plank-beds. The sky is full of innumerable stars. I sit on for a while without thinking of anything in particular. The moon, through drifting clouds, doesn't reveal more than vague outlines of our fairytale surroundings.

I'm not sure if I had been asleep or not when I feel someone touching my shoulder. Alarmed I jump up. A cool breeze caresses my bare skin. The moon has already set. There is a man standing in front of me. In the darkness I can only see his silhouette, not his face. He wants to know where we have come from.

'Nanga,' I say.

'Diamir?'

'Tike,' I nod, 'Diamir.'

The stranger takes a long look at me, as if he knew that was the only way to speak of something for which there are no words.

*The way to the summit
is like the way towards oneself —
a solo journey.*

Alessandro Gogna, climber from Milan.

NANGA PARBAT HISTORY

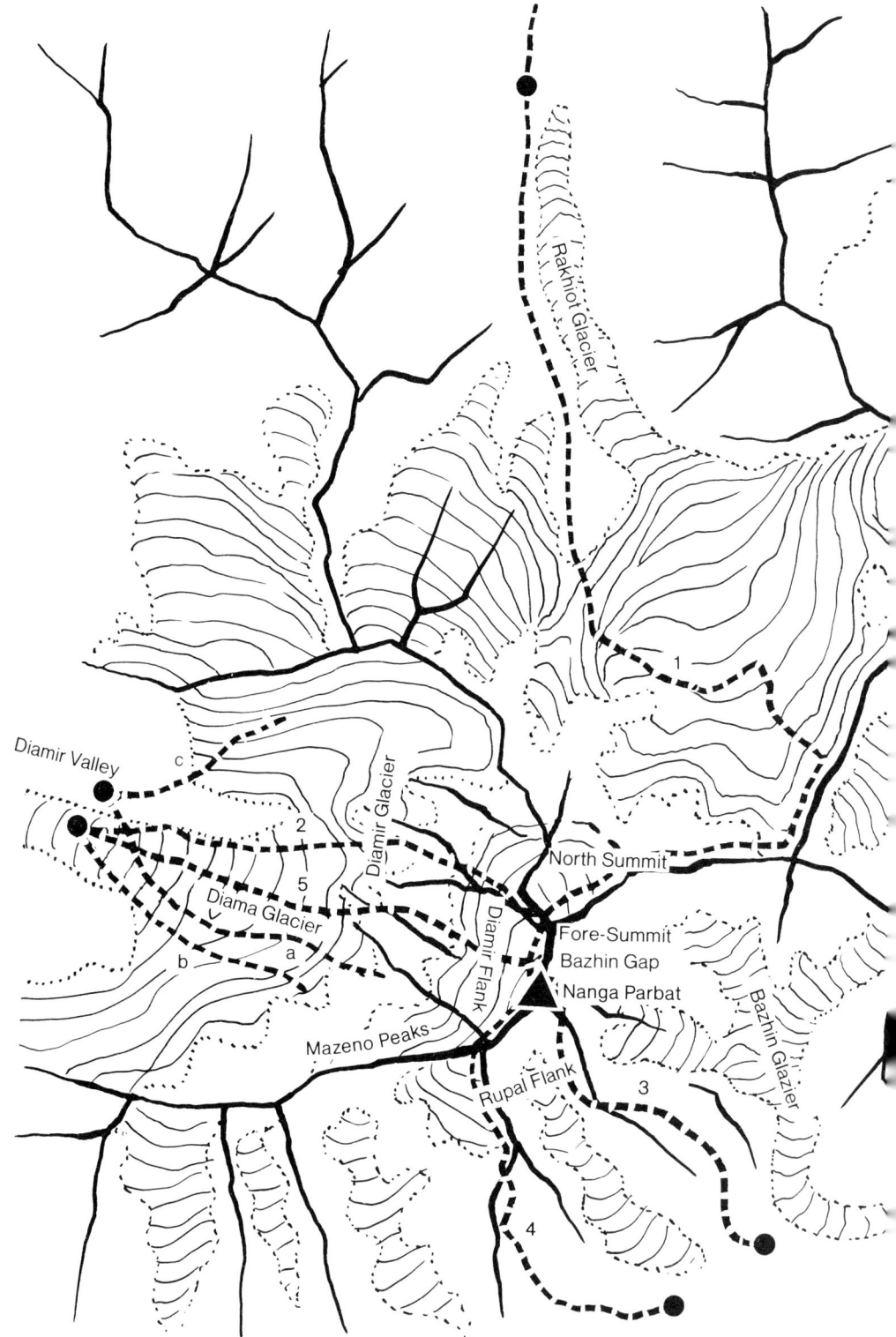

Nanga Parbat with the various climbing routes: 1 Rakhiot Face, Buhl-Route 1953; 2 Diamir Face, Kinshofer-Route 1962; 3 Rupal Face, Direttisima 1970; 4 Rupal Face, Schell-Route 1976; 5 Diamir Face, Messner-Solo Route 1978; a, b, c Reconnaissances by Mummery and Aufschnaiter.

NANGA PARBAT CHRONICLE

(Geographical location of Nanga Parbat: 35° 14' 32" N. Latitude, 74° 35' 40" E. Longitude.)

1841   An earthquake causes an immense rockslide from Nanga Parbat which blocks the flow of the Indus River causing a large lake to form. When the dam finally breaks there is a disastrous flood in the Indus Valley south of Nanga Parbat.

1845   Gulab Singh captures the previously Tibetan province of Baltistan, which includes the region of Nanga Parbat.

1850   Gulab Singh subdues Chilas and Gilgit (1852); continuing unrest.

1854   On the recommendation of Alexander von Humboldt, the Schlagintweit brothers undertake geographical and geological explorations in the Himalayan region.

1856   Adolf Schlagintweit advances to the foot of Nanga Parbat. First sketches and reports reach Europe.

1857   Adolf Schlagintweit assassinated in Kashgar. The Regent Wali Khan suspected the Asian explorer of being a spy.

1892   W. M. Conway passes Nanga Parbat on route for his Karakorum expedition and surmises that the Rakhiot Face promises to be the best climbing approach.

1895   First attempt to climb Nanga Parbat, indeed first attempt on any 8000 metre peak, by the British mountaineer Albert Frederick Mummery. His companions are G. Hastings and J. Norman Collie, joined later for a time by Major C. G. Bruce. With a Gurhka porter (Raghobir) Mummery, after a reconnaissance of the Rupal side of the mountain, reaches a height of about 6000 metres on the Diamir Flank (precise details unknown). My feeling is that Mummery climbed up the ice to the right of the rock ribs that now bear his name. Attempting to cross the Diama Col into the Rakhiot Valley, Mummery and his two porters disappear without trace.

The Schlagintweit brothers — left to right: Robert, Hermann and Adolf — who after exploratory work in the Western Alps, explored the Himalaya, Karakorum and Kunlun regions. Adolf pushed as far as Nanga Parbat.

1909	Luigi Amadeo, Duke of the Abruzzi, passes Nanga Parbat on his Karakorum expedition.
1910	The mountain writer and publisher Walter Schmidkunz purchases the German rights of Mummery's book, together with the right to publish the letters to his wife. Schmidkunz studies Nanga Parbat closely in the light of all the tangible evidence and advises Willo Welzenbach and Paul Bauer in the nineteen-twenties that Nanga Parbat should be possible from the northeast, from the Rakhiot Valley.
1913	An Englishman, E. Candler, circumnavigates Nanga but makes no attempt to climb it.
1914	The Himalayan pioneer, Dr Kellas, visits Astor and climbs the Ganalo Ridge. He considers the north side of Nanga could be climbed.
1930	Willo Welzenbach considers the ideas of Schmidkunz and Mummery and wants to attempt the west side of Nanga Parbat. He begins planning.
1931	Welzenbach's planned Nanga Parbat expedition fails to take

NANGA PARBAT HISTORY

place because this celebrated mountaineer cannot get leave of absence from the Munich authorities, for whom he works.

1932 German-American expedition under the leadership of Willy Merkl. Merkl, who has taken over the idea and planning from Welzenbach, disagrees over the western approach and sets his sights on the north side of the mountain. His team climb Rakhiot Peak and on 30 July reach the East Ridge. The expedition founders through lack of Himalayan experience.

1934 Willy Merkl leads his second expedition — the German Himalayan Expedition. Following the route reconnoitred in 1932, a large summit party (too large!) forge their way up to the Silver Plateau (five climbers and eleven Sherpas). Aschenbrenner and Schneider reach a height of about 7850 metres. A scientific group collect data for a Nanga Parbat map. In a blizzard lasting for more than a week, Wieland, Welzenbach, Merkl and six Sherpas perish. Another climber, Drexel, had already died of lung oedema at the beginning of the expedition. The dramatic course of this expedition is discussed internationally.

1937 In High Camp IV, below the Rakhiot Peak, the complete seven-man climbing team, including the leader Karlo Wien, and nine porters die under an avalanche. Only the two scientists survive. Paul Bauer organizes a rescue expedition and reaches the scene of the accident with the minimum of delay. But there is nothing to recover except bodies.

1938 The experienced expedition leader, Paul Bauer, takes a strong team to the north side of Nanga Parbat. Despite using an aircraft — a Junkers JU52 — to keep the expedition supplied with fresh food and equipment from Srinagar, success is modest. Rebitsch and Ruths reach a height of 7300 metres.

1939 A Reconnaissance expedition, led by Peter Aufschnaiter, makes two attempts on the Diamir Face, each time reaching just 6000 metres.

1950 A British expedition makes the first winter reconnaissance of Nanga Parbat. The leader, J. Thornley, becomes snowed in at Camp II with another climber, W. Crace. Both perish.

SOLO NANGA PARBAT

1953   First ascent of Nanga Parbat by Hermann Buhl on 3 July. Dr Karl Maria Herrligkoffer, organizer of the expedition, and Peter Aschenbrenner, one of the survivors from 1934, had previously ordered a retreat. Dr Walter Frauenberger, Hans Ertl and Hermann Buhl took responsibility on themselves for the summit bid. Apart from Hermann Buhl's achievement, which is quite remarkable, accomplishing 1300 metres of altitude on his own, Hans Ertl manages to shoot a unique film of this expedition. The subsequent dissension between the leadership on one hand and Ertl, Frauenberger and Buhl on the other, has not been fully resolved to this day.

1961   A new Herrligkoffer expedition reconnoitres the Diamir Flank of Nanga Parbat, and Toni Kinshofer finds a route up the left side of the face, difficult, certainly, but relatively safe and he follows it to a height of 7150 metres.

1962   Herrligkoffer's second expedition to the Diamir Face succeeds in making the second ascent of Nanga Parbat. Following the route reconnoitred in 1961, keeping to the right-hand section of the North Summit (a route of cracks, gulleys and icefields), Toni Kinshofer, Anderl Mannhardt and Siegi Löw successfully push to the summit. The new route is not a direct line but is in places extremely difficult. It is the first alternative route on any eight-thousander. During the descent Siegi Löw falls (he has doped himself with too much Pervitin) and is fatally injured.

1963   A reconnaissance expedition, again led by Herrligkoffer, investigates several possibilities on the south side of the mountain, the Rupal Face. A 'Direttissima' in the centre of the face which Kinshofer doesn't consider feasible; a route on the left-hand side and another following the South-east Ridge.

1964   An attempt on the Rupal Direttissima (Herrligkoffer) fails on the lower section of the face. Subsequently a Bavarian group under the leadership of the industrialist, Rosenthal, attempts the Mazeno Peak, west of Nanga Parbat.

1968   An extremely powerful team (Herrligkoffer again the leader) applies itself to a major attempt on the Rupal Face. Peter Scholz

NANGA PARBAT HISTORY

and Wilhelm Schloz press up to just above the Merkl Icefield.

1969 A Czechoslovakian Expedition under the leadership of I. Gálfy attempts Nanga Parbat by the Buhl-route.

1970 First and second ascents of the Rupal Face by Günther and Reinhold Messner (27 June) and Felix Kuen and Peter Scholz (28 June). The Messner brothers feel compelled to descend the west side of the mountain (by the Mummery Ribs) and thus accomplish an unplanned and unprepared first (and to date, only) traverse of the mountain. Günther Messner is killed by an avalanche at the foot of the face. As in 1953, bitter recriminations follow between the leadership and a section of the team.

1971 A strong Czech expedition, again under I. Gálfy, successfully make the fifth ascent of Nanga Parbat, the second ascent of the north side. A Japanese team is busy on the east side of the mountain and climb Chongra Peak.

1975 A new Herrligkoffer expedition ranges itself in three groups along the foot of the Rupal Face. One team attempts the Rakhiot Peak, another the South-east Ridge and the third the South-west Ridge reconnoitred by Toni Kinshofer — all with but modest success.

1976 With modest resources and the minimum of fuss, the Graz mountaineer Hanns Schell organizes and leads a small expedition (four members and a doctor) to test the feasibility of the route suggested by Toni Kinshofer on the left-hand side of the Rupal Face. All four climbers reach the summit. The new route (the Schell-Route) is the easiest route to date to the summit of Nanga Parbat, taking into consideration length, danger and difficulty. Even so, a few weeks later an Austrian/German/Polish team fail on the same route. At the same time a Japanese expedition is forced to abandon an attempt on the Diamir side.

1977 An American Explorers Club expedition attempt to repeat the Kinshofer-Route on the Diamir side of the mountain. A stone avalanche hits an occupied, unwisely-positioned camp in the first ice gulley killing two climbers.

The same summer an Austrian/Polish expedition fails on the Rupal Flank.

SOLO NANGA PARBAT

1978   The Pakistani authorities grant three permits for Nanga Parbat and a Czech team receive permission to attempt the unclimbed North Summit. This is successful taking a line up the ribs on the western side.

Reinhold Messner makes the first absolutely solo ascent of Nanga Parbat by a route on the Diamir Face (at the same time making the first solo ascent of any eight-thousander). He descends by a new route also.

A small expedition from Upper Austria (adopting the style set by Hanns Schell on Hidden Peak and on Nanga Parbat two years previously) repeat the difficult Kinshofer-route (its second ascent). Five of the six members reach the summit; above the Bazhin Basin the route differed in parts and was easier than that of 1962.

A German expedition attempts the Schell-route but fails.

R.M.

EXPEDITIONS TO NANGA PARBAT

No.	Year	Leader	Country/Expedition/Organization/Remarks	Route
1.	1895	A. F. Mummery†	British First ascent of Diamirai Peak (5568 m)	Reconnaissance of south side (Rupal Face); crossing of Mazeno Pass (5360 m) Attempt Diamir Face to 6100 m (?); lost attempting to cross the Diama Col (c. 6200 m)
2.	1932	W. Merkl	German/USA First ascents: South Chongra Peak (6448 m) Rakhiot Peak (7070 m)	Rakhiot Flank
3.	1934	W. Merkl†	German (plus three Austrians) Scientific party under Professor R. Finsterwalder	Rakhiot Flank Silver Saddle
4.	1937	K. Wien†	German DHS Expedition (Deutschen Himalajastiftung); plus two scientists	Rakhiot Flank
5.	1937	P. Bauer	German DHS Rescue Expedition after the catastrophe of expedition number 4	Rakhiot Flank
6.	1938	P. Bauer	German DHS Expedition	Rakhiot Flank

† Died during course of expedition.

SOLO NANGA PARBAT

No.	Year	Leader	Country/Expedition/Organisation/Remarks	Route
7.	1939	P. Aufschnaiter	German/Austrian Reconnaissance party (DHS)	Diamir Flank
8.	1950	J. W. Thornley†	British Winter Reconnaissance	Rakhiot Flank
9.	1953	K. M. Herrligkoffer W. Frauenberger	German/Austrian 'Willy-Merkl-Memorial Expedition' First ascent	Rakhiot Flank
10.	1961	K. M. Herrligkoffer	German DIAF Expedition (Deutschen Inst. für Auslandsforschung)	Diamir Flank
11.	1962	K. M. Herrligkoffer	German DIAF Expedition Second ascent	Diamir Flank via Bazhin Gap (Kinshofer-Route)*
12.	1963	K. M. Herrligkoffer	German DIAF Reconnaissance Expedition	Rupal Face
13.	1964	K. M. Herrligkoffer	German DIAF Expedition	Rupal Face
14.	1964	P. Rosenthal	German 'Bavarian Karakorum Expedition'	Rupal side, attempts on: Mazeno Peak (c. 7100 m), Mazeno Pass (5360 m)
15.	1968	K. M. Herrligkoffer	German 'Toni-Kinshofer-Memorial Expedition' (DIAF)	Rupal Face
16.	1969	I. Gálfy	Czechoslovakia	Rakhiot Flank

* *Translator's note:* Messner refers to the 1962 Diamir route (climbed by Kinshofer, Mannhardt and Löw) as the 'Kinshofer-Route'. It should not be confused with the 1976 South-west Ridge Route which is sometimes referred to as the 'Kinshofer Weg' since Kinshofer was the first to suggest its possibilities. Messner, quite sensibly, calls this South-west Ridge route (climbed by Schell/Schauer/Sturm and Gimpel) the Schell-Route.

NANGA PARBAT HISTORY

No.	Year	Leader	Country/Expedition/Organization/Remarks	Route
17.	1970	K. M. Herrligkoffer	German/Austrian 'Siegi-Löw-Memorial Expedition' (DIAF) Third and fourth ascent, and first traverse	Rupal Face 'Direttissima'
18.	1971	I. Gálfy	Czechoslovakia First ascent of Subsidiary Summit (Fore-peak 7910 m). First ascent of lesser Silberzacken (7530 m) Fifth ascent	Rakhiot Flank Buhl-Route
19.	1971	M. Kaitsu	Japan First ascent of Chongra Peak (6830 m)	East side
20.	1971	R. Messner	Italy Search action at foot of Diamir Flank where his brother Günther disappeared in 1970, probably under an avalanche	Diamir side
21.	1975	K. M. Herrligkoffer	German/Austrian/Swiss 'Felix-Kuen-Memorial Expedition' (DIAF)	Rupal Face and East side
22.	1976	H. Schell	Austrian Expedition from Graz Sixth ascent	Rupal Face South-west Ridge
23.	1976	H. Kato	Japan	Diamir Flank
24.	1976	M. Gradnitzer W. Rutkiewicz	Austrian/German/Polish Expedition under organization of DIAF	Rupal Face
25.	1977	G. Bogel† D. Bunce J. Hellman	USA	Diamir Flank
26.	1977	A. Zyzak	Polish/Austrian	Rupal Face

SOLO NANGA PARBAT

No.	Year	Leader	Country/Expedition/Organization/Remarks	Route
27.	1978	M. Sajncha	Czechoslovakia First ascent of North Summit (7816 m)	Diamir Flank
28.	1978	R. Messner	Italy First completely solo ascent Seventh ascent overall	Diamir Flank new route
29.	1978	R. Wurzer	Austria Upper Austrian Nature Friends Expedition Eighth and ninth ascents	Diamir Flank new route above 7200 m
30.	1978	A. Kraus	German Expedition from Schwäbisch Hall	Rupal Face Schell-Route

SUCCESSFUL ASCENTS

No.	Date	Climber	Route	Expedition/Leader Expedition Number
1.	3.7.1953	Hermann Buhl	Rakhiot side via Bazhin Gap Solo climb from Camp V (c. 6850 m) First ascent	German-Austrian Expedition (K. M. Herrligkoffer; Deputy Leader and organization of summit assaults by Dr H. Frauenberger) I
2.	22.6.1962	Toni Kinshofer Siegi Löw† Anderl Mannhardt	Diamir Flank via Bazhin Gap New route	German Expedition (K. M. Herrligkoffer) II
3.	27.6.1970	Reinhold Messner Günther Messner†	Rupal Face (direct route) New route and first traverse descending Diamir side	German-Austrian Expedition (K. M. Herrligkoffer) III
4.	28.6.1970	Felix Kuen Peter Scholz	Rupal Face	
5.	11.7.1971	Ivan Fiala Michal Orolin	Rakhiot side Second ascent of Buhl-Route	Czechoslovakian Expedition (I. Gálfy) IV
6.	11.8.1976	Hanns Schell Robert Schauer Hilmar Sturm Siegfried Gimpel	Rupal Flank South-west Ridge New route	Austrian Expedition (H. Schell) V
7.	9.8.1978	Reinhold Messner	Diamir Face New route First completely solo ascent	Solo-Expedition VI

SOLO NANGA PARBAT

No.	Date	Climber	Route	Expedition/Leader Expedition Number
8.	23.8.1978	Reinhard Streif Rudolf Wurzer Wilhelm Bauer	Diamir Flank, partly new route above 7200 m (similar number 2)	Austrian 'Nature Friends' Expedition (R. Wurzer) VII
9.	28.8.1978	Alfred Imitzer Alois Indrich	Diamir Flank as above	Austrian 'Nature Friends Expedition

Summary (to end of 1978):
- Nine successful ascents in the course of seven expeditions (of which one was a completely solo ascent).
- Nineteen climbers have reached the summit of Nanga Parbat by what is essentially five different routes. (Reinhold Messner has climbed the mountain twice by two different routes, including one traverse, each time his descent route was also a first.)
- Thirty expeditions in all, of which twenty-three were proper climbing attempts, three reconnaissances, two expeditions to neighbouring summits, one a recovery operation and one a search mission.
- One complete traverse (R. and G. Messner) — the second traverse of an 8000 metre peak (the first being on Everest in 1963).
- Nanga Parbat has claimed thirty-six victims, of which seventeen were European, two American, fifteen Sherpas and two Gurkhas.
- Nanga Parbat is better documented than most other eight-thousanders (apart from Everest); there are more than two dozen books, hundreds of reports and several dozen sketch maps. The best work to date remains Paul Bauer's, *The Siege of Nanga Parbat 1856–1953*.
- The Nanga Parbat map (R. Finsterwalder and W. Raechl), published jointly by the Deutschen Forschungsgemeinschaft and the German and Austrian Alpenvereins, is the best map of an eight-thousander yet produced.
- Despite all this excellent material, there are one or two points in the history of Nanga Parbat that remain unclear.
- The detailed structure of Nanga Parbat is well known and no other eight-thousander boasts a comparable variety of routes. There is one route from the north, two from the south/south-west, four and a variation on the west side, besides an independent route to the North Summit.
- However, there are still a few intriguing possibilities for the future: the South-east Spur to the right of the Direttissima (the 1970 Messner-Route); an ascent of Rakhiot Peak from the south; the north-west side from the Diama Glacier (you could get almost to the summit on skis by this route); less attractive, but equally possible, would be an ascent from the north to the Diama Gap, then following the North Ridge to the summit; a complete ascent of the 3000 metre North-east Face would be a dangerous undertaking, but might be possible for a fast-moving rope.

1932-9 THE GREAT TRAGEDIES

The story of the eight-thousanders begins with Nanga Parbat. At 8125 metres it ranks eighth in the list of the fourteen eight-thousanders. Its history is a dramatic one. Nanga Parbat, which means Naked Mountain — or to give it its less usual but more beautiful name, Diamir or King of the Mountains — is a massif forming the western cornerstone of the Himalayan chain. At its feet the Indus, one of the big holy rivers of Asia, changes its course from east–west to flow southwards. The vertical height from river bed to mountain top is in the region of 7000 metres.

First reports of the mountain, and the first picture, a panorama sketched from the north, came from the Munich explorer Adolf Schlagintweit. He made his drawing on 20 September 1856.

The first mountaineer to try and climb Nanga Parbat and who gave his name to the great rock ribs on the Diamir Flank of the mountain, was Albert Frederick Mummery. He is believed to have reached 6100 metres (19/20 August 1895). He was not only one of the boldest and most experienced British climbers of his day, his mountaineering principles were surprisingly modern. Soon after this attempt, Mummery and two Gurkhas set off to make a direct crossing to the north side of the mountain, leaving his friends Collie and Hastings to take a longer way around the base of Nanga Parbat. Mummery and his Gurkhas were not seen again.

It was thirty-five years after Mummery's death before thoughts again turned to Nanga Parbat. At the beginning of the nineteen-thirties Dr Willo Welzenbach, a municipal architect from Munich, and 'the leading climber of the interwar period' (Franz Grassler), began contemplating the possibility of climbing Nanga. Circumstances conspired against him and when he realized that he was not going to get his plans off the ground, he handed the idea and all his facts and figures over to his friend Willy Merkl. Willy Merkl organized a team and found the finance for the first German Nanga Parbat Expedition, later to become a German/American

Members of the 1934 German Nanga Parbat Expedition, from left to right, front row: Schneider, Welzenbach, Aschenbrenner, Merkl, Kapp, Müllritter, Kuhn; back row: Bernard, Wieland, Captain Sangster, Hieronimus, Bechtold.

expedition. Although they had a lot of bad luck, Merkl with Bechtold and Wiessner managed to climb the Rakhiot Ridge and the Moor's Head, just below the Silbersattel (to about 6900 metres). Aschenbrenner and Kunigk made the first ascent of Rakhiot Peak (7070 metres). Continuous bad weather forced the expedition to give up. The American climber, Rand Herron, was scrambling on the Cheops Pyramid in Egypt on the way home when he fell and was injured so badly that he died.

Willy Merkl returned home with the firm conviction that he had found the only possible route to the summit and was determined to go back and have another try. From the great moraine, Merkl's proposed route passed through the crevassed glacier and across the wide snow fields, then up the Rakhiot ice face, over the Silbersattel (the Silver Saddle), the Silver Plateau, the fore-summit, the Bazhin Gap (or Notch) and thus over the shoulder to the summit. It is the longest of all routes on any eight-thousander. The vertical height gain is 4625 metres, the horizontal distance 18 kilometres.

By dint of tireless effort, and eloquent, even passionate promotion, especially amongst work colleagues and the Sports Club of the German Railways, Willy Merkl succeeded in raising the money for a second expedition. Popular feeling was on his side — the *Kampf* for Nanga Parbat became a favourite theme in Germany and Austria. National pride was running high and there was an international race to see who would be the

NANGA PARBAT HISTORY

first to win an eight-thousander. The tremendous reputation earned at home and abroad by the mountaineers of Paul Bauer's two expeditions to Kangchenjunga (*Kantsch*) in 1928 and 1931, as well as the excellent photographs brought back by the Merkl expedition which were seen around the world, helped to bring the struggle for the world's highest mountains into the public eye.

Willy Merkl's 1934 team was one of first class climbers, many with expedition experience: Peter Aschenbrenner, Fritz Bechtold, Willy Bernhard, Alfred Drexel, Willy Merkl, Peter Müllritter, Erwin Schneider, Willo Welzenbach, Uli Wieland and Hanns Hieronimus as Camp Organizer. To these a scientific team was attached: Professor Richard Finsterwalder, Walter Raechl and Peter Misch (they were financed by national scientific organizations and the German and Austrian Alpine Clubs). Thirty-five Sherpas were employed as high-level porters.

Three weeks after setting off from Srinagar they had established Base Camp on the great moraine and briskly built up a chain of camps as far as Camp IV. Alfred Drexel was taken ill at Camp II and died of pulmonary oedema on 8 June. Everyone returned to Base Camp for the funeral ceremony. Precious days slipped away and it was not until 25 June that Camp IV (Advance Base at 6185 metres) was reoccupied. Now the expedition pushed their chain of camps on over the Silbersattel: Camp V (6690 metres) under the steep ice of Rakhiot Peak, Camps VI and VII (7050 metres) on the Rakhiot Ridge below the Silbersattel. Camp VIII was set up on 6 July at 7480 metres on the Silver Plateau 'behind' the Saddle. On this day Peter Aschenbrenner and Erwin Schneider had crossed the huge snow plateau and reached a point just below the subsidiary summit, the fore-peak (7850 metres). But in the night of 6/7 July a violent monsoon storm struck the mountain's upper slopes. A terrible day followed and an even more terrible second night. On the morning of 8 July they decided to retreat. Schneider and Aschenbrenner, following Merkl's instructions, went ahead to break trail through waist-deep powder snow. The others were to follow closely behind. Together with three porters, the two Tyroleans fought their way down to the lower camps. It was seven p.m. before they reached Camp IV, believing that the others — three Sahibs and eleven Sherpas — must be close on their heels. During

Paul Bauer led the first German expedition to an eight-thousander, to Kangchenjunga. Between the wars he was *the* expedition leader in Germany. He is also author of the definitive Nanga Parbat history.

the day in the blinding storm, visibility had been reduced to nil and it had not been possible to hang about and wait for the others. The fact was they had not been able to follow. The first to die was Uli Wieland; Welzenbach died during the night of the thirteenth and, after a last desperate bid to get down, Willy Merkl and his porter perished beneath the Moor's Head. The porter Angstering, alone of the Sherpas who had stayed behind with their Sahibs to the end, struggled down to Camp IV like a messenger from the past with news of the bitter drama that had taken place above. It was a complete tragedy. From that time on Nanga became known in Germany as Destiny Peak, and to climb it was a sacred trust in honour of those who had died.

The *Deutsche Himalaja-Stiftung*, under the organization of Paul Bauer, was set up to handle further expeditions. The team selected for 1937 comprised: Dr Karlo Wien as leader, Pert Fankhauser, Adolf Göttner, Dr Hans Hartmann, Dr Günther Hepp, Peter Müllritter and Arnold Pfeffer, as well as scientists, Professor Carl Troll and Uli Luft.

Everything ran smoothly to plan to start with and Camp IV was established at 6180 metres on 7 June. Bad weather then caused a delay. A renewed advance afterwards resulted in seven climbers and nine Sherpas being gathered together in Camp IV by the evening of 14 June. During that night a massive avalanche peeled off the North Flank of Nanga Parbat, burying the sixteen men sleeping peacefully in their tents. 'This enormous catastrophe is unparalleled in the checkered history of mountain-

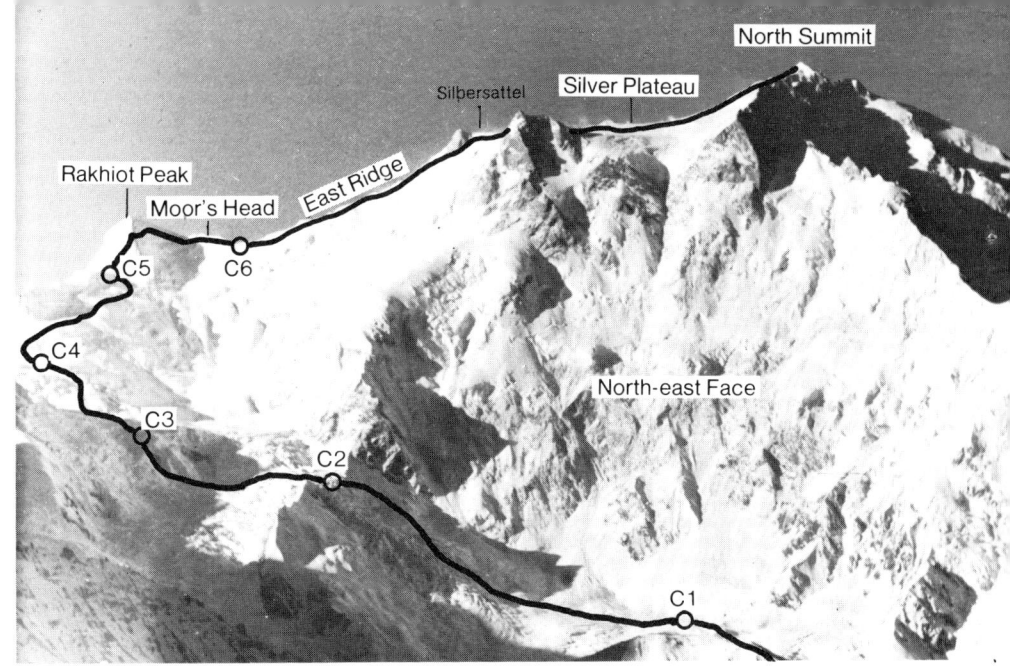

Nanga Parbat from the north-east with the lower camps of the 1934 expedition. In 1953 also, a similar line was followed.

eering' (Grassler). Uli Luft, alarmed, climbed up with a few porters on 18 June and discovered what had happened. With generous assistance from British military authorities, three of the most experienced German Himalayan climbers — Paul Bauer, Fritz Bechtold and Karl von Kraus — were able to reach the mountain in an incredibly short time and climbed to the grim scene of the accident. Four weeks after the event they had been able to uncover all but one of the tents from the debris and conducted last rites for their friends; important documentary material was recovered.

The very next year Paul Bauer led another expedition to the mountain. With him came Fritz Bechtold, Uli Luft, Rolf von Chlingensberg, Hias Rebitsch, Hans Herbert Ruths, Ludwig Schmaderer, Stefan Zuck, Dr Bruno Balke. Ernst Udet placed a light aeroplane at the disposal of the expedition, a Junkers 52, the crew of which were Alexander Thoenes (a climber with the 1929 Kangchenjunga expedition), Rudolf Mense as radio operator and Otto Spengler, mechanic. Albert Ebermann, another radio operator, maintained contact between the climbing team and the aircraft. This was the first time a mountaineering expedition had the benefit of air support, and in addition it was possible to obtain very valuable aerial photographs.

No attack on the summit was possible as the expedition again met with very heavy snowfalls and a lot of bad weather. On 22 July, however, Bauer, Bechtold, Luft and Zuck made a grim discovery on the Moor's Head. They found the preserved bodies of Willy Merkl and his porter Gay-Lay. In Merkl's pocket they found the last message from Willo Welzenbach. Franz Grassler rightly calls this letter 'one of the most emotive documents in mountaineering history'.

After this chain of futile attempts and fearful tragedies on the Rakhiot side, attention turned in 1939 back to the Diamir Flank of Nanga Parbat – for the first time since Mummery. A small reconnaissance expedition led by Peter Aufschnaiter with Heinrich Harrer, Hans Lobenhoffer and Lutz Chicken, looked at the possibilities of climbing the massive rock spur to the left of the Mummery Rib. But they only managed to reach a height of 6100 metres. War broke out and the mountaineers were interned in India. Harrer and Aufschnaiter succeeded in making an adventurous escape to Lhasa; Chicken and Lobenhoffer were only able to return home years later after the war.

1953 HERMANN BUHL'S SUMMIT CLIMB

Eight years after the end of the war the battle for Nanga Parbat was taken up again. The initiator and leader of the 1953 expedition was a Munich Doctor, Karl Herrligkoffer. His credentials were that he was the stepbrother of Willy Merkl and had inherited the legacy of Nanga Parbat. He was a completely unknown name in alpine circles, not a climber himself, nor with any experience of expeditions. Inevitably, therefore, his suitability was strongly contested. He demonstrated organizational abilities and exceptional doggedness when it came to collecting money. Members of the expedition, apart from Dr Herrligkoffer as leader and medic, were: Dr Walter Frauenberger from St Johann-im-Pongau, Salzburg (Deputy

NANGA PARBAT HISTORY

Expedition Leader); Peter Aschenbrenner from Kufstein, Tyrol, survivor of the 1934 summit party (Climbing Leader); Fritz Aumann, Munich, as Camp Administrator and Radio Technician; Albert Bitterling, a guide (Meteorology); Hermann Buhl, Kuno Rainer, both from Innsbruck; Otto Kempter and Hermann Köllensperger from Munich; and also Hans Ertl, Munich and La Paz, as cameraman with considerable experience of big expeditions and of the Himalaya — he was flown over from Bolivia.

The main camp on the great Rakhiot moraine (3967 metres) was established on 24 May. The build-up of high camps, up to Camp IV at 6185 metres was, as so often before, a wearisome, tough business, made more taxing by many snowfalls and difficulties with the Hunza porters. In the course of this process Kuno Rainer, who was Hermann Buhl's most proven and reliable partner, was exhausted to the point of collapse and later dropped out of any summit attempt.

On 21 June Buhl and Kempter became the first to reach the Rakhiot Ridge and the Moor's Head. But weather and supply difficulties delayed the preparation and rope-fixing on the Rakhiot ice face; a retreat to Camps III and II was unavoidable. The effect of this was that on 30 June the expedition leaders, Herrligkoffer and Aschenbrenner, ordered the summit team of Walter Frauenberger, Hans Ertl and Hermann Buhl to return to Base Camp. But the very same day the weather not only cleared but gave every sign of holding. The group at Camp III refused to come down as instructed, insisting on taking the chance to try and reach the summit.

They climbed up to Camp IV which had first to be dug out, then Hans Ertl and Hermann Buhl spent the whole afternoon equipping the Rakhiot ice face and the traverse to the Moor's Head with fixed ropes and ladders for the porters. Renewed instructions to retreat went unheeded. 'It was a strenuous and highly successful day,' noted Hermann Buhl. Early the next morning (2 July) there was a further call from Base Camp. Buhl, 'Perhaps we can go on now?' But the response was still the same — retreat. Half an hour of wrangling passed before Walter Frauenberger finally wrung from Base the desired permission, 'All right then. Go. In God's name; you have our blessing!'

Otto Kempter had moved up from Camp III in the meantime. On this

Left: Hermann Buhl after his first ascent of Nanga Parbat. Right: Dr Karl M. Herrligkoffer, organizer of the 1953 expedition.

day, 2 July, the four sahibs with four porters succeeded in reaching the Moor's Head. In the hollow behind it they placed Camp V, an assault camp with the bare essentials for two men. Frauenberger and Ertl then climbed back down with the porters. This was it. When assessing Buhl's subsequent achievement, it should not be forgotten how much effort he had put into the attempt during the two days previously. Camp V stood at about 6900 metres. There was still 1225 vertical metres to achieve before the summit could be reached, and a horizontal distance of some six kilometres. The weather was splendid, the sky cloudless. In the night of 2/3 July a violent wind blew up, forcing Buhl out of his tent to anchor it more securely. He slept little that night, if at all. He was ready to give his utmost, but if he needed any extra stimulus, the news of Hillary's and Tenzing's recent success on Everest provided it. What Hermann Buhl was about to do was, as Reinhold Messner wrote many years later, 'the act of a man obsessed by an idea in the face of almost certain defeat; a monstrous enterprise, seemingly contrary to all mountaineering logic and the possibility of success. It scoffed at all Himalayan experience.'

Buhl got up at one a.m. and set off at two. Otto Kempter followed a good hour later but was forced to give up on the Silver Plateau suffering from the effects of altitude. Hermann Buhl went on alone. The sections of the route with the relevant altitude gains, distances and times, were as follows: A good five hours to reach the Silbersattel (7400 metres – 500 metres of ascent, 1600 metres horizontal distance) where he took a short breakfast stop at about seven fifteen a.m. The route over the Silver Plateau, a gentle descent followed by a steady rise and finally a steep climb to the fore-summit covered a good 2200 metres of distance and brought a vertical gain of 500 metres. The wind had sculpted the surface of the

NANGA PARBAT HISTORY

snow on the high plateau into striations half a metre deep. With virtually no wind, the surface of the snow acted like a burning glass. From 7500 metres, the climbing took more and more out of Buhl, forcing him to take ever more frequent rests; it was as much as he could do not to just go on lying there in the snow. Where the slopes steepened towards the fore-summit, Buhl decided to leave his rucksack behind and stuffed what he needed into his pockets (a pennant for the summit, gloves, flask of Bolivian *Cocatee*) and tied his anorak around his waist. That brought some relief. In his new-found energy he quickly came to a notch less than 100 metres below the fore-summit. 'It must have been the upper Diamir Gap, 7840 metres high' (Bauer). From here he had to traverse down into the Bazhin Gap, steep rocks, bands of scree, snow, ice, and a sequence of climbing pitches which ended in a steep gully. Buhl reached the Bazhin Gap at about two in the afternoon (7812 metres). He had been going for twelve hours. It was exciting climbing.

The summit mass now lay ahead of him. It looked like a mountain in itself. Another 313 metres of height, a horizontal distance of 1000 metres. It is the hardest part of the climb – a steep rock ridge, barred by a series of towers, vertical saw-toothed crags, sharp cornices, and extremely exposed right up to the shoulder. Hermann Buhl felt that he had used too much strength getting as far as this and after some hesitation and, deliberation, took two Pervitin tablets. A snow ridge brought him out onto rocks. Step by step, from one rise to the next, from one temporary target to the next. When eventually he did catch sight of the summit still way above him, he began to doubt if he would ever stand upon it. He estimated the climbing difficulty of this rock ridge to be Grade IV or V. Just when he thought he was coming to the end of it, a huge gendarme, a free-standing rock tower, stood blocking his way. He made an awkward traverse round on the Diamir side, a delicate climb up a somewhat overhanging crack, until he was finally back on the ridge with a steep snow flank leading him to the shoulder (8060 metres). It was six o'clock. A series of rises, sometimes rock, sometimes ice, marked the rest of the ascent. He drank his last mouthful of *Cocatee* (there had been nothing left to eat for a long while). Now he literally struggled for each new step. He quite forgot – he wrote later – that he was climbing to the top of Nanga –

it could have been any mountain in his native Alps. The last few metres he crawled on all fours until finally he had reached the highest point (8125 metres). It was seven o'clock. Seventeen hours since he left his tent. 'I had not the slightest realization of the significance of that moment,' he wrote later, 'I felt no wave of overmastering joy, no wish to shout aloud, no sense of victorious exaltation . . . I was only thankful not to have to go uphill any more, not to have to think about the route ahead, not to have to keep on looking upwards with the frightful question "Would I get there?" always torturing my mind.' Going down would be easier. How long he stayed up there in the evening light under a flawless sky, we don't know. He took photographs to document his ascent, even reloaded his camera. Instinct prevented him from staying too long on the summit. He left his axe with the Pakistani pennant behind.

The descent began easily, he was much lighter of step. Somewhere near the shoulder he recovered the ski sticks he had left on the way up. He avoided the difficult ridge by traversing out onto the Diamir side towards the Bazhin Gap. It quickly grew darker. Working his way carefully down a smooth rib of rock, he reached a spot with room for both feet, though not big enough to sit down. He decided to spend the night here. The face had a slope of some forty-five to fifty degrees at this point; it was somewhere around 8000 metres high. He could have done with his second pullover which he had accidentally left behind in his rucksack. With no tent or food, he was forced to spend the night leaning against the rockface. He had hoped to be able to continue once the moon came up, but the face was in the moonshadow and he had to wait until four in the morning. These hours of inactivity cost him the toes of his right foot.

The new day, 4 July, was as clear and windless as the one before. Buhl was having trouble with one of his crampons and had to keep refixing it to his boot, this made the crossing of the gap even more difficult. The seemingly endless rise up to the fore-summit on the other side demanded enormous effort. Phantom voices and figures now seemed to accompany him, disturbing and confusing him. Searching for his rucksack proved a torment, but he finally found it only to discover that the dried fruit he thought it contained was not there. Thirst was becoming unbearable. He only had a couple of glucose tablets which he stuffed with a handful of

NANGA PARBAT HISTORY

snow into his parched, raw throat (blood and spittle were coming from his mouth). They helped only for a short while. Step by step he stumbled painfully down the vast snowfields of the Silver Plateau, often imagining he could see figures over on the Silbersattel. He imagined his companions were coming to meet him with flasks of tea. The figures turned out to be rocks over on the Rakhiot Peak. Before the final uphill stage from the plateau to the Silbersattel, Buhl again took Pervitin. 'It was my only chance; its effect might last long enough for me to get down to Camp V safely.'

At five thirty, thirteen hours after leaving his bivouac rock, he was standing on the Silbersattel, looking down. The tents looked forsaken. But then on the Moor's Head he was able to pick out two figures. His spirits lifted immediately and, fresher than at any time during that day, he climbed down from the saddle. Soon afterwards (about seven in the evening) he fell into the arms of Hans Ertl. The unbelievable summit climb was over.

Buhl wrote, 'Hans Ertl now came to meet me. He did not know how to hide his emotion and buried himself behind his camera.' The result was the now world-famous shot of a man who in the space of a few days had aged more than ten years, one of the most striking portraits in the story of mountaineering. It is impossible to put into words the joy these three men felt — Hermann Buhl, Walter Frauenberger and Hans Ertl. Buhl poured out his story until late into the night. He was saved.

Hermann Buhl's tremendous effort provided the climax for the *Ring of Nanga Parbat*. The sacred trust bequeathed by all those who had lost their lives on Nanga Parbat had now been fulfilled. Up till 1953 the mountain had claimed more lives than any other eight-thousander.

Amazement, celebration and worldwide publicity (but especially in Germany and Austria) followed, but the mountaineers' return was not one of unadulterated rejoicing. It was overshadowed by recriminations, disputes and lawsuits. This is not the place to go into all the details, but no-one suffered more or more acutely from it all than Hermann Buhl. He became very depressed by it, and this was the root cause for his decision to have nothing more to do with big expeditions. If he were to go to the Himalaya again, he would restrict himself to a small, mutually-

The Diamir Face with the various ascent and descent routes:
Buhl-Route 1953
Kinshofer-Route 1962
Messner brothers' descent route 1970
Messner solo descent route 1978
Messner solo ascent route 1978
Schell-Route 1976

compatible group, take the least possible amount of equipment, and hire only a small number of porters. He had, by this decision, taken the first step towards small West-Alpine-style expeditions, which he realized in 1957 on Broad Peak. (Herbert Tichy in 1954 had already paved the way with his Cho Oyu success, following Buhl's concepts.) Broad Peak was climbed by a four-man expedition: Markus Schmuck, Fritz Wintersteller, Kurt Diemberger and Hermann Buhl; it was Buhl's second eight-thousander. Shortly afterwards the career of this illustrious climber was prematurely curtailed when he fell to his death on Chogolisa.

1961-2 THE DIAMIR FLANK

The ascent of Nanga Parbat's Diamir Face, which Mummery had first attempted in 1895, is – and remains – inextricably bound with the name of Toni Kinshofer.

In 1961 Dr Karl M. Herrligkoffer led his second expedition to Nanga Parbat. Support for the undertaking came from the *Deutsche Institut für Auslandforschung*, a non-profit making trust set up and managed by Herrligkoffer in 1955 (replacing the *Gesellschaft zur Förderung deutscher Forschung im Ausland e.V*). There were ten in the team: Dr Herrligkoffer as expedition leader, Rudl Marek as Deputy, Ludwig Delp as Camp Administrator, Gerhard Wagner as Cartographer, Michl Anderl and Toni Messner (with considerable expedition experience), as well as Himalayan 'new-boys' Toni Kinshofer, Jörg Lehne, Siegi Löw and Harry Rost. Löw and Lehne were internationally renowned as one of the best climbing partnerships of the time, and Toni Kinshofer at twenty-seven had been amongst the climbing elite for years and a few months previously had hit the headlines again with the first winter ascent of the Eiger North Face.

The expedition set up main camp at about 4100 metres on the right-hand moraine of the Diamir Glacier. From 1 June Camp I stood at 5000

metres, safe from avalanches at the foot of a forty-five to fifty degrees snow and ice gully. The climbers had found a promising route running up between Mummery's 1895 Rib and the Aufschnaiter Rib of 1939. At the end of the gully, which eventually steepened to fifty-six degrees, they established a depot which they called the Eagle's Nest. Camp II was placed a little above 6000 metres. The ensuing 600 metres comprised a difficult rock face with five climbing pitches. This required 1400 metres of fixed rope, including wire hawsers. On 20 June Kinshofer, Löw and Lehne climbed to 7150 metres. This section up to Camp III led frequently over steep ice (Kinshofer Icefield) and was both hard and ticklish, especially with heavy rucksacks. Thus the territory of the Bazhin Basin was reached and the route to the summit open. The climbers found a bivouac site approximately in the fall-line of the fore-summit (7910 metres) and, as they had intended, quite near to the hollow leading up to the Bazhin Gap. The foreshortened summit bulk, now rising before them, misled them into underestimating the distance between them and the top. The three were new to the Himalaya. They firmly hoped to be able to reach the summit the following day.

But during the night the weather broke, lashing them with storms and snow, so that they had to retreat. There was no further chance that year.

From left to right: Toni Kinshofer, Siegi Löw, Anderl Mannhardt, the first to ascend the Diamir Flank.

Nevertheless, the outcome was excellent; they had found a route and partially equipped it.

The following year, 1962, the Second Diamir Expedition completed what was so encouragingly begun in 1961. The participants under Dr Herrligkoffer's leadership were: Michl Anderl, Toni Kinshofer, Siegi Löw, Anderl Mannhardt (Kinshofer's partner on the first winter ascent of the Eigerwand), Rudl Marek, Hubert Schmidbauer, Manfred Sturm and as medical/technical assistant, Sieglinde Ulbrich. The expedition reached the main campsite on 24 May. No time was lost — Base Camp and Camp I were immediately set up. The steep passages to the Eagle's Nest were safeguarded with steel ropes (more than 400 metres) and for the first time a cable lift was installed for transporting luggage, with a load line just short of 300 metres. The section between Camps II and III was slightly altered by Kinshofer from the previous year. By 19 June, Camp III (two tents at 6600 metres) was also erected. On 20 June the first thrust into the Bazhin Basin was made. 'A site for Camp IV was found in a kind of crater in the snow under a small ice wall,' according to Herrligkoffer's description (although he himself was never there), 'There were many crevasses around the tent.'

The climbers were prevented from setting out next day for the summit by snow and thick mist, and so remained in the tent. Was it going to be a repeat of last year's performance? But during the night of 22 June, the weather cleared promisingly. They didn't hesitate. At one a.m. they set off. The forty-seven year old Michl Anderl very quickly realized that at 7200 metres he had reached the limit of his powers, and turned back. After four hours Manfred Sturm also gave up, plagued by back pains and increasingly affected by the altitude. During the course of that day Anderl and Sturm made their way back to Camp III.

Toni Kinshofer, Anderl Mannhardt and Siegi Löw reached the Bazhin Gap, some 600 metres above Camp IV, at around nine o'clock. Here they met Hermann Buhl's route and, like Buhl nine years before, climbed to the North Shoulder along the difficult, pinnacled rock ridge with the giant gendarme at the end. The rock was verglased and dangerous with two rope's lengths of Grade V. There was a steep 4000 metre plunge on the Rupal side of the ridge. Siegi Löw was more affected by the exertion and the altitude than the others (he had also been frostbitten just prior to this), and at one time he broke through a snow bridge. His companions had to haul him up again. It was four in the afternoon before they reached the 8070 metre shoulder and gained access to the summit dome.

Just after five they stood on top, the first three German climbers on the summit of Nanga Parbat. Clouds encircled them, blocking all view. Just below the summit they made out the summit cairn Hermann Buhl had erected in the evening of 3 July 1953. It didn't occur to them to add stones to it.

As the sun went down it became bitterly cold. At 8080 metres the three men huddled into a tiny snowhole to bivouac, building a small protective wall of snow and stones around. They had nothing with them apart from the clothes they were wearing. Siegi Löw's feet were already frostbitten and he weakened noticeably during the night. The other two also lost feeling in their feet. At about six the next morning — 23 July — they set off and discovered a steep gully leading directly down into the Bazhin Basin from just below the shoulder. There was a biting wind which lashed their faces continually with blown snow. They were exhausted. In order to hasten their progress, they dispensed with the rope linking them together. Kinshofer and Mannhardt kept close together, but Siegi Löw dropped back during the course of the descent until he was some 200 metres behind the others. They were able to shout to each other.

Where the descent gully opened out into the Bazhin Basin, Siegi Löw,

SOLO NANGA PARBAT

replying to a call from Kinshofer, shouted, 'Come up here!' The cry sounded urgent, fearful. Toni climbed back up towards him, but before he had gone thirty metres, a shadow fell across him – Siegi Löw had fallen! With outstretched arms and legs, he slid on his back down the mountain without uttering a cry. At the end of the ice gully, the falling man bounced over a hump in the ground and hit his head so badly that he sustained injuries from which he later died. Here is Herrligkoffer's account of what happened:

> Toni and Anderl wanted to transport the injured man down right away – he had an open head wound and was unconscious. However, after a few metres they saw it was fruitless. Kinshofer stayed with Löw whilst Mannhardt set off for Camp III (!) to fetch help.
>
> Oblivious to any danger, Anderl took a direct line and got down to his goal in four hours; the shattering news was passed to Base Camp at about six in the evening. Before setting off, Anderl Mannhardt had placed his rucksack over the feet of the injured man – in it, amongst other things, was his camera with the summit shots.
>
> Toni Kinshofer kept vigil beside Siegi Löw, but he didn't regain consciousness. At some time between seven and eight o'clock he died.
>
> Shocked and exhausted, and already fighting symptoms of altitude, it was a slow business for Toni Kinshofer to get himself down. It was around eight thirty when he set off and he spent the whole night struggling back towards life. Everytime he rested, everytime he sat down, it became increasingly difficult to fight the mounting exhaustion. He was plagued by hallucinations, at one time believing he was wandering through the high green plants of a tobacco plantation. At nine o'clock the next morning, 24 June, he met his companions coming up towards him from Camp III. Since setting off at one a.m. on the 22 June, he had been away fifty-six hours. An incredible achievement!

1963-70 THE RUPAL FACE

Experiences and success on the Diamir Face provided the impetus to reconnoitre the Rupal side of the mountain. A unique precipice, the Rupal Face at 4500 metres is one of the highest mountain walls in the world.

NANGA PARBAT HISTORY

On 10 June 1963, a small camp was established in the high meadow of Shaigiri (3600 metres). The reconnaissance party under Herrligkoffer's leadership included Toni Kinshofer, Gerhard Haller and Klaus Scheck. Kinshofer's severe frostbite injuries to both feet had led to amputations. However, he had sufficiently recovered over the winter that he could now walk again and had retaught himself to climb. Thus, he was able to join the party.

The scouting party — but less so Kinshofer — were of the opinion that it should be possible to climb a 'Direttissima' route up the face, and photos were published of this line, on which Herrligkoffer had given the various sections of the face names to commemorate the unforgotten pioneers and victims of the Rakhiot Ridge: Wieland Glacier, Welzenbach Icefield, Merkl Gully. Toni Kinshofer also outlined another route to the left of the Rupal Face, in line with the West Ridge (which is a continuation of the Mazeno Peaks). This route was later climbed for the first time by a party from Graz under Hanns Schell.

The first big expedition to the Rupal Face left Munich on 31 January 1963 — a winter expedition. Why winter? For special climbing considerations? Was it expected that the objective dangers of this monstrous South Face would be less than than in spring or high summer? No — it wasn't that at all. Herrligkoffer: 'In autumn 1964 we were due to start on our Antarctic Expedition which had been planned for years, and to prepare for that we needed several months at home beforehand. Therefore, we had to go to Nanga Parbat in the winter.'

The nine-man expedition comprised: Dr K. M. Herrligkoffer, R. Hang, E. Hofmann, G. Lapp, P. Müller, R. Obster, G. Plangger, K. Reinhold, W. Schloz. The main Base Camp was established on 28 February. Camp I was placed at 4700 metres, Camp III at 5800 metres, 250 metres above an ice wall at the upper end of the Wieland Glacier. In five weeks on the mountain, the expedition experienced no more than ten days of fine weather. Climbing up to Camp II, six climbers were swept by an avalanche down a steep gully of more than 500 metres. What is amazing is that they all survived with only minor injuries.

Because of a mix-up by their liaison officer, the expedition found itself on a route for which they had no permission, and were obliged to abandon

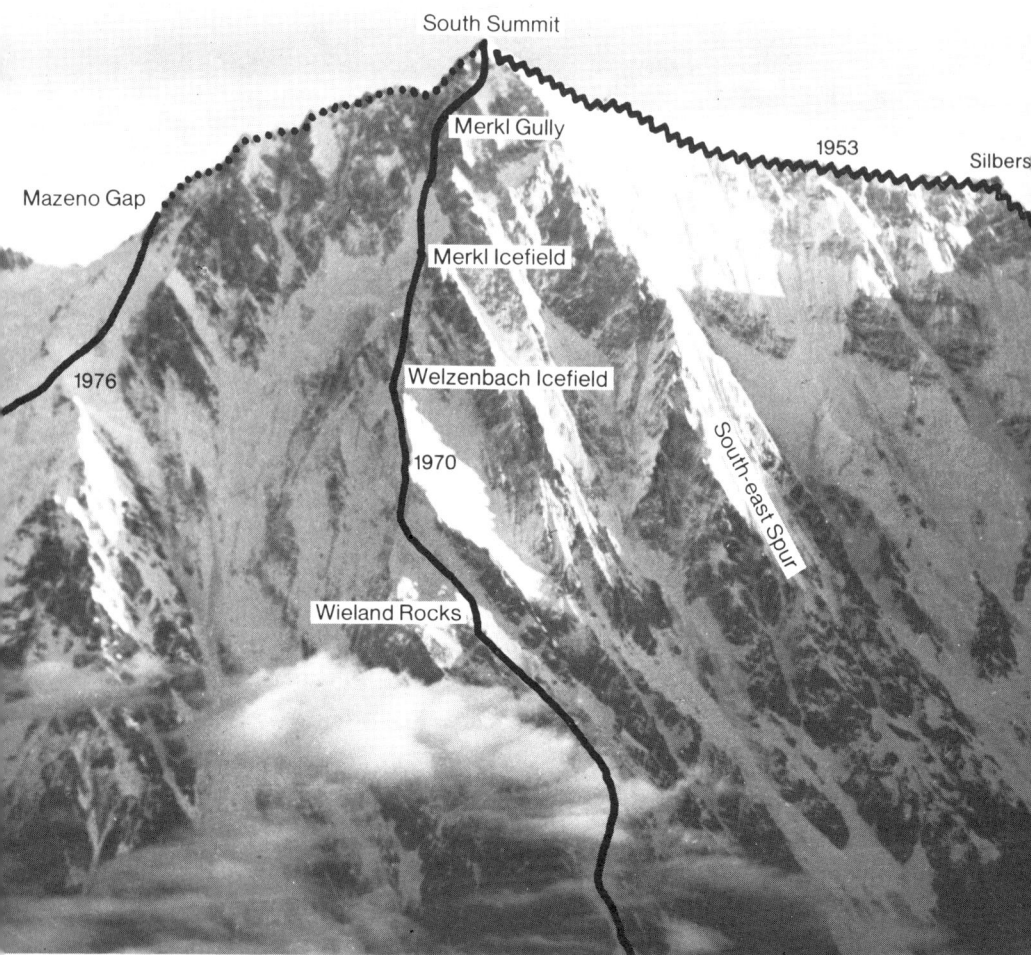

The Rupal Face: right (hidden) Buhl-Route; left (party hidden) Schell-Route; in the central section of the face, the Direttissima.

the attempt prematurely when the permit was withdrawn. The face had been climbed to about half-height, the difficulties and 'neuralgic' sections had been identified, locations of camps decided upon. And it was also known that winter conditions 'were not an insuperable handicap'.

Entitled the Toni Kinshofer Memorial Expedition (Kinshofer had been killed in a fall at Battert in 1964), the third Rupal Expedition set off with a very strong team of climbers in 1968: Wilhelm Dirmhirn, Karl Golikow, Siegi Hupfauer, Rolf Rosenzopf, Günther Schnaidt (Deputy Expedition Leader), Peter Scholz, Günter Strobel, Wolfgang Theurer, Roland Votteler, Wilhelm Schloz. Karl Breyer went as reporter (as far as 4700 metres) and scientific/medical assistant was Beatrice Kaltenbach. Six of the climbers (Golikow, Hupfauer, Rosenzopf, Schnaidt, Strobel and Votteler) had been participants in the spectacular Eiger Direct (Harlin Route) climb.

With five tons of equipment (seventeen jeeps, 230 porters) the expedition reached main camp on 7 June, and within four days Camp II had been erected at 5800 metres. By mid-June the fortress of the 250 metre ice wall was breached. A goods lift was installed above this by which loads of fifty kilograms could be winched up in flask-shaped containers; each 'bomb' took more than two hours to haul up — three hauls a day was the maximum. Camp III (5900 metres) was fully equipped as an (upper) 'acclimatization camp'

On 25 June when Scholz, Strobel and Golikow were 600 metres higher equipping a rising ice couloir which led out onto the Welzenbach Icefield where Camp IV was to be situated, they were halted by an abrupt drop in the temperature. Four days of continuous snowfall forced everyone back to base. A new assault was made during the first days of July and got as far as establishing Camp IV at 6600 metres. There was now another 1525 vertical metres to the summit.

On 19 July at six thirty in the evening Wilhelm Schloz and Peter Scholz set off for the first sortie into the Merkl Gully, and around midnight (there was a lot of climbing at night because during the day the radiant heat of the sun softened the snow until it seemed bottomless) they reached a height of 7100 metres, at a point where a crevasse cut right across the icefield. It was the last marginal crevasse before the rocky section of the Merkl Gully, which began some 300 metres higher. The two climbers bivouacked in the crevasse and finally turned back to Camp IV. It was the highest point reached during that year.

The same day, Gunter Strobel leaping over an awkward crevasse at Camp II sustained a complicated leg fracture. All climbers were required for the difficult rescue operation. 3500 metres of the Rupal Face had been climbed, but the most difficult section was yet to be attempted.

The fourth expedition to the Rupal Face in 1970 brought the final solution, it was the seventh year after the first reconnaissance. Eighteen members set off under the leadership of Dr Herrligkoffer, who was by this time fifty-four years old. They were: Michl Anderl, Gerhard Baur,

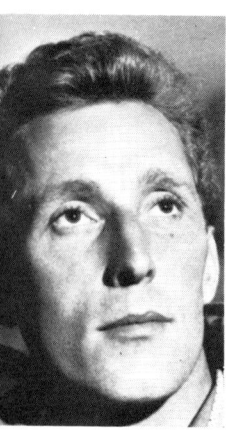

The second and first climbers of the Rupal Face, from the left: Felix Kuen, Peter Scholz, Reinhold and Günther Messner.

Wolf-Dietrich Bitterling, Werner Haim, Günther Kroh, Dr Hermann Kuhn, Gerd Mändl, Günther Messner, Reinhold Messner, Elmar Raab, Hans Saler, Peter Scholz, Peter Vogler, Jürgen Winkler, chemist Alice von Hobe as medical/scientific assistant, and Max von Kienlin as expedition guest. The expedition was dedicated to the memory of Siegi Löw.

Starting on 9 April, the expedition baggage was transported in three large lorries the 7500 kilometres to Pakistan, where we all met up in Rawalpindi on 26 April. The onward flights to Gilgit were delayed until 7/9 May. By mid-May the main camp had been set up on the old site on the Tap meadows, a veritable small town of fifteen tents. The rate of establishment of the high camps was brisk even though continuously hampered by snowfalls. On 21 May the Wieland Icefield was prepared. On 26 the old hauling apparatus was recovered from the snow and ice and after overhaul was found to still function perfectly. Finally, by the end of May, Camp III (5900 metres) was re-established in the old site, the safe ice hole. The route over the Welzenbach Icefield with its steep sixty degrees couloir at the end, was climbed and furnished with fixed ropes during the period up to 3 June.

A prolonged bad weather period with tremendous snowfall finally drove everyone back to base – the Messner brothers last of all. On 15 June, Günther Messner wrote in a letter home:

... For a good ten days here, all hell has been let loose ... Since 3 June we have had snowstorms practically without ceasing. In the high camps great quantities of new snow falls every day (a metre and more). Avalanches thunder down the incredibly steep slopes. The only good thing to say is that Reinhold

NANGA PARBAT HISTORY

and I have selected all the campsites (i.e. apart from Base and Winch Camps) and have taken care that they are protected from avalanche or stonefall danger ... With all the new snow, the face is extraordinarily treacherous right now ... Over the past twelve days all the high camps have had to be evacuated ... Initially Reinhold and I spent ten whole days in Camp III hoping for better weather. The 10 June was a better day, calmer and sunnier ... other members of the team climbed up to reoccupy the camps. On 11 June Reinhold and I wanted to climb up to Camp IV again, to finally locate a good spot for it on the lower edge of the Merkl Icefield, and erect a tent ... but in the morning we were greeted by a shower of sleet and there were black clouds encircling Nanga ... At eight o'clock all hell was let loose again. We felt pretty fed up. In the first place we would soon have spent two full weeks at Camp III at 6000 metres, and secondly, we felt it was now absolutely imperative that we soon make some sort of move ... On 13 June (two days later) we came down in the afternoon and – thanks to good acclimatization – were able to do so in a very few hours. The mist now hangs right down to the Tap Alpe and it drizzles most of the time. Avalanches are thundering away up on the mountain ... As a result of this filthy weather, hopes for the summit are getting smaller and several people are saying there is not much sense in going on with things ...

On 18 June a new attack was launched. By 25 June the two Messner brothers had reconnoited the Merkl Icefield to just below the Merkl Gully and found a spot for Camp V, the assault camp. The next day Felix Kuen and Peter Scholz carried up the necessary supplies. The tent for this assault camp stood 'under a spur of rock close to the start of the Merkl Gully' (Herrligkoffer) at 7350 metres. Scholz and Kuen turned back to IV, Gerhard Baur and the Messner brothers occupied the assault camp.

Before leaving Camp IV, Reinhold Messner had had the radio conversation with Dr Herrligkoffer that was later to become the subject of so much discussion, and during which it was agreed that the following signal would be used to transmit the last weather forecast (to Camp V which was out of radio contact): red rocket – bad weather, blue – good.

At five thirty in the evening Base Camp received the report 'Weather fair' for 27 June. At eight Michl Anderl fired a rocket with a blue banderole. But it turned out to be a red flare. A hasty check revealed that they had no rockets of any other colour at Base Camp. The decision was taken. How it turned out is world-famous.

Reinhold Messner got up at three a.m. on 27 June, took a look at the

SOLO NANGA PARBAT

weather and decided to make a lightning dash for the summit. Günther Messner followed Reinhold when the ropes he was supposed to be fixing in the Merkl Gully with Baur, got themselves tangled into a hopeless muddle, 'a rope salad'. Gerhard Baur, plagued with an altitude cough (bronchitis) climbed down to Camp IV that evening, where he met Kuen and Scholz coming up.

Günther Messner caught up with his brother in the Merkl Gully. With few words they continued together. At five p.m. they embraced each other on the summit. After an hour when they began their descent, Günther was showing signs of altitude sickness and was also suffering from hallucinations. The brothers spent the night without bivouac equipment in the Merkl Gap immediately below the South Shoulder, not far from the rocky drop to the Merkl Gully. On the morning of 28 June, Reinhold Messner held a shouted conversation with Felix Kuen and Peter Scholz across a distance of 80 to 100 metres. It resulted in a misunderstanding.

Kuen and Scholz reached the summit during that afternoon (four to five p.m.), bivouacked 'on the South Summit' and were back in Camp IV during the afternoon of the 29th. On 30 June at four p.m. Felix Kuen reached Base Camp.

The two Messner brothers risked a descent of the Diamir Face. Günther's only hope of survival was to get out of the 'Death Zone' and below 5000 metres as quickly as possible. It was a frightful decision, but not without logic, and taken entirely on survival grounds. 'Our will to survive was so great that we were able to find our way down the unknown Diamir side of the mountain. This was only possible because I scouted ahead for a passable route, step by step, retracing at least a thousand metres of height. Once when a serac blocked the way ahead, I climbed back, another time when a rock step seemed too risky for Günther, and a third time when crevasses barred all progress' (Reinhold Messner in *The Big Walls*). On the lower slopes of the Diamir Flank, Günther Messner lost his life under an avalanche.

The story of how Reinhold Messner — once he finally came to accept the death of his brother, bereft, exhausted, without food, with frostbitten toes but with an unswerving will to live, struggled down the

NANGA PARBAT HISTORY

Diamir Valley till he finally met some local people who helped him and eventually brought him to the Indus Road near Bunar Bridge, where an officer in a military jeep took charge of him and delivered him to a resthouse on the road to Gilgit — is a moving odyssey and one of the greatest achievements in all mountaineering history.

1969-71 CZECHOSLOVAKIANS ON THE BUHL-ROUTE

Eighteen years passed before the Buhl-Route on the Rakhiot side of Nanga Parbat was repeated. Czechoslovakian climbers finally succeeded on their second attempt in the summer of 1971.

In 1969 a big expedition travelled by lorry through six countries to reach their objective. The participants: Jozef Korsala, Frantisek Dostal, Juray Weincziller, Frantisek Mrazik, Jan Horan, Dr Juraj Janovsky, Vladimir Vacata, Ivan Urbanovic, Miroslav Jaskovsky, Arno Puskas, Ing. Zdeno Vasko, Milan Krissak, Miroslav Filip under the leadership of I. Gálfy. It was the first visit to the Himalaya for all of them. The course and tactics of their undertaking clearly revealed that they had done their homework and studied the accounts of their many predecessors on this, the longest of all routes on Nanga.

On 10 May they erected their Base Camp at 4470 metres on the great moraine of the Rakhiot Glacier. It took fifteen days before they had Camp II established at 5300 metres. To overcome the great icefall and to safeguard the constantly-changing route cost precious time and energy. The weather was unsettled with frequent snowfalls. Typical Nanga Parbat weather for this time of year. By 30 May, Camp III was standing at 6120 metres and on 16 June, Camp IV directly under the Rakhiot Ice Wall (6690 metres). The Czechs worked hard in the ensuing days and secured 350 metres of fixed rope.

SOLO NANGA PARBAT

A fall in temperature and a full week of tremendous falls of new snow condemned them to wait. Precious time trickled away. On 28 June an attempt was launched on the Rakhiot Ridge — unsuccessfully. There was nothing more they could do that year.

Two years later the Czechoslovaks came again. Under the leadership of Ivan Gálfy, they were sixteen-strong — eight from the first expedition and eight new faces. From 1969: Ivan Gálfy, Frantisek Dostal, Miroslav Filip, Miroslav Jaskovsky, Jozef Korsala, Milan Krissak, Arno Puskas, Ivan Urbanovic. The new men: Ivan Dieska, Ivan Fiala, Gejza Haak, Bohumir Kismak, Martin Mladon, Michal Orolin, Jozef Psotka, Ludovit Zahornasky.

This time they were successful. On 11 July 1971 Ivan Fiala and Michal Orolin stood on the summit. Ivan Fiala reported: ' "Misko (Michal), that little hill ahead, that's it, the celebrated Nanga Parbat!" We encouraged each other on. Greatest effort of will. One step, rest, two steps, another rest ... till we came to the last step which brought us onto the top — and we fell into each other's arms. "That's it, Misko, we're up! This is the top!" We couldn't hold back the tears.' It was the first time, according to the report in *Alpinismus* 3/72 that Czechoslovakian climbers — or any other alpinists from the Eastern block — had reached the summit of an eight-thousander.

The same day Ivan Urbanovic, Jozef Psotka and Arno Puskas climbed the 7910 metre south-east fore-summit and the 7530 metre south-east summit. Back home the climbers were awarded the honour of Meritorious Masters of Sport.

1976 FOUR GRAZ MOUNTAINEERS ON NANGA PARBAT

In the summer of 1976 four mountaineers from Graz made the sixth ascent of Nanga Parbat without any local high level porters — at the same time it was the first ascent of the South-west Ridge (Nanga-Mazeno

NANGA PARBAT HISTORY

Peak). The possibility of such a line on the wide flank west of the Rupal Face was first postulated by Toni Kinshofer many years earlier. The four men who set themselves the task of turning this route to reality were: Hanns Schell (37), Hilmar Sturm (37), Robert Schauer (22) and Siegi Gimpel (20)' With them was Dr Gerhard Mayer. Hanns Schell, who has been described by Wolfgang Nairz, leader of the Austrian Everest Expedition, as a man obsessed by mountains, is a very experienced mountaineer: six seven-thousanders (of which five were first ascents); first ski ascent of Mount Logan in Canada (6050 metres); Mount McKinley, Alaska; Aconcagua, highest mountain in all the Americas; and as his first eight-thousander, Hidden Peak in 1975.

The overland journey and march to Base Camp, after five week's preparation at home, was something of an adventurous odyssey in itself, not least because of the closing of the Karakorum Highway. By separate routes the five men met up on schedule at the Base Camp near the Tap Alpe in the upper Rupal Valley (3700 metres) on 11 July. Hanns Schell and Dr Mayer arrived from the Diamir side over the Mazeno Pass. From Diamirai up to the top of the pass was 3500 metres, but it presented no special difficulties and they described it as a splendid walk.

Together at last, the Graz mountaineers lost no time at all. The next morning, 12 July, Robert Schauer, Siegi Gimpel and Hilmar Sturm reconnoitred and prepared the route to Camp I, each carrying heavy loads. It was a fine start to gain 1400 metres of altitude from 3700 to 5100 metres. Taking account of the delays encountered on the approach, and the fact that the terrain allowed it, they made a certain compromise in as much as they made use of the valley porters to get eighteen loads up to Camp I in the shortest possible time. Whilst Schell and Mayer accompanied the porters, the others opened up and secured the next 1000-metre stage to Camp II (6100 metres). This compromise saved the climbers five days of load-carrying. From Camp I they worked completely without high porters.

The section from I to II, steep rock and ice and a couloir under constant threat of stonefall, proved to be the most difficult and dangerous part of the whole climb. Fixed ropes were essential here although several times they were torn away by stones. With four load-carries the climbers got

Nanga Parbat seen from the west; the 1976 Schell-Route with the upper campsites and bivouacs. On the right, the Rupal Face, on the left the upper section of the Diamir Flank.

all their necessary equipment over this 'panic section'. They came across remains of steel and perlon rope left by an expedition the previous year. Immediately below Camp II they also found an abandoned food dump.

The next stage to Camp III at 7000 metres is technically problem-free but with overloaded rucksacks fearfully energy-sapping. After this drudgery they resolved to have a rest day at Camp II. Suddenly on this day a strong wind got up, quickly increasing to storm intensity by evening. All the signs foretold a bad break in the weather and they therefore, all four, climbed back to Base Camp.

It rained for days on end without ceasing, finally also snowing right down to Base Camp. Had the monsoon already reached the Nanga Parbat massif? But the shepherds on the Tap Alpe told the visitors that such a long spell of stormy weather was not at all unusual in high summer. After six days it finally cleared and settled. But the mountain and their

NANGA PARBAT HISTORY

route were covered in deep snow. All the same they set off at once, leaving their doctor back in base. From then on, therefore, they were without medical aid at all.

In Camp I they found their tent, a Whillans box-tent with a flat roof, full of water. A day of bad weather confined them here then the next day they went on to find their Japanese dome tents only peeping a couple of centimetres out of the snow. It required several hours of shovelling to clear them, but they were undamaged and dry inside.

The next day the four met with a minor catastrophe. After endless energy-consuming burrowing they couldn't find their equipment dump below the Camp II site, although they had marked it well. They all dug and probed but it was fruitless — their personal trappings, bivouac sacks etc. as well as oxygen cylinders for medical emergency, were all lost.

Camp III itself had completely vanished in the snow. For more than two hours they dug at the exact spot and only after two metres of snow had been cleared, did they finally come upon their collapsed tunnel tent. It proved to be no longer usable and they had to put up the four-man Bishop tent intended for Camp IV. They slept well there. With renewed confidence they felt sure they could reach the summit, perhaps even the next day. But their enthusiasm was misplaced.

They found the climb a terrible effort in knee-deep snow, it was very steep and when they came to rocky patches they would sink in up to their bellies. At one time or another they all thought of turning back. It took eight hours to climb the 500 vertical metres they gained that day. Near a gap, they found a suitable site for their Bishop tent (which they had brought with them) under a backward-sloping rock. In a brief report such as this, it's only possible to say that the flank was climbed and the ridge separating them from the Diamir side, negotiated. (The place where the previous year's expedition had turned back was already behind them.) 675 more vertical metres separated them from their objective, but it was still a long way to the foot of the massive summit block.

After a small stretch of descent and an awkward traverse across an avalanche-prone slope, they came to a rising traverse on such steep rock that they fixed a rope there. Then another snow slope. Further hard trail-breaking and they reached 7700 metres, left their loads behind, and after

SOLO NANGA PARBAT

a rest, keeping to the left of the notch where the Merkl Gully meets the ridge (at the end of the Rupal Face climb), they reached the approximate spot where the Messners had bivouacked in 1970. Here they turned back and hacked out two little snowholes for the night. The tent they had obviously left behind at Camp V, so they were obliged to spend the night in the open. Hanns Schell wrote, 'The weather was excellent, windless and so warm that one had the impression of being in the Alps. Hilmar and I tucked ourselves into one snowhole, leaving our top halves out in the open. Robert forced himself into the second hole, whilst Siegi decided to sleep completely outside.' Thanks to their excellent American sleeping bags, they all slept well. Schell said he slept right through the night without waking – this at at least 7600 metres.

The next day, the third since leaving Camp IV, was their make-or-break day. They were within 400 vertical metres of the summit. The weather was completely clear, no clouds, but a strong, relentless wind blew up out of the clear blue sky forcing them back into their snowholes. Towards one p.m. the wind dropped as suddenly as it had come. New attempt. 'Across the notch, about 7800 metres,' noted Schell, 'then we climbed across a rock slope for 100 metres westwards, then snow, then a few patches of rock climbing. It was so steep that we preferred to belay,

Climbers who made the first ascent of the route reconnoitred by Toni Kinshofer over the left section of the Rupal Flank and the South-west Ridge of Nange Parbat. From the left: Siegfried Gimpel, Hilmar Sturm, Hanns Schell, Robert Schauer.

The South-west Ridge of Nanga Parbat above the Mazeno Gap. Immediately below the summit the South Shoulder rises in the mist to the right. Under the rock upswing below that is the end of the Merkl Gully which leads up from the Rupal Face on the right. That was where in 1970 the shouted conversation between Kuen and Messner took place. After that Reinhold Messner felt compelled to descend by the Diamir side with his brother who was suffering from the effects of altitude. Hanns Schell and his comrades also passed this way in 1976.

and finally we came out onto the flat snowfield, west of the South Shoulder at 8042 metres.'

It was seven p.m. What should they do? They conferred and after some hesitation, decided to bivouac again. They found a somewhat lower, even patch of snow under a small rock wall at 8020 metres. They only had one sleeping bag with them. They sat on their rucksack and managed to get their feet, legs, and lower bodies into the single sleeping bag. They watched the full moon trace its orbit across the black sky of this unique, almost windless Himalayan night, illuminating everything near and far. They didn't manage to get much sleep and feared frostbite, but succeeded in escaping serious damage.

Feeling 'astonishingly fresh' they set off next morning over the steep snow ridge directly to the highest point of Nanga Parbat which they reached in about an hour from their bivouac spot. Schell wrote, 'We were naturally very happy. I myself was amazed that we had managed to reach the top of dreaded Nanga on 11 August, exactly a month after arriving at Base Camp, despite all the bad weather. On 11 August a year ago, I stood with my friends (of whom only Robert Schauer is a member of this party) on 8086 metre-high Hidden Peak.'

After placing a piton in the summit rocks, they climbed down and had only gone a few steps before Hanns Schell found that he was suffering from a leaden tiredness. Fighting the impulse to lie down in the snow, the bivouac site was reached again about an hour later. His friends prepared a drink for him. He had to rest every few metres and it was night-time before he struggled back into Camp IV (we must remember Camp IV was at 7450 metres). Hanns Schell passed his fourth night above the dangerous 7000-metre mark. He didn't pick up in the night, his exhaustion went unrelieved. It took him as long to descend each stage between camps as it had to climb it, in all the descent from the summit to base took him four and three-quarters days. But he made it. In Base Camp he had a strong pain in his right lung which didn't go away until he was in Rawalpindi ten days later. Back in Graz the doctors told him he would suffer no lasting damage. It was assumed that he had suffered a minor pulmonary embolism as a result of changes in the blood. He was lucky to still be alive.

This little expedition, employing no porters (nor using oxygen), fulfills all the criteria with regard to style, endurance, drive, severity to make it a perfect example of a modern eight-thousander ascent.

1978 AUSTRIANS ON THE DIAMIR FLANK

August 1978 brought the second ascent of the Kinshofer-Route on the Diamir Face by a six-man group from the Upper Austrian Section of the Club *Naturfreunde*. One man had to withdraw after being injured in a

NANGA PARBAT HISTORY

stonefall, five others climbed to the summit in two parties. Without porters, without artificial oxygen, with carefully calculated, streamlined equipment, they made a swift, direct assault, a further success for a small expedition on this celebrated eight-thousander.

The six climbers were: Rudolf Wurzer (Expedition Leader), Wilhelm Bauer, Alfred Imitzer, Alois Indrich, Karl Pfeifer and Reinhard Streif. For several years Rudolf Wurzer and his companions had been planning quite a different expedition, to the 7500 metre Yuksin Garden in the Karakorum, close to the Chinese border. But the Pakistani authorities were unable to grant permission for Yuksin Garden and offered the Austrians Nanga Parbat as an alternative. The readjustment to their plans and partial re-equipment of the expedition (already almost complete) created problems.

Wurzer and his friends first thought of trying a new variation on the great rock pillar to the left of the Diamir Flank, but once there, changed their minds quickly in favour of the Kinshofer-Route, which runs to the

The Upper-Austrians who in 1978 climbed Nanga Parbat by the Kinshofer-Route. From the left: Alfred Imitzer, Karl Pfeifer, Alois Indrich, Sir Blanc (Liaison Officer), Rudolf Wurzer, Wilhelm Bauer, Reinhard Streif.

SOLO NANGA PARBAT

left of the pillar up a crack and couloir system, which is in places very steep and presents considerable objective danger. With steady and exceptionally strenuous effort, the six Austrians built up their chain of camps: Base Camp 4300 metres, Camp I 5000 metres, Camp II 6000 metres (c.), Camp III 6800 metres, Camp IV at 7300 metres above the spur in the snowfield under the Bazhin Gap. The first summit attempt by Alfred Imitzer and Alois Indrich had to be cut short on 20 August after attaining the summit ridge when stormy conditions set in. Both climbed right back to Base Camp. On 23 August (setting off at five thirty a.m.) Reinhard Streif reached the summit at two p.m. with Wilhelm Bauer and Rudolf Wurzer following at three thirty. Alois Indrich and Alfred Imitzer successfully reached the top on 28 August.

Only one of the six, Karl Pfeifer, was denied the summit. He had been badly injured by a stonefall in the gully and suffered 'an enormous flesh wound to his left leg in the hollow of his knee, with considerable loss of blood'. Pfeifer's evacuation over very steep terrain turned out to be difficult and hazardous. One of the team was a trained ambulance man. He stitched the wound with a normal needle and thread, and it healed well.

The team had a few cylinders of oxygen for medical emergency (altitude sickness, pulmonary oedema) and carried these as far as Camp III.

Ferrying their own equipment supplies to a height of 7300 metres must have been a tremendous slog, 'Climbing at 6000 metres with a heavy rucksack of between fifteen and eighteen kilograms is extremely difficult,' Wurzer recorded.

He tells of the summit success,

... Reinhard (Streif) — who has been cooking tea and soup steadfastly since one thirty a.m. — set off at five fifty and went out ahead over the Ice Gully (on the summit buttress), which was the way Alois (Indrich) and Alfred (Imitzer) hoped to reach the summit. Willi (Bauer) and I followed an hour later. Wearily we struggled up the steep gully. Later it eased off, but we kept encountering a lot of powder snow. The last few metres up the summit ridge were very strenuous indeed. Icy winds and fierce cold accompanied us. Reinhard reached the summit at two p.m. after eight and half hours. After a short while he was forced to descend. In this wind a longer stay on the summit was not possible. We met up in a sheltered hollow and exchanged a few words. Around three

NANGA PARBAT HISTORY

thirty p.m. (after nine hours) we too came to the highest point. A dream is realized. Dumbly we clasped hands, mittened still because of the intense cold. We saw the metal container left by Reinhold Messner and added our own date inside.'

This short report by Rudolf Wurzer is precise and important. For the descent to Camp IV both climbers took five hours. With the half hour spent on the summit they were out for a total of fourteen hours on their summit day.

This little expedition typifies a modern eight-thousander undertaking.

SOLO NANGA PARBAT

BIBLIOGRAPHY

Paul Bauer, *The Siege of Nanga Parbat 1856-1953*, Rupert Hart Davis (1956). Chris Bonington, *Annapurna South Face*, Cassell (1971). Hermann Buhl, *Nanga Parbat Pilgrimage*, Hodder & Stoughton (1956). G. O. Dyhrenfurth, *To the Third Pole*, Werner Laurie (1955) (and revised edition *Der dritte Pol* Munich, 1960); *Das Buch vom Nanga Parbat* (Munich, 1954, both Nymphenburger Verlagshandlung). Dr Franz Grassler, *Der Kampf um die Achttausender*, Bergverlag Rother, Munich. Dr Karl M. Herrligkoffer, *Nanga Parbat — Sieben Jahrzehnte Gipfelkampf in Sonnenglut und Eis*, Verlag Ullstein (Frankfurt/Berlin, 1967); *Kampf und Sieg am Nanga Parbat*, Spectrum-Verlag (Stuttgart, 1971); *Nanga Parbat* in *The Mountain World 1954*, Allen and Unwin (1954). Ulrich Link, *Nanga Parbat*, Bergverlag Rother (Munich, 1953). Reinhold Messner, *The Big Walls*, Kaye and Ward (1978). Magazine, *Der Bergsteiger*, Bruckmann Verlag, Munich, issues 1958-1978. Magazine, *Alpinismus*, Heering-Verlag, Munich, issues from 1964. *Nachrichten der Sektion Graz*, issues 7-9, 1976.

Numerous other newspaper and magazine articles covering the whole period, as well as letters and personal notes.

ACKNOWLEDGEMENTS

Photographs:

Archive R. Messner: Endpapers, frontispiece as well as pages 11, 13, 17, 20, 29 (3), 30-31, 32 (2), 35, 40, 44, 51, 57 (2), 58-59, 60, 67, 69, 71, 77 (2), 78-79, 80 (3), 86, 89 (2), 90-91, 92 (2), 94, 101 (2), 102-103, 104 (2), 109, 113, 114-115, 116 (2), 123, 133, 136, 141, 149, 151, 152-153, 154 (2), 156 (lower), 161, 169, 171 (2), 172-173, 174 (2), 178, 184-185 (6), 186-187 (6), 188-189 (6), 191 (2), 192-193, 194, 196-197 (6), 198-199 (6), 218-219, 220, 232, 255, 262 (2).

A. Chen: pages 18-19.

Deutsche Himalaja-Stiftung: pages 15, 23 (2), 75, 126, 177, 201, 205, 244, 246, 247, 260, 271.

Deutsches Institut für Auslandsforschung: pages 250 (2), 256 (3), 262 (1).

U. Grether: pages 131, 134-135, 147, 156 (upper), 157 (2), 159, 212, 214, 215, 217 (3).

A. Indrich: pages 225, 270.

Archive H. Schell: pages 268, 270 (4).

R. Stummhofer: page 262 (left).

Graphics:

Hellmut Hoffmann, Munich. Diagrams on pages 54-55 and 62 were prepared from originals by Tomoya Iozawa in *Trekking in the Himalayas*.

The Author and Publisher wish to thank:

Anders Bolinder, Switzerland, for the preparation of pages 237-242; Ulrich Link, Munich for pages 243-275 (compiled in association with Anders Bolinder).

The 'Deutsche Himalaja-Stiftung' as well as the 'Deutsche Institut für Auslandsforschung' for placing material at their disposal.

The Deutsche and the Osterreichische Alpenverein for permission to reproduce part of their Nanga Parbat map (pages 278-279).

During the five days in which I undertook my solo climb, our escort officer, Terry, sat continually at the telescope in Base Camp, following my progress. He would be up before five and only put the glass away when darkness came. He plotted all my essential changes of direction on the face, so far as they were visible to him and Nanga was not enshrouded in mist and cloud. The result was this sketch which is exact to the minute in places. Terry gave it to me when I returned to the valley and I have photographed the original for this book.

Endpaper
Nanga Parbat in late afternoon light, seen from the west. On the right, in shade, the Mazeno Ridge; and on the left, covered in mist, the North Summit; above, the trapezoid summit and the South-west Ridge. From this angle, my route up and down takes the form of a triangle. When I got back to Base Camp after my 120-hour solo adventure, and saw this face from below, it looked just as mysterious and secretive as it had always done. I had difficulty in believing that I had really and truly been to the summit of Nanga Parbat again.

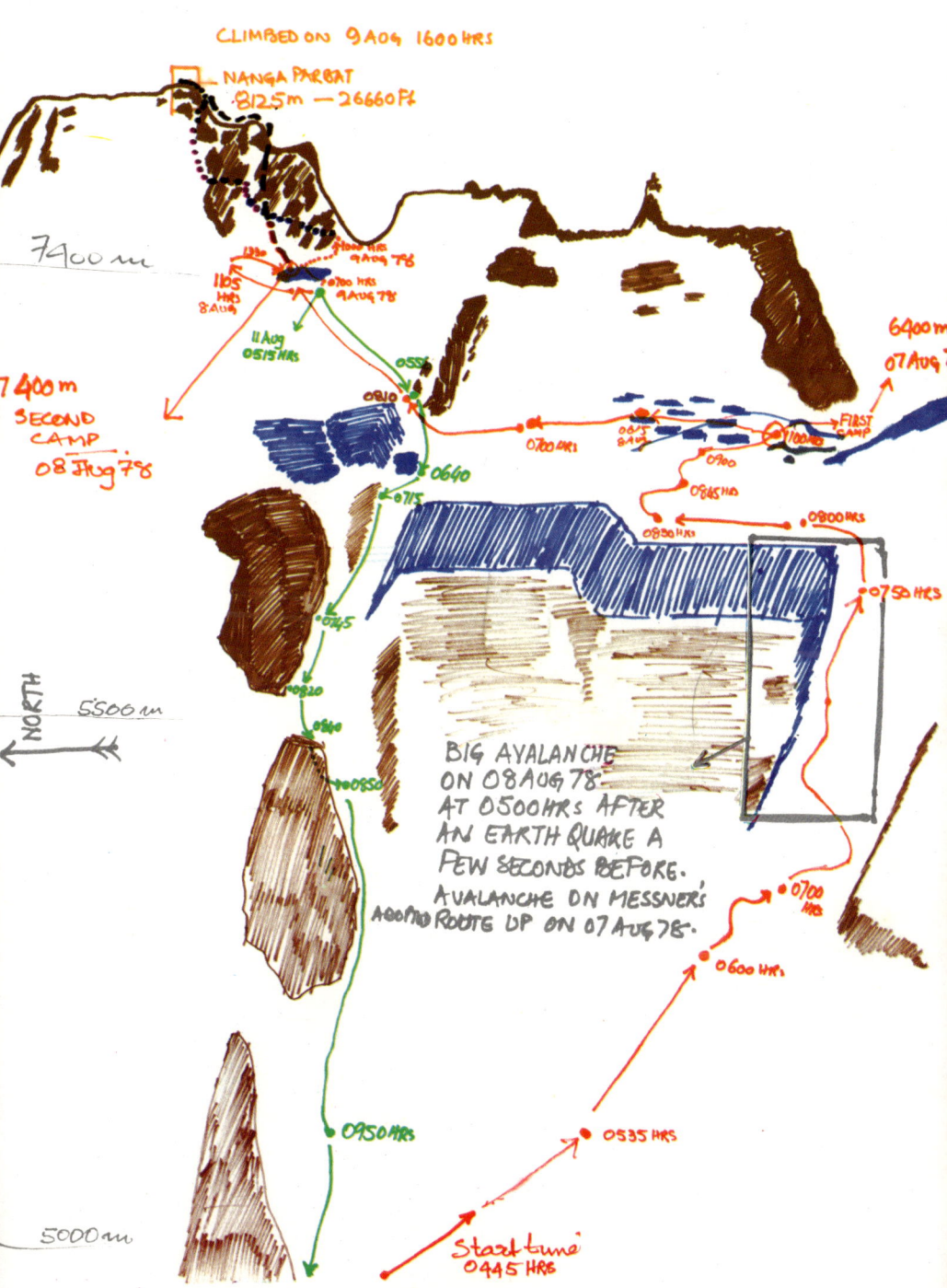